THE NEW GLUTEN-FREE
Recipes, Ingredients, Tools & Techniques

Demystifying
Gluten-Free Baking

–A RESOURCE GUIDE–

LISA DIAMOND, RD
ARELI HERMANSON, RD

CONTENTS

THE NEW GLUTEN-FREE™

Acknowledgements.. xi

About The Guide: How it is set up and why................................. xiii

Introduction xvi

Lisa's Story xx

SECTION 1: ABOUT GLUTEN-FREE FLOURS AND STARCHES
UNDERSTANDING GLUTEN-FREE FLOURS.................................1

CHAPTER 1: GLUTEN-FREE FLOURS BY FLOUR GROUPS
(FLOURS WITHIN THESE GROUPS CAN BE INTERCHANGED 1-FOR-1) 3

Flour Group 1: Brown Rice, White Rice, Corn, Buckwheat, and Pure Oat* Flours..............3

Flour Group 2: Sorghum, Teff, and Fonio Flours...11

Flour Group 3: Millet Flour 16

Flour Group 4: Quinoa, Black Bean, White Bean, Whole Bean,
Lentil, Garfava Bean, Chickpea, and Soy Flours...18

Flour Group 5: Amaranth Flour 28

Flour Group 6: Coconut Flour...30

Flour Group 7: Rice Bran..32

Flour Group 8: Nut and Seed Meals..33

Flour Group 9: Cocoa Powder, and Defatted Legume, Nut and Seed Flours 45

Summary Table Chapter 1: Gluten-Free Flours by Flour Group................................55

CHAPTER 2: STARCHES BY STARCH GROUP
UNDERSTANDING STARCHES AND STARCH-LIKE FLOURS..............64

Summary Table Chapter 2: Starches and Starch-like Flours 65

Starch Group 1: Tapioca Starch...65

Starch Group 2: Arrowroot Starch 65

Starch Group 3: Potato Starch..65

Starch Group 4: Corn Starch..65

Starch Group 5: Sweet Rice Flour..65

CHAPTER 3: NUTRIENT ANALYSIS OF GLUTEN-FREE FLOURS AND STARCHES..........67

    Category 1: Nutrient Analysis Graphs..67

    Category 2: Nutrient Analysis: Frequency of Flour in Top 3 for Vitamin and Mineral Content ...82

**SECTION 2: LIQUIDS, BINDERS, FOAMS,
LEAVENING AGENTS, AND SWEETENERS** 87

CHAPTER 1: INTRODUCTION TO LIQUIDS...88

    Chapter 1 Summary Table: Liquids..89

    Liquid Group 1: Water..89

    Liquid Group 2: Juices...89

    Liquid Group 3: Grain "Milks"...90

    Liquid Group 4: Nut "Milks"...90

    Liquid Group 5: Seed "Milks" non-protein-containing....................................90

    Liquid Group 6: Mashed vegetables and fruit..91

    Liquid Group 7: Seed "Milks" – protein-containing 91

    Liquid Group 8: Legume "Milks"...91

    Liquid Group 9: Dairy Milks..91

    Liquid Group 10: Partially-solid Dairy..91

    Liquid Group 10: Partially-solid Dairy-free...91

**CHAPTER 2: INTRODUCTION TO BINDERS
– INGREDIENTS THAT "STICK" OR "BIND"** 93

    Hydrophilic Binders..93

    Summary Table Chapter 2: Hydrophilic Binders..95

    Hydrophilic Binder Group 1: Xanthan and Guar Gum 95

    Hydrophilic Binder Group 2: Methylcellulose...96

    Hydrophilic Binder Group 3: Psyllium Husk...96

    Hydrophilic Binder Group 4: Chia Seeds..97

    Hydrophilic Binder Group 5: Flax Seeds..97

    Protein Binders..98

    Category 2: Protein Binders..98

    Protein Binder Group 1: Egg White...98

    Protein Binder Group 2: Gelatin...98

    Protein Binder Group 3: Agar 99

CHAPTER 3: LEAVENING AGENTS AND FOAMS – INGREDIENTS THAT MAKE "GAS" AND "AIR" 100

    Category 1: Leavening Agents 100

    Baking Powder 101

    Baking Soda 101

    Cream of Tartar 102

    Egg Replacer 102

    Yeast 103

    Vinegar, Lemon and Lime Juice 103

    Carbonated Liquids 104

    Category 2: Foams 104

    Summary Table Chapter 3: Foams 105

    Foam Group 1: Egg White 105

    Foam Group 2: Methylcellulose 105

    Foam Group 3: Gelatin 106

    Foam Group 4: Egg Yolk 106

    Foam Group 5: Whipping Cream 106

    Foam Group 6: Coconut Cream 107

    Foam Group 7: Evaporated Milk 107

CHAPTER 4: INTRODUCTION TO SWEETENERS 108

    Category 1: Liquid Sweeteners 108

    Category 2: Crystal Sweeteners 112

    Summary Table Chapter 4: Sweeteners 118

SECTION 3: ABOUT SOLID AND LIQUID FAT 121

    Introduction to Solid and Liquid Fat 122

    Summary Table Section 3: Solid Fat 123

    Fat Group 1: Butter 124

    Fat Group 2: Macadamia Nut Butter 124

    Fat Group 3: Lard and Shortening 125

    Fat Group 4: Hard Margarine 125

    Summary Table Section 3: Semi-Solid and Liquid Fat 126

Fat Group 5: Cream Cheese..126

Fat Group 6: Mashed Avocado..127

Fat Group 7: Soft Margarine..127

Fat Group 8: Low-fat Margarine...127

Fat Group 9: Oils..128

SECTION 4: SUMMARY OF GLUTEN-FREE BAKING BY BAKED GOOD 129

Summary of Gluten-Free Baking by Baked Good Including Trouble Shooting Tips............130

CHAPTER 1: WATER-BASED BATTERS AND DOUGH 131

Recipe Group 1: Yeast Breads...131

Recipe Group 2: Flat Breads..135

Recipe Group 3: Pasta Dough..138

Recipe Group 4: Crêpes...140

Recipe Group 5: Non-yeast Breads and Loaves..............................142

Recipe Group 6: Waffles and other items made with electric maker.........145

Recipe Group 7: Pancakes...148

Recipe Group 8: Muffins, Cakes, Cupcakes, and Cake-style Loaves..........151

CHAPTER 2: FAT-BASED AND/OR EGG-BASED BATTERS AND DOUGH 155

Recipe Group 9: Biscuits, Scones and Soft Cookies........................155

Recipe Group 10: Foam Cake...158

Recipe Group 11: Crispy Cookies and Chewy Cookies........................160

Recipe Group 12: Pastry..163

SECTION 5: PUTTING IT ALL TOGETHER 165

CHAPTER 1: GLUTEN-FREE BAKING - PUTTING IT ALL TOGETHER 166

Summary Table Section 5: Putting It All Together.........................167

CHAPTER 2: RECIPES THAT DEMONSTRATE GLUTEN-FREE INGREDIENTS, TOOLS AND TECHNIQUES 171

- Basic Yeast Bread - Egg White Foam 172
- Basic Yeast Bread - Gelatin Foam 174
- Basic Yeast Bread - Agar and Methylcellulose Foam 176
- Tortillas 178
- Pasta Dough 180
- Basic Crêpes 182
- Irish Soda Bread 184
- Basic Buttermilk Waffles 186
- Cornmeal Cheddar Lunch Waffles 188
- Chocolate Snack Balls 190
- Basic Buttermilk Pancakes 192
- Mock Bran Muffins 194
- Banana Muffins 196
- Basic Biscuits 198
- Chocolate Biscuit or Foam Cake 200
- Ginger Spice Cookies 202
- Quinoa Flake Bars 204
- Traditional Pie Dough 206

NUTRITION FACTS LABELS FOR EACH RECIPE 208

SECTION 6: TOOLS AND TECHNIQUES 217

CHAPTER 1: TOOLS 218

- Mixers and Beaters 220
- Bowl, Measuring Tools and Baking Pans 222
- Electric Makers 222
- Bread Machines 222
- Storage 222

CHAPTER 2: TECHNIQUES 223
　　Beating 223
　　Time 223
　　Heat 223
　　Cold 223
　　Chop size 224
　　Sifting 224

SECTION 7: BAKING BEYOND THE GUIDE 225
　　Baking Beyond The Guide 226
　　The Recipe Equation 226/227
　　The Last "ah-ha"... for now! 228

SECTION 8: APPENDICES 231
　　Appendix 1: Kitchen Must-Haves 232
　　Appendix 2: Basic Pantry List 234
　　Appendix 3: Sources of Information and Reference Materials 237

Copyright © 2014
by Lisa Diamond, RD & Areli Hermanson, RD
First Edition — April 2014

ISBN
978-1-4602-3745-8 (Hardcover)
978-1-4602-3746-5 (Paperback)
978-1-4602-3747-2 (eBook)
All rights reserved.

No part of this publication may be reproduced in any form, or by any means, electronic or mechanical, including photocopying, recording, or any information browsing, storage, or retrieval system, without permission in writing from the publisher.
Produced by:
FriesenPress
Suite 300 – 852 Fort Street
Victoria, BC, Canada V8W 1H8
www.friesenpress.com
Distributed to the trade by The Ingram Book Company

"The New Gluten-Free™ offers an expert view on the nutritional benefits of incorporating gluten-free products in your everyday living, just for the health of it."

– ERICA MESSING, RD

"This is so much more than a cookbook! It is unique because it is so educational and the details are arranged in such a logical way"

– RUTH IRVING, BC TEACHER AND SENSITIVE TO GLUTEN

"Lisa Diamond and Areli Hermanson – these two Registered Dietitians have used their knowledge and expertise of Food Science to research all the various ingredients that celiacs have to use to bake gluten-free and then proceeded to test and develop fail-safe recipes. Now they have developed and written a reliable book with so much useful information – The New Gluten-Free™... has delivered the best information for celiac baking and food preparation that I have ever seen or heard of so far."

– SANDRA LUND, RD

Revolutionary! Lisa and Areli have effectively deconstructed gluten-free baking into ingredient categories, then put them back together for exquisite taste and perfect texture!

Say goodbye to gluten-free baking disasters. Learn the 'mechanics' of baking without gluten and save precious dollars by getting gluten free right, every time! 'The New Gluten-Free™' is a must-have for anyone interested in gluten free - from beginners to professional bakers!"

– ELLEN BAYENS, FOUNDER, THE CELIAC SCENE™

ACKNOWLEDGEMENTS

Lisa and Areli would like to thank the following people for their support in the making of this reference guide whose dedication, contribution, commitment and enthusiasm have been greatly appreciated.

Lisa:

My parents, Naomi and Chris Diamond, who always supported me to use the kitchen to create the latest and greatest thing and for understanding that to learn to create a new item or recipe took not one batch, but much re-iteration. Through it they smiled, encouraged and provided kind and helpful suggestions. Their never-ending enthusiasm to support the interests and efforts of their kids – which in my case meant slogging in knee deep, baking my latest gluten-free recipe, sending me photos and full product evaluations, with attention to texture, smell, taste, mouth-feel, crumbliness, browning along with anything else I had decided needed to be critiqued. My mom received the less-mature side of me after I "discovered" I could no longer eat wheat - ever again! She was the one who quietly coaxed me along with my attempts at gluten-free baking, recipes and ingredients, knowing that my curiosity and love of food would eventually get the better of me.

My sisters Ruth and Christie, who like me, need gluten-free food have cheered me on, inspiring me to create festive baked goods for all holidays and celebrations.

My husband Rob Schuckel and my girls, Madailein and Maria, have lived and breathed my "experimental baking and cooking roller-coaster" on a daily basis. There have been many highs (delicious) and lows (disasters) in my gluten-free baking journey. They have provided me with great feedback and suggestions as well as demands of what I should try to make next. They have eaten many, many, many items over and over again - some more happily than others! They have whole-heartedly embraced the love of food and nutrition and are my greatest supporters.

My friend and colleague, Areli Hermanson, who invited me to do a few workshops with her on gluten-free ingredients and baking at a local natural foods market. The response from participants was exceptionally positive, with many participants stating that they had never heard gluten-free baking talked about in the way I had presented it. It was after those workshops that Areli convinced me that I should create this resource and that she would help me every step of the way. Without Areli this resource guide would not be in print. I cannot forget Areli's family, Craig, Benjamin and William, who over the past year have lost Areli to the world of gluten-free baking for hours at a time.

ARELI:

My friend and colleague, Lisa, for bringing your expertise and creative ideas to *Eat it Up!* and *The New Gluten-Free*™. Thank you for sharing your knowledge, experience and expertise of gluten-free baking with me. I was quite possibly your worst student so far making me the ideal co-creator in this resource! Well done, my friend.

My husband, Craig, for "holding down the fort" while I worked with Lisa on *The New Gluten-Free*™ and my two sons, Benjamin and William, for giving your dad "a run for his money" while saving your best behaviour and cuddles for me.

Lisa and Areli would also like to recognize:

Ellen Bayens of the Celiac Scene, in her role as Vice-President of the Victoria Chapter of the Canadian Celiac Association. Kathy McAree with Taste, Victoria Wine and Food Festival for their encouragement in bringing *The New Gluten-Free*™ to fruition.

The folks at Bob's Red Mill for replying to our many, many emails requesting product information and nutrient breakdown.

The reviewers who spent a significant number of hours reading our final drafts and providing feedback: Rob Schuckel; Chris, Naomi and Christie Diamond; Erica Messing; Lisa McKellar, and Geoff Robards.

We would like to acknowledge that the nutrient analysis of the recipes included in this guide was *Powered by the ESHA Research Nutrient Database©*.

ABOUT THE GUIDE:
HOW IT IS SET UP AND WHY

THE RECIPE EQUATION

The secret to successful gluten-free baking is getting the right combination and proportion of seven key components: flours, starches, liquids, binders, foams and leavening agents, sweeteners and fats. It is important to understand the contribution each component makes to the qualities of the final product: structure, strength, moisture, rise, and tenderness. Unknowingly, these characteristics are what we evaluate when we determine whether or not we think something is good and worth making and eating again.

In order to get the "right" combination and proportion of these seven key components, it helps to understand the science behind the ingredients - what they are made of, how they work, what they need to do their job, and how they interact with other ingredients to bring out their best qualities. The first step in baking is to determine the characteristics of the item you want to bake – do you want cake-like, or crispy, crunchy cookies? The second step is to identify the predominant moisture source that is being used in your recipe – is it water-based (water, juice, and milk) or fat-based (butter, oil, and lard)? It is from the moisture base, along with the characteristics of texture, taste, moisture, crumb, chew and mouth-feel that the remaining components (flours, starches, liquids, binders, foams and leavening agents, sweeteners and fats) tools and techniques are chosen.

THE RECIPE EQUATION

Although The Guide is large and detailed The Recipe Equation is simple and speaks to the principles of gluten-free baking.

THE RECIPE EQUATION

Determine what it is you want to bake: is it crunchy, chewy, tender? + **Consider the moisture base of the recipe: is fat- or water-based moisture being added?** + **Build on the moisture base with the "right" combination and proportion of the 7 key components: flours, starches, liquids, binders, foams and leavening agents, sweeteners, and fats.** + **The right equipment, tools and some very important techniques.** = **Gluten-Free products that turn out every time!**

The Guide has been laid out so that you will go through each of the seven key components of gluten-free baking, starting with flours and ending with fats. Once you have determined the item you want to make, the characteristics you want in the final product and the moisture base that is required to create these characteristics, you choose the flours, starch, liquid, binders, foams and leavening agents, sweeteners and fats. This resource breaks the seven key components down into categories based on function and properties. Summary tables are included to highlight important information and identify ingredients from within groups that can be substituted one-for-one.

The first half of *The Guide* speaks to the chemistry and science of gluten-free baking. The second half looks at the gluten-free baking principles of yeast breads, flat breads, pasta, crêpes, non-yeast breads, waffles, pancakes, muffins, cakes, loaves, biscuits, scones, cakes, foam cakes, and pastry.

It may be tempting to skip through the book; however, each section builds to the next shedding light on how the ingredients work together. You will learn how to choose them specifically for the baked good you are trying to make. Read through each section of *The Guide* fully to expand your gluten-free baking knowledge.

Sample recipes are included at the end of the resource guide so that you can see how the ingredients, tools and techniques are put together to create delicious gluten-free baked goods. Visit thenewgluten-free.ca or thenewgluten-free.com for more information.

INTRODUCTION

Welcome to the new world of gluten-free baking. Have you ever wanted to make a favourite family recipe gluten- free or bake gluten-free without a recipe? Whether you have just begun baking or have been doing it for a while, *The New Gluten-Free™: Recipes, Ingredients, Tools & Techniques* (*The Guide*) will help you to demystify the expanding world of gluten-free ingredients and recipes. The reference tables and summaries found within *The Guide* will provide you with the information on the ingredients, tools, techniques and know-how required to look at a recipe to see if it is going to work - to adapt a favourite recipe to a gluten-free one or to create your own recipes with consistent results and success every time.

Embracing gluten-free eating often requires a significant lifestyle adjustment. That being said, it also affords an excellent opportunity to leave behind and/or expand on a "mono-grain" wheat-based diet and to incorporate a greater variety of grains and flours into your everyday choices, thereby enhancing your nutrition. Using gluten-free ingredients together with healthy protein, fat and fibre in proportion and combinations that work yields the most delicious and nourishing baked goods. Home baking allows you to create new baked goods and adapt family favourites at lower cost and with better nutrition. Using the ingredients, tools and techniques specific to gluten-free baking makes all the difference.

Bringing healthy eating principles to gluten-free baking and cooking is one of our goals.

First and foremost we love to eat good-tasting food. Next, we want our food to be nutritious. Being dietitians, many of our friends assumed that we would eat foods just because they are "good for us". It is well-proven that having the knowledge does not make one do the right thing. Humans need positive reinforcement for consistent follow through. If it tastes bad or the texture is wrong - we just will not eat it. So adding healthy eating principles into the mix just adds to the *fun* of gluten-free baking. We have a desire to enhance the palatability, quality and nutrition content of gluten-free baking at home and commercially around the world. Yes, we realize that it is a bit of a lofty goal.

We think that it is also worth mentioning that there are two main groups of people who eat gluten-free: those who are *required to* be gluten-free due to celiac disease or gluten sensitivity and those who *choose* to be gluten-free for other reasons. Those who are *required* to be gluten-free need to ensure that flours and baking products are marked as gluten-free and are free from possible cross-contamination. Those who *choose* to be gluten-free have more "wiggle room" and can choose products that theoretically do not contain gluten but may have been packaged in a facility that also manufactures gluten-containing products. If unsure, read labels and ask questions.

The grain debate and the quest for the perfect flour

Before we dive into gluten-free flours and ingredients, let's look at wheat. There are many different varieties of wheat with some pretty amazing characteristics that bakers of gluten-free products work hard to recreate. Many gluten-free bakers are looking for one flour (in the form of a single or multi-flour mix) that can do everything, a desire that stems from an inherent wish for simplicity and convenience. They want something that is easy to work with, convenient, cost-effective, available, tastes good, produces great texture and mouth-feel, and takes on almost any flavour. Well, wheat pretty much fits the bill and it is these characteristics which have led it to become a staple in people's diets. With the incorporation of wheat into so many foods, along with its convenience and other attributes, many people find themselves eating a mono-grain diet comprised of wheat. "Mono" anything (grain or otherwise) lacks at least some of the nutrients required for health and puts people at risk for intolerances and other less desirable health outcomes. Let the quest for "the" perfect flour lead you to knowing how to use and enjoy a variety of flours in your daily eating.

Over the last century, great debate has surrounded the recommended number of servings of grain products, both in Canada and abroad. Recommended intakes for the Canadian population have ranged from 2-3 servings per day up to 10-12 servings per day. Perhaps on a population level, the optimal amount lies somewhere in-between, though on an individual level genetics, environment, lifestyle, health status and other factors come in to play, the amount is individual. Although there is recognition of whole grains in optimal health, eating fewer, higher quality and nutrient-dense grains tailored to one's individual needs is best. Think of it as getting as "big a bang for your buck" as possible. It is far better to derive high quality nutrition in the form of energy-providing carbohydrate, healthy fat, quality protein, vitamins, minerals and fibre from 2-3 servings of grain products per day than from 8 servings of highly processed grain products that contain refined sugar, and missing or low levels of protein, vitamins, minerals and fibre. Eating high-quality grain, prepared with maximum nutrient density per serving, means the number of servings you have to eat to meet your nutrient needs is reduced.

The New Gluten-free

Increasing your repertoire by including gluten-free flours along with add-ins like chia seed, psyllium, flax meal, nut and seed meals and flours into your food choices increases diversity and nutrition in your diet.

Gluten-free flours are more diverse

Every flour has its strengths and its weaknesses – both nutritionally and functionally.

Flours fit into one of two food groups as outlined in *Eating Well with Canada's Food Guide* - Grain Products (wheat, rye, rice, barley, couscous, quinoa, etc.) or Meats and Alternatives (bean flours, nut and seed meals and flours). Inherent to each food group is a set of nutrients most often found in those foods (carbohydrate, protein, fat, vitamins, minerals as well as antioxidants and fibre). As outlined in *The Guide*'s comparison charts and summary tables, many gluten-free flours are as nutritious as, or even more nutritious than, wheat flour.

When flours are combined, the strengths of each come together to increase desirability in the baked product and enhance the nutrition for you.

In short, whatever grains, flours and/or meals you can eat, we encourage you to include them in your baking and cooking in whole form. If you can eat wheat, continue to do so in moderation but abandon the culture of mono-grain/flour cooking and baking. It will do your body good.

Pure oats and oat products

Oats are inherently gluten-free however, all commercially available oats are cross contaminated with gluten-containing grains in the fields where they are grown, in processing and in packaging. As a result, Health Canada mandates that oats sold in Canada may never be labelled as 'gluten-free.' That said, there are oat products on the market that are carefully grown, processed and tested to be free of gluten. Oats prepared in this way are labelled, "wheat-free / pure / uncontaminated / free of wheat, rye or barley / safe for the celiac diet" and are allowable for celiacs and those choosing to follow a strictly gluten-free diet. In the United States, such oats can be labelled 'gluten-free.' 3-5% of the general population, with or without a diagnosis of celiac disease, experience an adverse reaction to oats. For information on the suitability of oats in a gluten-free diet, visit the Canadian Celiac Association website at www.celiac.ca. We have included oats in this resource for those people who can and choose to use pure oats. All references to pure oat(s) are marked with an asterisk (*) to remind you that oat(s) is an exception and is not part of the recognized gluten-free flours/products list.

eat it up!
Nutrition Counselling & Consulting

Lisa Diamond, RD and Areli Hermanson, RD
Life is delicious ... eat it up!

LISA'S STORY

When I was first diagnosed with anaphylaxis to wheat in 1994, I refused to believe it, so much so that I challenged the finding, not once, but twice! Needless to say, I ended up in the emergency department both times. Having proved it to myself without a doubt, I was determined to expand my world beyond rice cakes. I tried non-wheat grains such as rye and barley only to discover that I felt really bad after eating them. This led me to eat completely gluten-free.

Since that day, almost two decades ago, I have employed my love of baking, my knowledge of food science and nutrition, some creativity and a good bit of guessing to create nutrient-rich gluten-free recipes from yeast breads to pastry which has fed my family and me deliciously and nutritiously.

As with trying anything new, sometimes I would have great success and other times I would think to myself, *the last time I did this recipe it was great. This time I swear I did basically the same thing and it is a total failure.* This puzzle drove me to analyze the ingredients, the tools, and the techniques that I used to understand "what went right" and "what went wrong". Today I know the ingredient combinations for each product as well as the tools and techniques I need to use to have success every time. I do not even think twice about placing my home baked pastries, cookies, muffins, cakes, snack balls, brownies, waffles, yeast breads, pasta, etc., on the table for all to share. Kids and adults alike devour and love my baking and no one is the wiser that the items are both gluten-free and packed with healthy goodness.

When I look back, I see myself more like the mad scientist than a food scientist - or perhaps an explorer, except I am discovering the secrets of gluten-free baking instead of the West! I think that anyone who has attempted gluten-free baking and has been puzzled by the outcome of their efforts will appreciate the story of my journey, my learning and the revelations I have had along the way.

My Adventure in the World of Gluten-Free Baking ... Mysteries Uncovered

What do instant pudding, play dough, marshmallows, homemade volcanoes, gingerbread house-making and going to the gym have in common? Why, gluten-free baking of course! It's true! During the course of my almost 20-year history of gluten-free baking, these six experiences have expanded the ingredients, enlightened my knowledge and refined the tools and techniques I use to improve my gluten-free baking and cooking.

I started cooking and baking gluten-free in 1994 – in the days when gluten-free options were few and the knowledge about gluten-free was even less. There were some desperate times and some truly horrible products made in my kitchen - but I am tenacious and love good food so I forged on and continued my quest for delicious gluten-free baked goods!

MYSTERY 1: It all started with instant pudding. I was craving a *real* chocolate chip cookie, not one that fell apart, tasted only so-so and left my mouth feeling like it had just been sandpapered. In an effort to do something, I added a package of chocolate instant pudding. The unexpected outcome was a less crumbly cookie that had an improved mouth-feel, and yes, the taste improved, too. Today I know that it was due to the xanthan gum and the starch in the instant pudding mix. The xanthan gum was the glue I needed to hold the cookie together and the starch filled in the spaces between the particles (flour) of ground rice and a better cookie resulted! I think those cookies were one of my first successes back in the early days. That success led me to study the use of starch and xanthan gum as ingredients on their own. Twenty years ago cornstarch was easy to find - xanthan gum on the other hand - not so easy. That is why I continued to use instant pudding in those early days until xanthan gum was more readily available. Although the instant pudding mix provided the starch and xanthan gum I needed, it also contained ingredients I didn't want, namely additives and artificial colours, flavours and a large amount of sugar.

Instant pudding also taught me another important lesson of gluten-free baking: the importance of agitation, or beating. I quickly learned that I could not just stir instant pudding into the milk; I needed to beat it in to achieve the thick glossy "pudding" consistency I was looking for. This is also true when using xanthan gum and some of the other hydrophilic (water-absorbing) binders to maximize their function. You need to beat your product vigorously for at least 1 minute. The best way to do this is to use an electric mixer or electric beaters. They are quick and easy and the results are better than when I use a bowl, mixing spoon and good old-fashioned brute strength.

MYSTERY 2: My journey of learning continued with play dough. Play dough was a big hit in my house and my kids used a lot of play dough. In an effort to have the high volumes of play dough I needed at low cost I made my own. In the process of making play dough, one important technique is to use boiling water and the other is to beat the play dough until it is cool enough to handle and then knead the dough until it is cool and elastic. The boiling water cooks the starches which thicken the dough and improve the dough's elasticity which adds to the dough-like consistency of play dough. The kneading creates non-granular and smooth elastic dough. This inspired me to utilize boiling water in my flat bread and pasta dough, and I even used it for cookie dough that I wanted to roll out and cut into shapes. It worked like a charm. My dough rolled better.

MYSTERY 3: Another "ah-ha" moment came to me one beautiful evening around the campfire. My kids were playing with large marshmallows – squishing them and watching them spring back, stretching them into long strings and so on. What great structure marshmallows have – strong and soft and they cling together. Funny, that was something I had been trying to create in my baked goods, particularly in my yeast breads. I could hardly wait to get home to my kitchen to look at incorporating the science of marshmallows into my gluten-free baking. I did not want to use marshmallows themselves as they would have added more sugar or sweetness than I wanted and so I looked elsewhere: gelatin.

Making marshmallows without sugar (essentially gelatin foam) turned another light on – the use of foams in general: gelatin foam, egg white foam, and methylcellulose foam all provide structure, air and improved texture. They truly created a "wow" difference in my baked goods. The use of these strong structural foams turned my dense crumble-apart-if-not-toasted bread into an amazing loaf of bread that held together, rose up, was lighter and did not need to be toasted to be palatable.

MYSTERY 4: Homemade volcanoes turned on some more lights for me in my quest for great gluten-free baking. I had not made a volcano in years, but one of my girls brought home a science project and my kids and I started in with enthusiasm. The volcano was beautiful! When it was time to make it erupt, we placed baking soda and dye into the cup positioned inside the volcano and then poured in a vinegar solution. What a thrill! What a mess! Happily, I was explaining the chemical reaction when a light went off – to maximize gas formation in my baking I needed to maximize leavening. Sure, I had played with leavening agents early on, but without the use of hydrophilic binders, protein and protein binders, and foams, my batters were just not strong enough to hold up the rise and my products would fall. With a good structure in place, the gas-producing agents have something to work against – the air pushes up the cell structure and lighter, more desirable texture results. Thinking about air and gas in my baked goods made me re-look at foams. Some foams such as whipped cream, coconut cream or evaporated milk assist by adding air to the baked good. These foams do not help with structure, but do help in adding air. Similarly, carbonated drinks help by adding gas to baked goods. An example of this is the "cola-cake". So, I took yet another look at my recipes through a new lens, one that would maximize air and gas production in my baked goods. The outcome was really positive.

MYSTERY 5: Every year we make a gingerbread house for Christmas. We really get into it. We create our own design, make the pattern, make the dough, the icing and the candies to decorate it. It is a week-long process at least. During one of the gingerbread house-making seasons, I started thinking about the science of sugar. Sugar or other sweeteners are an important element in gluten-free baking. They add moisture, provide taste, texture, binding, energy and preservation to the baked product. Depending on which sweetener is used – sugar, honey, or syrup – they add differing amounts of liquid, crispness, flavour, browning, and so on because the compositions of the sweeteners are different. And like fats, there is much research about what sweeteners are healthier for human consumption. Regardless of the type, all sources agree that less is best. So using the right sweetener for the job is important. When agave syrup first came onto the market, I tried to make my quinoa flake granola bars with it instead of corn syrup or honey. The result was a soft bar that fell apart. So, on to sweetener experimentation I went. Some are stronger binders than others – corn and cane syrups are stronger binders than honey. Agave syrup and maple syrup have larger amounts of water in them and do not result in crispy baked goods. I discovered that if the water is reduced from the syrup, the syrup thickens and then they have greater capacity to bind. Like hydrophilic binders, sweeteners cannot be exchanged one-for-one for sweetness, for binding, or for moisture content. In revising my recipes, I determined what the role of the sweetener was, what options I had to accomplish that role, and then which of my options was the "best" choice. During this process I was looking at function and health and then went for it using as little as I needed to get a delicious baked good.

MYSTERY 6: After a bit of a hiatus - having small kids and a husband who worked nights will do that - I returned to the gym. My personal trainer was talking to me about the importance of protein in muscle repair and in the building of strong healthy muscles and so on. This inspired me to do a review of my baking and apply the protein theory to my baked goods. The original gluten-free baking "gurus" utilized significant amounts of starches mixed with rice flour for gluten-free flour mixes. Doing so dilutes the protein content of the flours which is detrimental to the product structure.

In the old days when rice flour was really the only readily available gluten-free flour, starch was a must. Today, with a great number of gluten-free flours on the market, starches are not needed in the same way or in the same quantity as before.

Protein is vital to the cellular structure and strength of the baked product. If the baked good does not have enough protein content, there is not enough structure to allow for the product to rise, or the product may rise but the rise will not be maintained. The rise impacts the overall look and texture of the product. It is easy to increase the protein content in gluten-free baking with the number of bean flours and nut/seed flours or meals on the market. Protein powders are also plentiful and can be used. Even old-fashioned skim milk powder works to increase the protein content. Other protein binders such as egg white, gelatin or agar can also be used. I learned quickly that the composition of the protein used will impact the outcome of the baked good (using a defatted protein such as skim milk powder, defatted pumpkin seed protein powder or even cocoa powder works to add strength to the structure whereas fat-containing protein such as nut and seed meals interfere with structure development). In all, my return to the gym made me experiment with different protein sources and teamed with my desire to lower my overall carbohydrate content through the reduction of starch and sugar, I further revised my recipes which led to an improvement in the balance of carbohydrate, protein, and fat in my recipes.

DEMYSTIFYING BINDERS: I have applied other learnings from my life to my gluten-free baking. Being a registered dietitian, I am no stranger to fibre. Psyllium husks are one agent that I have used routinely. When psyllium husks are mixed with -water; the water gels. This creates issues for healthcare staff who try to offer this source of fibre to clients in a way that is palatable. The psyllium dilemma at work inspired me to look deeper into hydrophilic (water absorbing) binders. Hydrophilic binders are ingredients such as xanthan gum, guar gum, methylcellulose, psyllium, chia seeds, and flax seeds. All of these that can be mixed with water to form gels, or that can be added to products to absorb liquid, provide thickening and binding. So, for gluten-free baking, hydrophilic binders have some real benefit. However, in my learnings I have discovered that they are not interchangeable – at least not completely. There are concentrated hydrophilic binders such as methylcellulose and the gums (xanthan, guar gum, and locus bean gum) that do not mix well with water, require agitation for maximum benefit, and are flavourless. This is perfect for items like bread where you require greater quantities of these binders to achieve the desired end product without the impact on taste, texture or gut happiness. Whereas, the fibrous hydrophilic binders such as psyllium husk, chia seed (ground or whole), and flax seed (ground or whole) are required in larger amounts to get the same effect and tend to be weaker in the structure development.

I had a number of successes and failures before I decided to put my food science hat on again to see how much of each binder was required to create the same viscosity or thickness when added to ½ cup of water. I discovered that varying amounts were required to achieve the same degree of viscosity; specifically, it takes ½ tsp xanthan gum or 1 tsp methylcellulose or 1 tbsp psyllium or 3 tbsp ground chia seeds or 8 tbsp ground flax seeds to create the same degree of viscosity when mixed with ½ cup of water. This clarified my understanding of hydrophilic binders and how to utilize and exchange them in my baking.

My final learning on binders came when I questioned some of the teachings I had learned from the past "gurus" of gluten-free baking. I had always based the amount of xanthan gum (hydrophilic binder) used proportional to the amount of flour I was using in my recipe. I think the funniest "ah-ha" moment I had was when it occurred to me to question this recommendation thinking, *why am I basing the volume of my hydrophilic binder on my flour volume and not my liquid volume when xanthan gum is hydrophilic?* I was at a loss. Of course, I should have been basing my volumes of hydrophilic binder on the amount of liquid in my recipe, not on the amount of flour. So, back to my recipes I went. With this adjustment in thinking and technique, I have been able to produce a desirable batter 100 % of the time.

DEMYSTIFYING FAT: As a dietitian I am very familiar with fats – reducing total fat and saturated fats and increasing unsaturated fats while maintaining adequate fat, without too much fat! Fats are also important to the end product of a gluten-free recipe. Fats are not created equal for nutritional health, as well as for end results of your gluten-free baking. Solid fats help maintain stronger structure for more tender and flakier end products, whereas, oils coat the flours and interfere with the binders; thus, creating moister, softer, and heavier baked products. Both can have their advantages depending on what you are making. There are some natural foods that are gifted with high "better" fat content that can be used as fat replacements to enhance the fat quality, create a delicious end product and improve nutrition quality of the baked good. Mashed avocados and super-smooth macadamia nut butter have proven to be very beneficial in dairy-free and gluten-free baking.

THE SECRET OF TIME: I am a working mom and I often feel I need more time in my life to accomplish the things I want to accomplish. Cutting corners to speed up processes can lead to less desirable outcomes some times. I have found this to be true in life, as well as in gluten-free baking. I have learned that taking the time to beat batters or dough that extra minute; allowing the muffins to sit on the counter 15 to 20 minutes before baking to let the leavening agents get into action; letting the dough rise in a warm place so the yeast can do its job, or letting my batter sit for a few minutes to let the hydrophilic binders maximize their thickening capacity makes the difference between an "okay" product and a "wow" product. Quite frankly, if I am making the effort to bake, I am all about the "wow" product. So, planning for time to allow the ingredients to do a good job has become a cardinal rule.

THE NEW
GLUTEN-FREE

Like a modern day food "explorer", discovering the art and science of gluten-free baking has been a bumpy and enlightening journey, one of curiosity, analysis, surprise, puzzlement, discovery, research, knowledge, trial and error, disasters and thankfully, success! It has been a reminder that learning comes from a variety of places and circumstances. If we allow ourselves to be inquisitive we truly can make new discoveries. Being hungry for delicious nutritious gluten-free foods kept my quest alive and today there is little I cannot make to meet my food and nutrition needs and desires. I am glad that I did not give up or settle for the so-so. I hope that you find this guide useful in understanding how to create your own delicious, nutritious gluten-free foods.

SECTION 1

About Gluten-Free Flours and Starches

GLUTEN-FREE
FLOURS AND STARCH

Gluten-free flours and starches rely on each other for their different properties and produce the best results when used together In the right quantities.

Understanding Gluten-Free Flours

Today there are many different flours to choose from. Flours no longer come from just the Grain Products Group. Flours also come from the Meats and Alternatives Group. Flours derived from products found in the Meat and Alternatives Group offers bakers the ability to add additional nutrients, vitamins, and minerals that are not available to the same extent when using flours solely from the Grain Products Group. It has been my experience that all flours work best when used in combination with other flours. Combining flours results in delicious baked goods that have ideal mouth-feel and texture as well as a balanced nutrient content. When combining flours it is important to understand the flour's fundamentals: function (characteristics, use, and taste) and composition (nutrient breakdown). These elements assist in choosing the right flour combinations for your product.

On the pages that follow, the information on flours has been broken down into two different parts. The first part outlines the flour's function and is arranged in groups as such. The flours in these groups can be used interchangeably one-for-one within the same group. The second part provides the flour's vitamin, mineral, and nutrient composition.

CHAPTER 1:
GLUTEN-FREE FLOURS BY FLOUR GROUPS 1 THROUGH 9

FLOUR GROUP 1:
THE FLOURS WITHIN THIS GROUP CAN BE INTERCHANGED 1-FOR-1

FLOUR GROUP 1	**BROWN RICE FLOUR**
CHARACTERISTICS	• Brown rice flour is milled from unpolished brown rice, contains rice bran (the outer layer of the rice kernel) and is higher in nutrients than white rice flour. • Brown rice flour is known for its granular mouth-feel and dry texture. • When 2 tbsp brown rice flour is added to ½ cup water and brought to a boil, it produces a firm and very thick "cereal" that is pudding like in consistency. It is useful to understand what happens to brown rice flour when it is cooked to appreciate how the flour is going to respond in a baked product. • The thick consistency and firm structure produced from brown rice flour is useful for creating stronger structures in baked goods. Rice flour on its own produces a drier product due to its ability to absorb a greater amount of liquid as a result of its high carbohydrate content, leaving your baked product drier in texture.

FLOUR GROUP 1 | BROWN RICE FLOUR

- Brown rice flour is a good flour to add to flour mixes to assist in structure and liquid absorption.
- Add brown rice flour to other flours with lower carbohydrate content and higher protein, fat and fibre content.
- Brown rice flour is missing the "gluey" characteristic of wheat flour. This has to be created by use of binders and "gluey" starches such as tapioca or arrowroot. It is not necessary to use "pudding-like" starches such as potato or corn or sweet rice flour as brown rice flour itself will produce this effect.

TASTE
- Brown rice flour has a mild nutty flavour.
- Brown rice flour takes on the flavour of the other ingredients used.
- Brown rice flour is ideal for those products that need a mildly-flavoured flour to allow the desired flavour, such as vanilla, to come through in the final product.

USE
- Use brown rice flour in combination with flours that are lower in carbohydrate content and higher in protein, fat and fibre content such as quinoa, bean flours, amaranth, coconut flours, and nut/seed flours.
- Brown rice flour can be used in all baked goods, such as: breads, pizza dough, muffins, loaves, cakes, biscuits, pancakes, crêpes, waffles, cookies, pie dough, and pasta.
- Brown rice flour is ideal to add to flour mixes for baked goods including yeast breads, yeast buns, pizza crusts, and other products that have liquids that are water-based and coarse crumb and chewier consistency is desired.

FLAVOUR PAIRING
- Brown rice flour pairs with and is complementary to any flavour and any flour due to its neutral, mild flavour. Useful for mild-flavoured baked items, such as vanilla cake and shortbread cookies.
- Brown rice flour pairs well with all nutrition enhancers such as ground flax, rice bran, nutritional yeast and hemp hearts.

STORAGE
- Due to the fat content in the bran, brown rice flour has a shorter shelf life than white rice flour.
- Purchase brown rice flour in smaller amounts and use while it is fresh.
- Store brown rice flour in glass canning jars with plastic screw-top lids to keep the product fresh for an extended period of time.

FLOUR GROUP 1 | WHITE RICE FLOUR

CHARACTERISTICS

- White rice flour is milled from polished rice, does not contain bran and is far less nutritious than brown rice flour.
- White rice flour is known for its granular mouth-feel and dry texture.
- When 2 tbsp white rice flour is added to ½ cup water and brought to a boil, it produces a firm, very thick "cereal" that is pudding-like in consistency. It is useful to understand what happens to white rice flour when cooked in order to appreciate how the flour responds in a baked product.
    - The firm, thick structure is useful for creating strong structures in baked goods.
    - White rice flour on its own will produce a drier product due to its ability to absorb a greater amount of liquid as a result of its high carbohydrate content, leaving your baked product drier in texture.
- White rice flour is missing the "gluey" characteristic of wheat flour. This has to be created by use of binders and "gluey" starches such as tapioca or arrowroot. Starches that produce a pudding-like consistency, such as potato or corn or sweet rice, are not necessary as white rice flour will produce this effect.

TASTE

- Very mild flavour.
- Does not alter the taste of flavourings used in the recipe.
- Ideal flour to highlight mild flavours like vanilla.

USE

- Can be used as part of a gluten-free flour mix.
- If choosing to use white rice flour, use in the same manner as brown rice flour. See Brown Rice Flour for details.

FLAVOUR PAIRING

- This flour goes with any flavour and any flour (grain, bean, nut or seed) due to its neutral, mild flavour. Useful for mild flavoured baked items such as vanilla cake or shortbread cookies.

STORAGE

- White rice flour has a long shelf life. Store in a glass or plastic airtight jar or metal container in a dry, cool place. Glass canning jars with plastic screw-top lids work well.

NOTES

- There is limited nutritional benefit to using white rice flour. Brown rice flour does not alter the taste or the texture of the product and is the preferred flour of the two for its nutritional benefits. The New Gluten-Free™ does not incorporate white rice flour in its recipes for this reason.

FLOUR GROUP 1 | BUCKWHEAT FLOUR

CHARACTERISTICS

- Buckwheat is not related to wheat, but to rhubarb and sorrel.
- Buckwheat is darker-coloured flour made up of a beige base with dark flecks.
- When 2 tbsp buckwheat flour is added to ½ cup water and brought to a boil, it produces a very thick, sticky and dense "cereal". It is useful to understand what happens to buckwheat flour when it is cooked to appreciate how the flour responds in a baked product.
    - The firm, thick structure is useful for creating strong structures in baked goods.
    - Buckwheat flour on its own will produce a dense, dry product because it absorbs liquid well due to the amount and type of carbohydrate in the flour.
    - It is a good flour to add to flour mixes to assist in structure and liquid absorption. It needs to be added to flours lower in carbohydrate content and higher in protein, fat and fibre content.
- Buckwheat flour has a sticky quality but is missing the "gluey" texture of wheat flour. This has to be created with the use of binders and "gluey" starches such as tapioca and arrowroot.

TASTE

- Buckwheat has a strong flavour that is slightly bitter, similar to darkly toasted bread with a hint of earthiness.

USE

- Combine buckwheat with flours that are lower in carbohydrate content and higher in protein, fat and fibre content such as quinoa, bean flours, amaranth, and nuts/seed flours.
- It is also wise to combine buckwheat with lighter flours such as sorghum flour, fonio flour, teff flour, and millet flours. Buckwheat works well with rice bran, brown rice flakes, pure oat* products, flax seeds, hemp hearts, and other nutrition enhancers to create a hearty end product.
- Buckwheat can be used in all baked goods such as breads, muffins, loaves, cakes, biscuits, pancakes, crêpes, waffles, cookies, pie dough, and pasta.
- Buckwheat is an ideal flour for use in pancakes, mock bran muffins or mock rye products and other hearty items such as German black bread.

FLAVOUR PAIRING

- Buckwheat pairs well with brown rice flour, corn flour/meal, sorghum flour, teff flour, fonio flour, black bean flour, white bean flour, whole bean flour, garfava bean flour, oat* flour/flake/bran, millet flour, quinoa flour/flake and nut/seed flours.

- Buckwheat pairs well with and is complementary to flavours including chocolate, coffee, molasses, spices, maple, and brown sugar.
- Buckwheat pairs well with nutrition enhancements such as flax seed, rice bran, oat bran, hemp hearts, and many protein powders.
- Buckwheat's strong flavour clashes with and overpowers flavours like citrus, cheese, and peanut.

STORAGE

- Buckwheat has a good shelf life. Buy in smaller amounts and store in an airtight container in a dry, cool place. Glass canning jars with plastic screw-top lids work well.

FLOUR GROUP 1 | CORN FLOUR

CHARACTERISTICS

- Corn flour is a yellow flour milled from corn.
- When 2 tbsp corn flour is added to ½ cup water and brought to a boil it produces a very thick and sticky "cereal" with a dense consistency. It is useful to understand what happens to corn flour when it is cooked to appreciate how the flour is going to respond in a baked product.
    - The firm, thick structure is useful for creating stronger structures in baked goods.
    - Corn flour on its own produces a denser, drier product because it absorbs greater amount of liquid due to the higher carbohydrate content and the type of carbohydrate.
    - It is a good flour to add to flour mixes to assist in structure and liquid absorption. Needs to be added to flours that are lower in carbohydrate content and higher in protein, fat and fibre.
- Corn flour has a sticky quality but is missing the "gluey" texture of wheat flour. This has to be created by use of binders and "gluey" starches such as tapioca or arrowroot.

TASTE

- Corn flour has a mild, slightly sweet, corn-like flavour. Takes on other flavours in baked goods.

USE

- Corn flour can be used in all baked goods such as breads, tortilla, muffins, loaves, cakes, biscuits, pancakes, crêpes, waffles, cookies, pie dough, and pasta.
- Corn flour is ideal to add to yeast breads and baked goods desiring a coarse crumb and sturdier structure.

FLAVOUR PAIRING

- Corn flour works well with brown rice flour, sorghum flour, fonio flour, quinoa flour/flakes, millet flour, white bean flour, chickpea flour, lentil flour, garfava flours, tree nut flours, pumpkin seed meal/protein powder, sunflower seed meal, peanut flour.
- Corn flour pairs well with and is complementary to flavours like cheese, onion, pepper, hot pepper or sauces, tomato, avocado, herbs, and garlic.

STORAGE

- Corn flour has a good shelf life. Store in an airtight container in a dry, cool place. Large glass canning jars with plastic screw-top lids work well.

FLOUR GROUP 1 | PURE OAT* FLOUR

REMINDER: Please refer to page xviii for information about oats* and the gluten-free diet.

CHARACTERISTICS

- Pure oat* flour is a fine and granular flour made from steamed, cleaned oat* groats.
- When 2 tbsp oat* flour is added to ½ cup water and brought to a boil, it produces a firm "cereal" with a thick, "gluey" consistency. It is useful to understand what happens to oat flour when it is cooked to appreciate how the flour is going to respond in a baked product.
  - Think of cold oatmeal* to get an understanding of cooked oat* flour. The firm, thick and gluey structure is useful for creating strong structures in baked goods.
  - Oat* flour works best when combined with brown rice flour. On its own, it produces too moist, too heavy and too chewy a product. It is a good flour to add to flour mixes to assist in structure, liquid absorption, and chewiness.
  - It is good to add to flours that are either high or low in carbohydrate content and that can absorb liquid and produce a more pudding-like consistency.
- Oat* flour is one of the grain flours that has a "gluey" consistency (like wheat) and can assist in adding a "chew" factor to the baked good. This allows for a reduction or an elimination of "gluey" starches such as tapioca or arrowroot starch.
  - The addition of "pudding-like" starches such as potato or corn or sweet rice flour adds to the pudding-like consistency which can assist in softening the crumb for items such as cakes and muffins.

TASTE

- Oat* flour has a mild and pleasant, creamy and slightly sweet, nutty taste. Picks up the flavours of the baked product.

USE

- Oat* flour can be used in all baked goods such as breads, muffins, loaves, cakes, biscuits, pancakes, crêpes, waffles, cookies, pie dough, and pasta.
- Oat* flour assists in holding moisture and increasing chewiness. Ideal to add to yeast breads and baked goods when a chewy texture is desired.

FLAVOUR PAIRING

- Oat* flour works well with all flours (grain, bean, nut or seed) and all flavours. There are very few flours and flavours that do not work well with oat*.

STORAGE

- Buy oat* flour in smaller amounts and store in an airtight container in a dry, cool place. Glass canning jars with plastic screw-top lids work well.

NOTES

- The Canada Celiac Association recommends that children with celiac disease consume no more than 20-25 grams per day of oat* flour and adults with celiac disease consume no more than 50-70 grams per day. For people choosing to avoid gluten for other reasons, there is no limitation on pure or uncontaminated oat* products. REMINDER: Please refer to page xviii for information about oats*.

FLOUR GROUP 2:
THE FLOURS WITHIN THIS GROUP CAN BE INTERCHANGED 1-FOR-1

FLOUR GROUP 2	SORGHUM FLOUR
CHARACTERISTICS	• Sorghum is also know as "Jowar" and is grey-white with beige overtones in colour. • Sorghum flour is not ground as fine as other flours. Baked goods that contain sorghum flour brown well due to the types of carbohydrate found in sorghum flour. • When 2 tbsp sorghum flour is added to ½ cup water and brought to a boil it produces a thick "cereal" that is pudding-like in consistency. It is useful to understand what happens to sorghum flour when it is cooked to appreciate how the flour is going to respond in a baked product. • Sorghum flour on its own produces a dry product because it absorbs liquid well due to type and amount of carbohydrate in the flour, leaving your baked product drier in texture. It is a good flour to add to flour mixes to assist in structure and liquid absorption. • Sorghum flour is missing the "gluey" characteristic of wheat flour. This has to be created by use of binders and "gluey" starches such as tapioca or arrowroot. The addition of "pudding-like" starches or flours may be useful to enhance the firmness of the pudding consistency and to strengthen the batter.
TASTE	• Sorghum has a nutty, hint-of-sweet flavour. It is very neutral-tasting flour that takes on the flavour(s) of the other recipe ingredients.
USE	• Sorghum flour needs to be added to flours that are lower in carbohydrate content and higher in protein, fat and fibre. • It is good to combine sorghum flour with flours that have greater fluid absorbency and stronger "pudding-like" consistency (e.g. brown rice flour) as well as flours that are lower in carbohydrate content and higher in protein, fat and fibre such as quinoa, bean flours, nuts/seed flours, and amaranth. • For breads and other baked goods requiring a stronger structure, sorghum flour is best mixed with brown rice, corn, buckwheat, or pure oat* flour.

- Sorghum flour can be used in all baked goods such as breads, muffins, loaves, cakes, biscuits, pancakes, crêpes, waffles, cookies, and pie dough.

FLAVOUR PAIRING

- Sorghum flour pairs well with buckwheat flour, brown rice flour, quinoa flour/flakes, teff flour, pure oat* flour/flakes/bran, fonio flour, whole bean, garfava bean flour, white/black bean flour, and nut/seed flours.

- Sorghum pairs well with and is complementary to sweet flavours such as vanilla, chocolate, nut, coconut, seed, spice, molasses, coffee, apple, banana, citrus, pear, and other flavours.

- Sorghum flour adds sweetness to savoury items like onion, cheese and herb which may not be desired; taste is individual.

- Sorghum flour imparts a flavour that may be too distinct when very mild-flavoured flour is desired or required such as in a mild vanilla cake.

STORAGE

- Sorghum flour stores well in an airtight container in a dry, cool place. Glass canning jars with plastic screw-top lids work well.

FLOUR GROUP 2 | TEFF FLOUR

CHARACTERISTICS

- Teff is an ancient, minute grain.
- Teff is grown in India, Ethiopia, and Australia. Because it is so small it contains mostly bran and germ.
- Teff looks more like a poppy seed than a grain and can be used like one, too.
- When 2 tbsp teff flour is added to ½ cup water and brought to a boil it produces a thick "cereal" that is pudding-like in consistency. It is useful to understand what happens to teff flour when it is cooked to appreciate how the flour is going to respond in a baked product.
  - Teff flour on its own produces a drier product because it absorbs greater amounts of liquid due to the higher carbohydrate content leaving your baked product drier in texture. It is a good flour to add to flour mixes to assist in structure and liquid absorption.
  - Teff flour needs to be added to flours that are lower in carbohydrate content and higher in protein, fat and fibre content.
- Teff flour is missing the "gluey" characteristic of wheat flour. This has to be created by use of binders and "gluey" starches such as tapioca or arrowroot. Addition of "pudding-like" starches or flours such as potato, corn or sweet rice may be useful to enhance the firmness of the pudding-like consistency and to enhance the strength of the end product.

TASTE

- Teff has a mild nutty flavour and a slightly molasses-like sweetness. Teff ranges in colour from white to brown; white teff has a chestnut-like taste and the darker grains have a hazelnut-like taste.

USE

- Combine teff flour with flours that have a greater absorbency and produce a stronger "pudding-like" consistency such as brown rice as well as flours that are lower in carbohydrate content and higher in protein, fat and fibre, such as quinoa, bean flours, nut/seed flours, and amaranth flour.
- For breads and other baked goods requiring a stronger structure, teff flour is best mixed with brown rice, corn, buckwheat, or oat* flour.
- Use teff flour in breads, muffins, loaves, cakes, biscuits, pancakes, crêpes, waffles, and cookies.

FLAVOUR PAIRING

- The flavour of teff flour pairs well with buckwheat flour, brown rice flour, sorghum flour, amaranth flour, quinoa flour/flakes, pure oat* flour /flakes/bran, fonio flour, whole bean flour, garfava bean flour, white/black bean flour, and nut/seed flours.

- Teff pairs well with and is complementary to vanilla, chocolate, nut, coconut, seed, spice, molasses, coffee, and other flavours.
- Teff clashes with some flavours such as banana, apple, citrus, pear, cheese, onion, and herb.
- Teff dominates the flavour of the flour and may be too distinct a flavour when neutral-flavoured flour is required as is the case with a plain vanilla cake.

STORAGE

- Teff stores well in an airtight container in a dry, cool place. Glass canning jars with plastic screw-top lids work well.

Recipes, Ingredients, Tools, & Techniques

FLOUR GROUP 2 | FONIO FLOUR

CHARACTERISTICS

- Fonio is the oldest African cereal and is a species of millet that is often referred to as "hungry rice".
- Fonio is a beige coloured flour that is easy to digest.
- When 2 tbsp fonio flour is added to ½ cup water and brought to a boil it produces a thick "cereal" with a pudding-like consistency. It is useful to understand what happens to fonio flour when it is cooked to appreciate how the flour responds in a baked product.
  - Fonio flour on its own produces a drier product because it absorbs a greater amount of liquid due to the higher carbohydrate content leaving your baked product drier in texture.
  - It is a good flour to add to flour mixes to assist in structure and liquid absorption.
  - Needs to be added to flours that are lower in carbohydrate content and higher in protein, fat and fibre.
- Fonio flour is missing the "gluey" characteristic of wheat flour. This has to be created by use of binders and "gluey" starches such as tapioca or arrowroot. Addition of "pudding-like" starches such as potato, corn and sweet rice flour may be useful to enhance the firmness of the pudding consistency.

TASTE

- Mild with a slightly nutty flavour. Often referred to as the "best tasting" cereal.

USE

- Good to combine with flours with greater absorbency and stronger pudding-like consistency such as brown rice flour, as well as with flours lower in carbohydrate content and higher in protein, fat and fibre such as quinoa flour, bean flours, nuts/seed flours, and amaranth flour.
- For breads and other baked goods requiring a stronger structure, it is best mixed with brown rice flour, corn flour, buckwheat flour, or oat* flour.
- Use in breads, muffins, loaves, cakes, biscuits, pancakes, crêpes, waffles, and cookies.

FLAVOUR PAIRING

- Fonio flour is very versatile and pairs well with and is complementary to all flours (grain, bean, and nut/seed) and flavours.

STORAGE

- Fonio flour stores well in an airtight container in a dry, cool place. Glass canning jars with plastic screw-top lids work well.

FLOUR GROUP 3:
THE FLOURS WITHIN THIS GROUP CAN BE INTERCHANGED 1-FOR-1

FLOUR GROUP 3	**MILLET FLOUR**

CHARACTERISTICS	• Millet flour is a yellowish, tan-coloured flour milled from a small cereal grain that is closely related to corn.
	• When 2 tbsp millet flour is added to ½ cup water and brought to a boil it produces a moderately thick "cereal" with a custard-like consistency. It is useful to understand what happens to millet flour when it is cooked to appreciate how the flour is going to respond in a baked product.
	    • Even though millet flour has a greater amount of carbohydrate, it does not absorb liquid like other flours with similar carbohydrate content.
	    • Millet flour on its own produces a relatively moist, soft-structured product.
	    • Millet is a good flour to add to flour mixes to assist in moisture and a soft crumb texture.
	    • Add millet flour to flours that have greater liquid absorbency as well as to flours that are lower in carbohydrate content and higher in protein, fat and fibre such as quinoa flour, bean flours, nuts/seed flours, and amaranth flour.
	• Millet is a true "companion" flour as it needs to be paired with flours with both lower carbohydrate and higher carbohydrate content to produce the best results.
	• Cooked millet flour is custard-like in consistency. When the ratio of millet flour to water increases the consistency becomes more "gluey". Depending on how much millet flour is used, and what other flours it is combined with, the addition of a "gluey" starch such as tapioca may be useful.

TASTE	• Millet flour has a slightly nutty aroma and taste. It is a more neutral tasting flour and takes on the flavour of other stronger flavoured ingredients.

Recipes, Ingredients, Tools, & Techniques

USE
- Good to combine millet flour with flours that have greater absorbency and a stronger pudding-like consistency as well as flours lower in carbohydrate, higher in protein, fat and fibre.
- The addition of "pudding-like" starches such as corn or potato, or stronger pudding-like flours such as flours from Flour Group 1 and 2, to millet flour may be useful to enhance the firmness of the batter.
- Use millet flour in breads, muffins, loaves, cakes, biscuits, pancakes, waffles, cookies, pie dough, and pasta.

FLAVOUR PAIRING
- Millet flour pairs well with most other flours such as brown rice flour, corn flour/meal, quinoa flour/flake, pure oat* flour/flake/bran, amaranth flour, nut/seed flours, white bean flour, garfava flour, chickpea flour, and lentil flour.
- Millet flour pairs well with and is complementary to citrus flavours, apple, banana, pear, cranberry, berry, coffee, chocolate, caramel, spices, pumpkin, herbs, onion, bacon, and cheese.
- Millet flour does not clash with many flavours; however, millet flour is not generally paired with teff, black bean or whole bean flours.

STORAGE
- Millet flour stores well in an airtight container in a dry, cool place. Glass canning jars with plastic screw-top lids work well.

FLOUR GROUP 4:
THE FLOURS WITHIN THIS GROUP CAN BE INTERCHANGED 1-FOR-1

FLOUR GROUP 4	QUINOA FLOUR
CHARACTERISTICS	• Quinoa is a grain-like crop grown primarily for its edible seeds. • Quinoa flour is tan coloured. • The dense and heavy texture of quinoa is referred to as truffle-like. • Because quinoa is neither a grain nor part of the grass family, quinoa flour is useful for people on a grain-restricted diet. • Quinoa is not a grain but is in the same family as spinach, Swiss chard and beets. It is in the category of pseudo-cereals and it can be ground into flour. • When 2 tbsp quinoa flour is added to ½ cup water and brought to a boil it produces a soft "cereal" with a pudding-like consistency. It is useful to understand what happens to quinoa flour when it is cooked to appreciate how the flour is going to respond in a baked product. 　• Quinoa flour on its own produces a soft and moist product because it has lower carbohydrate content and absorbs less liquid. The structure resulting from the use of quinoa is not as strong as a product made from flour with higher carbohydrate content. Some baked products leave a "wet" mouth-feel even though the baked good is thoroughly cooked. Quinoa is a good flour to add to flour mixes as it assists in enhancing the moisture content to the baked good. 　• Quinoa flour needs to be added to flours that are higher in carbohydrate content and lower in protein, fat and fibre to develop a flour mix with a better balance of characteristics to create ideal textured baked goods. • Quinoa flour is missing the "gluey" characteristic of wheat flour. This has to be created by use of binders and "gluey" starches such as tapioca or arrowroot. The addition of "pudding-like" starches or flours with higher carbohydrate content such as brown rice may be useful to enhance the firmness of the pudding consistency.

Recipes, Ingredients, Tools, & Techniques

TASTE
- Quinoa flour has a mild, slightly bitter flavour that takes on the flavour of the ingredients in the recipe and imparts a bitter aftertaste in some baked goods.

USE
- It is good to combine quinoa flour with other flours with a greater absorbency and stronger pudding-like consistency that are higher in carbohydrate content, and lower in protein, fat and fibre to improve crumb consistency.
- Use quinoa flour for breads and other baked goods requiring a stronger structure, it is best mixed with brown rice, corn, buckwheat, or oat* flours.
- Use quinoa flour in breads, muffins, loaves, cakes, biscuits, pancakes, waffles, cookies, pastries, and pasta.
- If unable to use bean flour in a recipe, quinoa flour can be used as a substitute 1-for-1.

FLAVOUR PAIRING
- Quinoa flour pairs well with brown rice flour, buckwheat flour, sorghum flour, fonio flour, millet flour, pure oat* flour/flake/bran, amaranth flour, and coconut and nut/seed flours, garfava bean flour, chickpea flour, lentil flour, and white bean flour.
- Quinoa flour pairs well with and is complementary to citrus, apple, banana, pear, cranberry, berry, coffee, chocolate, caramel, spices, pumpkin, herb, onion, and bacon.
- Quinoa flour does not tend to clash with many flavours; however, it is not generally paired with teff, black bean, whole bean flours.
- Quinoa flour may have too distinct a flavour when neutral or mild flavoured flour is desired.

STORAGE
- Buy quinoa flour in smaller amounts and store in airtight container in a dry, cool place. Glass canning jars with plastic screw-top lids work well.

FLOUR GROUP 4	**BLACK BEAN FLOUR**

CHARACTERISTICS	• Black bean flour is made from black turtle beans.
	• Black bean flour is a dark flour that is grey in colour with a hint of purple.
	• When 2 tbsp black bean flour is added to ½ cup water and brought to a boil it produces a "mash" with a pudding-like consistency. It is useful to understand what happens to black bean flour when it is cooked to appreciate how the flour is going to respond in a baked product.
	    • Black bean flour is lower in carbohydrate content and higher in protein and fat so it does not absorb as much liquid or thicken to the extent of some grain flours.
	    • Black bean flour assists in holding moisture and produces a softer crumb and more desirable mouth-feel and texture. Black bean flour also assists in reducing the glycemic index of the flour mix by increasing the protein, fat and fibre content. For all these reasons it is a good flour to add to flour mixes.
	• Black bean flour needs to be added to flours that are higher in carbohydrate content and lower in protein, fat and fibre.
	• Black bean flour is missing the "gluey" characteristic of wheat flour. This has to be created with the use of binders and "gluey" starches such as tapioca and arrowroot. Addition of "pudding-like" starches such as potato, corn and sweet rice flour may be useful to enhance the firmness of the pudding consistency.

TASTE	• Black bean flour has a distinct, yet subtle, black bean taste. • Prior to baking, batters containing black bean flour will have a raw bean flavour that is not appealing. This flavour disappears with baking to an appealing flavour that works well in stronger flavoured baked goods. See Flavour Pairing below.
USE	• Black bean flour can be used in all baked goods such as breads, muffins, loaves, cakes, pancakes, waffles, cookies, snack balls, and bars.
FLAVOUR PAIRING	• Black bean flour combines well with sorghum flour, teff flour, buckwheat flour and pure oat* flour. • Black bean flour pairs well with chocolate, coffee, molasses, cinnamon, cloves, and ginger.
STORAGE	• Buy black bean flour in small quantities and store in an airtight container in a dry, cool place. Large glass canning jars with plastic screw-top lids work well.

Recipes, Ingredients, Tools, & Techniques

FLOUR GROUP 4	WHITE BEAN FLOUR

CHARACTERISTICS	• White bean flour is made from small white beans such as navy bean or lima bean.
	• White bean flour is off-white in colour with a slight grey tone. It is light and powdery in texture.
	• When 2 tbsp white bean flour is added to ½ cup water and brought to a boil it produces a "mash" with a pudding-like consistency. It is useful to understand what happens to white bean flour when it is cooked to appreciate how the flour is going to respond in a baked product.
	    • White bean flour is lower in carbohydrate content and higher in protein and fat so it does not absorb as much liquid or thicken as well as some grain flours. White bean flour assists in holding moisture and produces a softer crumb and more desirable mouth-feel and texture. White bean flour also assists in reducing the glycemic index of the flour mix by increasing the protein, fat and fibre content.
	    • For all these reasons white bean flour is a good flour to add to flour mixes. Bean flours need to be added to flours higher in carbohydrate content and lower in protein, fat and fibre.
	• White bean flour is missing the "gluey" characteristic of wheat flour. This has to be created by use of binders and "gluey" starches such as tapioca and arrowroot. Addition of "pudding-like" starches such as potato, corn or sweet rice flour may be useful to enhance the firmness of the pudding consistency.

TASTE	• Baked in a product, white bean flour has a neutral taste and takes on the flavour of the other ingredients in the baked product. • Prior to baking batters containing white bean flour will have a raw bean flavour that is not appealing. This flavour disappears with baking.
USE	• Use white bean flour as part of a gluten-free flour mix. • Use white bean flour in all baked goods including breads, muffins, loaves, cakes, biscuits, pancakes, crêpes, waffles, cookies, pie dough, and pasta.
FLAVOUR PAIRING	• White bean flour pairs well with and is complementary to all flours and flavours.
STORAGE	• Buy in small amounts and store in an airtight glass container in a dry, cool place. Glass canning jars with plastic screw-top lids work well.

FLOUR GROUP 4 | LENTIL FLOUR

CHARACTERISTICS

- Lentil flour is made from lentils.
- Lentil flour is somewhat greyish-yellow and tan in colour.
- When 2 tbsp lentil flour is added to ½ cup water and brought to a boil it produces a "pudding" that is gluey and gelatinous in consistency. It is useful to understand what happens to lentil flour when it is cooked to appreciate how the flour is going to respond in a baked product.
  - Lentil flour is lower in carbohydrate content and higher in protein and fat content so it does not absorb as much liquid or thicken as well as some grain flours.
  - Lentil flour assists in holding moisture and produces a softer crumb and more desirable mouth-feel and texture.
  - Lentil flour also assists in reducing the glycemic index of the flour mix by increasing the protein, fat and fibre content.
  - For all these reasons lentil flour is a good flour to add to flour mixes. Bean flours need to be added to flours that are higher in carbohydrate content and lower in protein, fat and fibre.
  - Addition of "pudding-like" starches such as potato, corn and sweet rice flour may be useful to enhance the firmness of the pudding consistency.

TASTE

- Lentil flour is a stronger-flavoured flour that works well in savoury products or as an ingredient In products with strong flavours.

USE

- Use lentil flour as part of a gluten-free mix to provide structure in breads, muffins, and cookies.
- Lentil flour can be substituted for other bean flours.

FLAVOUR PAIRING

- Lentil flour pairs well with quinoa flour, millet flour, rice flour, corn flour, and taro flour.
- Lentil flour pairs well with and is complementary to nutritional yeast, cheese, savoury herbs and spices, Eastern or Indian spices, as well as flavours such as peanut, sesame, pumpkin seed, onion, garlic, parsley, and cilantro.

STORAGE

- Follow manufacture's directions. Remove from plastic bags as oils stick to the bag over time.
- Buy in smaller amounts and store in an airtight glass container in a dry, cool place. Glass canning jars with plastic screw-top lids work well.

FLOUR GROUP 4	WHOLE BEAN FLOUR

CHARACTERISTICS	• Whole bean flour is made from the Romano bean (also known as the cranberry bean).
	• Whole bean flour is darker in colour.
	• When 2 tbsp whole bean flour is added to ½ cup water and brought to a boil it produces "mash" that is pudding-like in consistency. It is useful to understand what happens to whole bean flour when it is cooked to appreciate how the flour is going to respond in a baked product.
	   • Whole bean flour is lower in carbohydrate content and higher in protein and fat so it does not absorb as much liquid and does not thicken as well as grain flours.
	   • Whole bean flour assists in holding moisture and producing a softer crumb and more desirable mouth-feel and texture.
	   • Whole bean flour also assists in reducing the glycemic index of the flour mix by increasing the protein, fat and fibre content.
	   • For all these reasons whole bean flour is a good flour to add to flour mixes.
	   • Whole bean flour needs to be added to flours higher in carbohydrate content and lower in protein, fat and fibre.
	• Whole bean flour is missing the "gluey" characteristic of wheat flour. This has to be created by use of binders and "gluey" starches such as tapioca and arrowroot starches. Addition of "pudding" starches such as potato, corn and sweet rice flour may be useful to enhance the firmness of the pudding consistency.

TASTE	• Baked in a product whole bean flour has a neutral taste and takes on the flavour of the baked product. • Prior to baking, batters that contain raw whole bean flour will have a bean flavour that is not appealing. This flavour disappears with baking.
USE	• Use whole bean flour as part of a gluten-free flour mix. • Whole bean flour can be used in all baked goods including breads, muffins, loaves, cakes, pancakes, waffles, cookies, snack balls, and bars.
FLAVOUR PAIRING	• Whole bean flour combines well with sorghum flour, teff flour, buckwheat flour, and pure oat* flour. • Whole bean flour pairs well with and is complementary to chocolate, coffee, molasses, cinnamon, cloves, and ginger spices.
STORAGE	• Whole bean flour has a good shelf life. Buy in small amounts and store in an airtight container in a dry, cool place. Glass canning jars with plastic screw-top lids work well.

FLOUR GROUP 4 | GARFAVA BEAN FLOUR

CHARACTERISTICS

- Garfava bean flour is made from garbanzo and fava beans which are ground and combined into a flour mix.
- Garfava bean flour is light yellow in colour.
- When 2 tbsp garfava bean flour is added to ½ cup water and brought to a boil it produces a "mash" with a pudding-like consistency. It is useful to understand what happens to garfava bean flour when it is cooked to appreciate how the flour is going to respond in a baked product.
  - Garfava bean flour is lower in carbohydrate content and higher in protein and fat so it does not absorb as much liquid or thicken as well as some grain flours. Garfava bean flour assists in holding moisture and producing a softer crumb and more desirable mouth-feel and texture.
  - Garfava bean flour also assists in reducing the glycemic index of the flour mix by increasing the protein, fat and fibre content.
  - For all these reasons garfava bean flour is a good flour to add to flour mixes.
  - Garfava bean flours need to be added to flours higher in carbohydrate content but lower in protein, fat and fibre.
- Garfava bean flour is missing the "gluey" characteristic of wheat flour. This has to be created by use of binders and "gluey" starches such as tapioca and arrowroot. The addition of "pudding-like" starches such as potato, corn and sweet rice flour may be useful to enhance the firmness of the pudding consistency.

TASTE

- Baked in a product garfava bean flour has a mild taste and takes on the flavour of the baked product.
- Prior to baking, batters that contain garfava bean flour will have a raw bean flavour that is not appealing. This flavour disappears with baking.

USE

- Use garfava bean flour as part of a gluten-free flour mix.
- Garfava bean flour can be used in all baked goods such as breads, muffins, loaves, cakes, biscuits, pancakes, crêpes, waffles, cookies, pie dough, and pasta.

FLAVOUR PAIRING

- Garfava bean flour can be used with all flours and all flavours.
- When preparing a mild-flavoured item such as vanilla cake, it is better to use white bean flour instead of garfava bean flour as the garfava bean flour is notable in the final product.

STORAGE

- Garfava bean flour has a good shelf life. Buy in small amounts and store in an airtight glass container in a dry, cool place. Canning jars with plastic screw-top lids work well.

FLOUR GROUP 4	**GARBANZO BEAN (CHICKPEA)**

CHARACTERISTICS	• Garbanzo bean flour is made from ground chickpeas (also called garbanzo beans).
	• Garbanzo beans produce yellow-coloured flour.
	• When 2 tbsp garbanzo bean flour is added to ½ cup water and brought to a boil it produces a "mash" with a thick, gelatinous pudding-like consistency. It is useful to understand what happens to chickpea flour when it is cooked to appreciate how the flour is going to respond in a baked product.
	    • Garbanzo bean flour is lower in carbohydrate content and higher in protein and fat so it does not absorb as much liquid or thicken as well as some grain flours.
	    • Garbanzo bean flour assists in holding moisture and producing a softer crumb and more desirable mouth-feel and texture. Garbanzo bean flour also assists in reducing the glycemic index of the flour mix by increasing the protein and fat and fibre content.
	    • For all these reasons it is a good flour to add to flour mixes.
	    • Garbanzo bean flour needs to be added to flours that are higher in carbohydrate content and lower in protein, fat and fibre content.
	• Garbanzo bean flour is missing the "gluey" characteristic of wheat flour. This has to be created by use of binders and "gluey" starches such as tapioca and arrowroot. Addition of "pudding-like" starches such as potato, corn and sweet rice flour may be useful to enhance the firmness of the pudding consistency.

TASTE	• Baked in a product garbanzo bean flour has a mild taste that is slightly stronger in flavour than garfava bean flour. • Prior to baking, batters that contain garbanzo bean flour will have a raw bean flavour that is not appealing. This flavour disappears with baking as the flour takes on the flavour of the other ingredients in the baked product.
USE	• Garbanzo bean flour can be used in all baked goods such as breads, muffins, loaves, cakes, biscuits, pancakes, crêpes, waffles, cookies, pie dough, and pasta.
FLAVOUR PAIRING	• Garbanzo bean flour pairs well with quinoa flour, millet flour, rice flour, corn flour, and taro flour.

- Garbanzo bean flour pairs well with and is complementary to nutritional yeast, cheese, savoury herbs and spices, Eastern or Indian spices and flavours including peanut, sesame, pumpkin seed, garlic, parsley, cilantro, and onion.

STORAGE

- Follow the manufacture's directions. Remove from plastic bags as oils stick to the bag over time. Buy in small amounts and store in an airtight glass container in a dry, cool place. Glass canning jars with plastic screw-top lids work well.

Recipes, Ingredients, Tools, & Techniques

FLOUR GROUP 4 **FLOUR GROUP 9**	**FULL FAT SOY FLOUR** **DEFATTED SOY FLOUR**
CHARACTERISTICS	• Soy flours are yellow in flour and have a high protein content. Full fat soy flour is also high in fat.
TASTE	• Soy flour has a strong nutty flavour and combines well with other stronger or matched flavours such as fruit, nuts, and chocolate. • Full fat soy flour comes debittered for a more neutral flavour. • Defatted soy flour has had fat removed and has a milder flavour.
USE	• Full fat soy flour is high in protein and fat and low in carbohydrate and fibre as compared with other bean flours. • Defatted soy flour is high in protein and low in carbohydrate and fat. • Note: Full fat soy flour is heavy due to fat content and it needs to be used in smaller amounts (up to 25-30% of your flour mixture). Defatted soy flour can be used in all baked products like other flours in Flour Group 9.
FLAVOUR PAIRING	• Soy flour pairs well with rice flour, corn flour, quinoa flour, and millet flour. • Soy flour pairs well with nutritional yeast, Eastern and Indian spices and strong flavoured items such as coffee, chocolate or nuts including almonds, pecans, walnuts, and peanuts.
STORAGE	• Remove from plastic bags as oils stick to the bag over time. • Full fat soy flour turns rancid quickly due to its high fat content. • Buy smaller amounts; store in an airtight glass container for up to 3 months in the refrigerator or up to 6 months in the freezer. Glass canning jars with plastic screw-top lids work well.

FLOUR GROUP 5:
THE FLOURS WITHIN THIS GROUP CAN BE INTERCHANGED 1-FOR-1

FLOUR GROUP 5	**AMARANTH FLOUR**
CHARACTERISTICS	• Amaranth flour is cream-coloured.
	• Amaranth flour browns well when baked and gives baked goods a beautiful golden colour.
	• Amaranth is not a grain but is in the same family as spinach, Swiss chard and beets. It is in the category of pseudo-cereals and it can be ground into flour.
	• When 2 tbsp amaranth flour is added to ½ cup water and brought to a boil it produces a thin "cereal" with a pudding-like consistency. It is useful to understand what happens to amaranth flour when it is cooked to appreciate how the flour is going to respond in a baked product.
	• Amaranth flour has lower carbohydrate content and it does not absorb liquid as well as other flours with similar carbohydrate content. Because amaranth does not absorb liquid well or thicken, it does not work well in baked products whose moisture is derived from liquids such as water and milk.
	• It is a good flour to add to flour mixes in baked goods where the moisture predominantly comes from fat and/or eggs.
	• Needs to be added to flours that have greater liquid absorbency and thickening ability.
	• Amaranth flour is missing the "gluey" characteristic of wheat flour. This has to be created by use of binders and "gluey" starches such as tapioca or arrowroot.
	• The addition of "pudding-like" starches such as potato, corn and sweet rice flour, to amaranth flour mixes may be useful to enhance the firmness of the pudding consistency.
	• Note: If you use amaranth flour in a baked good that uses liquid for moisture as found in muffins, pancakes, cakes and breads, do not allow more that 10-12 % of your flour mixture to come from amaranth. Greater than that and your baked product does not bake to form a solid "baked" crumb.

TASTE	- Amaranth flour has a nutty and slight earthy taste. In larger amounts it can be slightly sweet.
USE	- It is good to combine amaranth flour with other flours that are higher in carbohydrate content and lower in protein, fat and fibre to improve crumb consistency.
- Amaranth does well in baked goods where the moisture content is fat-based such as in cookies, pastries, granola, and biscuits, as it assists in making shorter, crispier or flakier products.
- Amaranth flour tends to do well in mixtures where the main ingredients are egg white-based foam, sugar, and small amounts of flour. When these batters are baked into a thin sheet cake or biscuit they can be used to create layer cakes such as tortes or even jelly rolls. When making an egg white foam-based cake such as jelly roll or torte, amaranth or any flour can be used exclusively as the egg white is what forms the structure and airiness versus the flour.
- Use amaranth flour in breads, muffins, loaves, cakes, biscuits, pancakes, waffles, cookies, pastries, and pasta.
FLAVOUR PAIRING	Amaranth flour pairs well with buckwheat flour, brown rice flour, sorghum flour, teff flour, fonio flour, quinoa flour/flakes, pure oat* flour/flakes/bran, millet flour, white bean flour, garfava bean flour, chickpea flour, coconut flour, and nut/seed flours.

Amaranth flour pairs wonderfully with and is complementary to flavours such as chocolate, coffee, molasses, spices, maple, brown sugar, honey, and vanilla. Also pairs well with savoury flavours. |
| **STORAGE** | Buy amaranth flour in small amounts and store in an airtight container in a dry, cool place. Glass canning jars with plastic screw-top lids work well. |
| **NOTES** | Amaranth is an excellent thickener for gravies as it does not easily over thicken. |

FLOUR GROUP 6

FLOUR GROUP 6	COCONUT FLOUR
CHARACTERISTICS	• Coconut is actually not a true nut – it is the seed of the palm tree, botanically know as a drupe. Coconut produces cream-coloured flour. It does not respond like other nut flours in that it absorbs liquid "like a sponge".
TASTE	• Coconut flour tastes like coconut: sweet and nutty.
USE	• Can be added to a gluten-free flour mix to increase protein content and add flavour. • Can be used in granola cereals, cookies, pastries, or egg white foam-based cakes including torte. • Coconut flour is best used in recipes with fat or egg-based moisture (as with cookies and torte), not water-based liquid. If you choose to add coconut flour to water-based liquid items such as pancakes, waffles, muffins or cakes, use a very small amount (10% or less of the flour mix) so as not to impact the product's ability to cook. • Coconut flour, like other nut flours, shines in fat-based baked goods. Coconut flour adds flavour and tenderness to pastries and cookies. • Coconut flour does well in homemade granolas. Quantities added are to personal preference.
FLAVOUR PAIRING	• Coconut flour pairs well with rice flour, sorghum flour, fonio flour, teff flour, millet flour, quinoa flour, pure oat* flour, white bean flour, garfava bean flour, whole bean flour, almond flour, and macadamia nut meal. • Coconut flour pairs well with and is complementary to cranberry, banana, pineapple, mango, other tropical fruits and flavours, honey, agave syrup, chocolate, vanilla, cinnamon, cardamom, ginger, curry, and other hot spices.
STORAGE	• Buy or make coconut flour in small quantities and store in an airtight glass container for up to 3 months in the refrigerator or up to 6 months in the freezer. Glass canning jars with plastic screw-top lids work well.

NOTES

TOASTED NUT MEAL: Put a single layer of coconut shreds on a baking sheet and toast at 350°F for 3-4 minutes. Stir frequently. Flakes should be fragrant and light brown when done. Remove from oven and let cool completely. Place into a food processor and process until desired consistency is reached.

- To make finely-ground coconut meal requires a high quality grinder. Regular household grinders generally make coarse meals.

- Commercial coconut flour has been partially-defatted.

FLOUR GROUP 7

FLOUR GROUP 7 | **RICE BRAN**

- Rice bran has not been broken down in detail as it is a component of brown rice flour. However, it is classified in its own group as it absorbs very little liquid so does not need to be counted as part of the dry ingredients when creating your recipe.

FLOUR GROUP 8:
THE FLOURS WITHIN THIS GROUP CAN BE INTER CHANGED 1-FOR-1

Flour Group 8 is made up of nut and seed full-fat flours and meals. Full-fat flours are coarse flour as it is difficult to flour nuts/seeds due to their higher fat content. When the particles get smaller or fine enough for flour the fat leaks out and clings the particles together forming clumps and eventually butter. Almonds are lowest in fat and are the most successful full fat nut flour. For simplicity we refer to all full fat nut and seed flours as "meals". The exception to this is almonds. Almond flour refers to skinned almonds that have been ground into fine flour and almond meal is almonds with skins ground into coarse "flour" or meal.

FLOUR GROUP 8	SUNFLOWER SEED MEAL
CHARACTERISTICS	• Sunflower seed meal is made from raw or roasted sunflower seeds; sunflower seeds make an excellent "nut" meal. Sunflower seeds are truly a seed and are great to use as a replacement for nut flours for people with nut allergies. Defatted sunflower seeds can produce flour. • Sunflower seed meal is low in carbohydrate content and higher in protein and fat so it does not absorb much liquid or thicken like grain or bean flours. Sunflower seed meal can assist in adding protein needed for increasing structure strength. It also adds to the texture, flavour, and mouth-feel of the product. • Sunflower seed meal assists in reducing the carbohydrate content of a baked good as well as in lowering the glycemic index of the flour mix by increasing the protein, fat and fibre content. Seed meals are heavier due to the protein and fat content and can weigh a flour mixture down if used in higher quantities.
TASTE	Sunflower seed meal is fairly neutral in flavour and is mildly sweet and nutty.
USE	• Sunflower seed meal adds weight to baked products. Muffins, cakes, pancakes, and waffles rise better and have a lighter crumb when smaller volumes of seed flours are used.

- Sunflower seed meals tend to do well in mixtures where the main ingredients are egg white-based foam mixed with sugar and a small amount of flour. When this is baked into a thin sheet cake or biscuit, it can be used to create layer cakes such as torte or even jelly roll. With these items, some lighter seed meals can be used exclusively with great success.

- Defatted sunflower seed flours have reduced fat making it easier to incorporate into baking.

- Sunflower seed meals add flavour and tenderness to pastries and cookies.

FLAVOUR PAIRING

- Due to its fairly neutral flavour, sunflower seed meal pairs with all flours and flavours.

STORAGE

- Buy or make sunflower seed meal in small amounts and store in an airtight glass container for up to 3 months in the refrigerator or up to 6 months in the freezer. Glass canning jars with plastic screw-top lids work well.

NOTES

RAW SEED MEAL: Wash seeds thoroughly under running water. Drain seeds and place on a clean tea towel to remove excess water. Dehydrate the nuts in a 170°F oven for about 2 hours. Remove from oven and let cool completely. Place washed/dried seeds into a food processor and process until desired consistency is reached. Be careful not to over process as the seeds turn to butter.

TOASTED SEED MEAL: Put a single layer of dehydrated seeds on a baking sheet and toast at 350°F for 6-8 minutes. Stir frequently. Seeds should be fragrant and light brown when done. Remove from oven and let cool completely. Place into a food processor and process until desired consistency is reached.

- 1 cup of seeds makes about 1 cup of meal.
- To make finely-ground sunflower seed meal takes a high quality grinder. Regular household grinders generally make coarser meal.
- Defatted sunflower seed flours have reduced fat making it easier to substitute in recipes for a portion of the flour mix and can be added to gluten-free flour mixes.

FLOUR GROUP 8 | ALMOND FLOUR AND ALMOND MEAL

CHARACTERISTICS

- Almond flour and meal are made from almonds. To produce almond flour the almonds are blanched to remove the skins and ground into fine flour. Almond meal tends to use the whole almond, including skin, processed into flour. Almond flour is a creamy, off-white colour and almond meal is more beige in colour. Almond flour is the finest flour of all the nut flours and tends to be favoured for use in baked products.

- Almond flour and meal are low in carbohydrate content and higher in protein and fat content so they do not absorb much liquid or thicken like grain or bean flours. Almond flour assists in adding protein needed for increasing structure strength. It also adds to texture, flavour and mouth-feel.

- Almond flour/meal assists in reducing the carbohydrate content of a baked good as well as lowering the glycemic index of the flour mix by increasing the protein, fat and fibre content. Nut flours are heavier due to their protein and fat content and can weigh a flour mixture down if used in higher quantities.

TASTE

- Almond flour/meal is mild in flavour. The almond flavour can be enhanced by toasting the flour or meal prior to baking or if making your own almond flour by toasting the nuts prior to processing.

USE

- Baking to increase the protein content and add flavour. Due to the short shelf-life, almond flour should not be added to flour mixes in advance.

- Almond flour is the most flexible of all the nut flours as it is lower in fat and neutral in flavour and grinds finely. The finer the grind, the lighter the final product will be and the better the crumb. If you are making cakes, a baked item where texture is key, use a fine grind blanched almond flour.

- Almond flour/meal can be used in granola cereals, cookies, pastries, pancakes, waffles, muffins, and cakes.

- Almond flour/meal adds weight to baked products. Muffins, cakes, pancakes, and waffles rise better and have lighter crumb when smaller volumes of nut flours are used. Almond flour is lighter and is more successful in these items.

- Almond flour/meal can be added to a gluten-free flour mix at the time of baking to increase protein content and add flavour. Almond flour/meal tends to do well in mixtures where the main ingredients are egg white-based foam mixed with sugar and a small amount of flour. When this is baked into a thin sheet cake or biscuit, it can be used to create layer cakes, including torte or even jelly roll. With these products some lighter nut flours can be used exclusively with great success.

FLAVOUR PAIRING

- Almond flour/meal adds flavour and shortness to pastries and cookies. If you can find partially-defatted almond flour, it can easily be substituted into recipes for a portion of the flour mix and can be added to gluten-free flour mixes.

- Almond flour is the most versatile nut flour as it is mild in flavour and pairs well with all flavours.

- Almond flour and meal pairs well with rice flour, sorghum flour, teff flour, quinoa flour, millet flour, fonio flour, oat* flour, white bean flour, garfava bean flour, and coconut flour.

- Almond flour/meal pairs with and is complimentary to apple, banana, pear, lemon, honey, agave syrup, vanilla, chocolate, and carob.

STORAGE

- Buy or make almond flour/meal in small amounts and store in an airtight glass container for up to 3 months in the refrigerator or up to 6 months in the freezer. Glass canning jars with plastic screw-top lids work well.

NOTES

RAW NUT MEAL: Blanch almonds by boiling for 10 minutes and then plunging in very cold water. Drain nuts and place on a clean tea towel. Rub the skins off the nuts. Remove the nuts leaving the skins on the towel. Dehydrate the nuts in a 170°F oven for about 2 hours. Remove from oven and let cool completely. Place raw nuts into a food processor and process until desired consistency is reached.

TOASTED NUT MEAL: Put a single layer of dehydrated nuts on a baking sheet and toast at 350°F for 6-8 minutes. Stir frequently. Nuts should be fragrant and light brown when done. Remove from oven and let cool completely. Place into a food processor and process until desired consistency is reached.

- To produce finely-ground almond flour requires a high quality grinder. Regular household grinders generally produce nut meal.

FLOUR GROUP 8 | PECAN MEAL

CHARACTERISTICS

- Pecan "flour" is made from high quality pecans that have been ground into fine flour-like meal. Pecan meal is the bits left in the grinder which is then ground into finer meal. Pecan meal is darker in colour and drier than pecan flour.

- Pecan meal is low in carbohydrate content and higher in protein and fat so it does not absorb much liquid or thicken like grain or bean flours. Pecan meal can assist in adding protein content. It also adds texture, flavour and mouth-feel to the final product

- Pecan meal assists in reducing the carbohydrate content of a baked good as well as lowering the glycemic index of the flour mix by increasing the protein, fat and fibre content. Pecan meal is heavier due to the protein and fat content and can weigh a flour mixture down if used in higher quantities.

TASTE

- Pecan meal has a distinct pecan flavour. The flavour can be enhanced by toasting the flour or by toasting the pecans prior to making pecan meal at home.

USE

- Pecan meal can be added to a gluten-free flour mix at the time of baking to increase the protein content and add flavour. Due to the short shelf life, pecan meal should not be added to flour mixes in advance.

- Pecan meal can be used in granola cereals, cookies, pastries, pancakes, waffles, muffins, and cakes.

- Pecan meal adds weight to baked products. Items such as muffins, cakes, pancakes, and waffles rise better and have a lighter crumb when smaller volumes of nut meals are used.

- Pecan meal tends to do well in mixtures where the main ingredients are egg white-based foam mixed with sugar and a small amount of flour. When this is baked into a thin sheet cake or biscuit it can be used to create layer cakes including torte or even jelly roll. With these items some lighter nut meals can be used exclusively with great success.

- Pecan meals add flavour and tenderness to pastries and cookies.

- If you can find partially-defatted pecan flour, it can easily be substituted into recipes for a portion of the flour mix and can be added to gluten-free flour mixes.

FLAVOUR PAIRING

- Pecan meal goes well with all grain flours, white bean flour, and garfava bean flour.

- Pecan meal pairs with and is complimentary to maple, brown sugar, caramel, banana, apple, pear, berry, pumpkin, yam, and spices including cinnamon, clove, nutmeg, ginger, cardamom, and allspice.

STORAGE

- Buy or make pecan meal in small amounts and store in an airtight glass container for up to 3 months in the refrigerator or up to 6 months in the freezer. Glass canning jars with plastic screw-top lids work well.

NOTES

RAW NUT MEAL: Wash nuts thoroughly under running water. Drain nuts and place on a clean tea towel to remove excess water. Dehydrate the nuts in a 170°F oven for about 2 hours. Remove from oven and let cool completely. Place raw nuts into a food processor and process until desired consistency is reached.

TOASTED NUT MEAL: Put a single layer of dehydrated nuts on a baking sheet and toast at 350°F for 6-8 minutes. Stir frequently. Nuts should be fragrant and light brown in colour when done. Remove from oven and let cool completely. Place into a food processor and process until desired consistency is reached.

- To produce finely ground pecan meal requires a high quality grinder. Regular household grinders generally produce a coarser meal.

FLOUR GROUP 8 | HAZELNUT OR FILBERT MEAL

CHARACTERISTICS

- Hazelnut meal is made from raw hazelnuts. Unlike almonds, the skins are not removed but are ground into meal. The meal tends not to be as fine as almond meal/flour, yet is aromatic and full of flavour.

- Hazelnut meal is low in carbohydrate content and higher in protein and fat so it does not absorb much liquid or thicken like grain or bean flours. Hazelnut meal can assist in adding protein needed for increasing structure strength. It also adds to texture, flavour, and mouth-feel of the product.

- Hazelnut meal assists in reducing the carbohydrate content of a baked good as well as in lowering the glycemic index of the flour mix by increasing the protein, fat and fibre content.

- Hazelnut meal adds weight to a product due to its protein and fat content and can weigh a flour mixture down if used in higher quantities.

TASTE

- Hazelnut meal has a distinct, sweet hazelnut flavour. The flavour can be enhanced by toasting the nuts and making your own meal.

USE

- Hazelnut meal can be added to a gluten-free flour mix at the time of baking to increase the protein content and add flavour. Due to the short shelf life, hazelnut meal should not be added to flour mixes in advance.

- Hazelnut meal can be used in granola cereals, cookies, pastries, pancakes, waffles, muffins, cakes, pastry.

- Hazelnut meal adds weight to baked products. Muffins, cakes, pancakes, and waffles rise better and have lighter crumb when smaller amounts of hazelnut meals are used.

- Hazelnut meal tends to do well in mixtures where the main ingredients are egg white-based foam mixed with sugar and a small amount of flour. When this is baked into a thin sheet cake or biscuit it can be used to create layer cakes including torte or even jelly roll. With these items, some lighter nut meals can be used exclusively with great success.

- Hazelnut meals add flavour and tenderness to pastries and cookies.

- If you can find partially-defatted hazelnut flour, it can easily be substituted into recipes for a portion of the flour mix and can be added to gluten-free flour mix.

FLAVOUR PAIRING

- Hazelnut meal pairs with and is complimentary to many flavours such as chocolate, vanilla, toffee, caramel, coffee, orange, apple, banana, pumpkin, squash, bacon, as well as garlic, herbs, and spices.

STORAGE

- Buy or make hazelnut meal in small amounts and store in an airtight glass container for up to 3 months in the refrigerator or up to 6 months in the freezer. Glass canning jars with plastic screw-top lids work well.

NOTES

RAW NUT MEAL: Wash nuts thoroughly under running water. Drain nuts and place on a clean tea towel to remove excess water. Dehydrate the nuts in a 170°F oven for about 2 hours. Remove from oven and let cool completely. Place raw nuts into a food processor and process until desired consistency is reached.

TOASTED NUT MEAL: Put a single layer of dehydrated nuts on a baking sheet and toast at 350°F for 6-8 minutes. Stir frequently. Nuts should be fragrant and light brown when done. Remove from oven and let cool completely. Place into a food processor and process until desired consistency is reached.

- To make finely ground hazelnut meal takes a high quality grinder. Regular household grinders generally make coarser hazelnut meal.

FLOUR GROUP 8	**MACADAMIA NUT MEAL OR BUTTER** |око

FLOUR GROUP 8 — MACADAMIA NUT MEAL OR BUTTER

Macadamia nut meal/butter is approximately 77% fat and it makes a better butter substitute than it does a nut meal. However, it can be used successfully in baking where higher fat is desired.

CHARACTERISTICS

- Macadamia nut meal/butter is made from raw or roasted macadamia nuts. Fine grind macadamia nut flour is impossible to achieve due to its high fat content.
- Macadamia nut meal/butter is low in carbohydrate content and higher in protein and fat so it does not absorb much liquid or thicken like grain or bean flours. Macadamia nut meal/butter can adds protein and fat. It also adds to texture, flavour, and mouth-feel of the product.
- Macadamia nut meal/butter assists in reducing the carbohydrate content of a baked good as well as in lowering the glycemic index of the flour mix by increasing the protein, fat, and fibre content.
- Macadamia nut meal/butter is heavy due to its high fat and protein content and will weigh a flour mixture down.

TASTE

- Macadamia nut meal/butter has a neutral "buttery" flavour that is very pleasant.

USE

- Macadamia nut meal/butter cannot be added to a gluten-free flour mix but can be added as an ingredient in the recipe at the time of creation and baking.
- Can be used in granola cereals, cookies, pastries, pancakes, waffles, muffins, cakes and pastry. Because of its rich buttery flavour it tends to enhance the richness of baked products to which it is added.
- Macadamia nut meal adds weight to baked products. It is so high in fat that it is better to use macadamia nut butter as a fat replacement than a flour replacement.

FLAVOUR PAIRING

- Macadamia nut is neutral tasting and pairs well with all flavours - savoury, sweet, spicy or herbed.

STORAGE

- Buy or make macadamia nut meal/butter in small amounts and store in an airtight glass container for up to 3 months in the refrigerator or up to 6 months in the freezer. Glass canning jars with plastic screw-top lids work well.

NOTES

It is very difficult to make macadamia nut flour due to its high fat content. Macadamia nut meal is more successful as the oil clumps together and the finer powder to form a paste or butter.

RAW NUT MEAL/BUTTER: Wash nuts thoroughly under running water. Drain nuts and place on a clean tea towel to remove excess water. Dehydrate the nuts in a 170°F oven for about 2 hours. Remove from oven and let cool completely. Place raw nuts into a food processor and process until desired consistency is reached.

TOASTED NUT MEAL/BUTTER: Put a single layer of dehydrated nuts on a baking sheet and toast at 350°F for 6-8 minutes. Stir frequently. Nuts should be fragrant and light brown when done. Remove from oven and let cool completely. Place into a food processor and process until desired consistency is reached.

FLOUR GROUP 8
FLOUR GROUP 9

WALNUT MEAL
PARTIALLY DEFATTED WALNUT FLOUR

CHARACTERISTICS

- Commercial walnut flour is made after walnuts are pressed to expel the walnut oil. This would be considered defatted nut flour. Defatting nuts assists in making the flour lighter and finer when ground. Homemade walnut "flour" contains all the oil and thus is heavier and more meal-like in consistency.

- Walnut meals are low in carbohydrate content and higher in protein and fat so they do not absorb much liquid or thicken like grain or bean flours. It also adds to texture flavour and mouth-feel. Walnut meal assists in reducing the carbohydrate content of a baked good as well as in lowering the glycemic index of the flour mix by increasing the protein, fat and fibre content.

- Walnut meal is heavier due to its protein and fat content and can weigh a flour mixture down if used in higher quantities.

- Defatted walnut flour can assist in adding protein content needed for increasing structure strength of the baked good. Defatted walnut flour can be used in greater amounts improving product quality and lowering glycemic index.

TASTE

- Walnut meal has a distinct walnut flavour with a bitter aftertaste. You can enhance the walnut flavour by toasting the nuts and making your own meal. Defatted walnut flour has a milder flavour than walnut meal which makes it more versatile.

USE

- Walnut meal can be added to a gluten-free flour mix at the time of baking to increase the protein content and add flavour. Due to the short shelf life, walnut meal should not be added to flour mixes in advance.

- Defatted walnut flour can be added to gluten-free flour mixes in advance.

- Walnut meal and defatted walnut flour can be used in granola cereals, cookies, pastries, pancakes, waffles, muffins, cakes, and pastry.

- Walnut meal adds weight to baked products. Muffins, cakes, pancakes, and waffles rise better and have lighter crumb when smaller volumes of walnut meal is used.

- Walnut meal tends to do well in mixtures where the main ingredients are egg white-based foam mixed with sugar and a small amount of flour. When this is baked into a thin sheet cake or biscuit, it can be used to create layer cakes including torte or even jelly roll. With these items some lighter nut meals can be used exclusively with great success.

- If you can find partially-defatted walnut flour, it can easily be substituted into recipes for a portion of the flour mix and can be added to gluten-free flour mixes.

- Walnut meal/flour adds flavour and shortness to pastries and cookies.

FLAVOUR PAIRING

- Walnut meal has a distinct flavour and is bitter so must be paired with complimentary ingredients. Walnut flour goes well in both savoury and sweet dishes. Defatted walnut flour has a milder flavour hence making pairing with other flavours more possible.

- Walnut meal/flour pairs well with sorghum flour, teff flour, oat* flour, amaranth flour, garfava flour, whole bean flour, and white bean flour.

- Walnut meal/flour pairs well with and is complementary to, cinnamon, cardamom, nutmeg, ginger, cloves, allspice, banana, apple, pear, berries, pumpkin, honey, brown sugar, maple, caramel, onions, garlic, bacon, tomatoes, parsley, herbs, mustard, and cheese.

STORAGE

- Buy or make walnut meal in small amounts and store in an airtight glass container for up to 3 months in the refrigerator or up to 6 months in the freezer. Glass canning jars with plastic screw-top lids work well.

NOTES

RAW NUT MEAL: Wash nuts thoroughly under running water. Drain nuts and place on a clean tea towel to remove excess water. Dehydrate the nuts in a 170°F oven for about 2 hours. Remove from oven and let cool completely. Place raw nuts into a food processor and process until desired consistency is reached.

TOASTED NUT MEAL: Put a single layer of dehydrated nuts on a baking sheet and toast at 350°F for 6-8 minutes. Stir frequently. Nuts should be fragrant and light brown when done. Remove from oven and let cool completely. Place into a food processor and process until desired consistency is reached.

- To make finely ground walnut meal requires a high quality grinder. Regular household grinders generally produce coarser walnut meal.

- **DEFFATTED WALNUT FLOUR:** Can be purchased commercially.
  - If you can find partially-defatted walnut flour, it can easily be substituted into recipes for a portion of the flour mix and can be added to gluten-free flour mixes.

FLOUR GROUP 9:
THE FLOURS WITHIN THIS GROUP CAN BE INTERCHANGED 1-FOR-1

FLOUR GROUP 8 FLOUR GROUP 9	PUMPKIN SEED MEAL DEFATTED PUMPKIN SEED PROTEIN POWDER
CHARACTERISTICS	• Pumpkin seed meal is made from raw or roasted pumpkin seeds. Pumpkin seeds are truly a seed and are great to use as a replacement for nut meals for people with nut allergies. Pumpkin seed meal is greenish in colour and alters the colour of light coloured baked goods if present in large quantities. • Pumpkin seed meal is low in carbohydrate content and higher in protein, fat and fibre and does not absorb as much liquid or thicken like grain or bean flours. Pumpkin seed meal is heavier due to the protein and fat content and weighs down the flour mixture. Pumpkin seed meal adds texture, flavour, and mouth-feel to baked goods. It assists in reducing the carbohydrate content of a baked good as well as in lowering the glycemic index of the flour mix by increasing the protein, fat, and fibre content. • Pumpkin seed protein powder is partially-defatted pumpkin seeds ground into flour often called powder. Pumpkin seed protein powder is defatted pumpkin seed flour. • Pumpkin seed protein powder is high in protein and low in fat making it versatile. It can assist in adding protein needed for adding structure and strength to baked goods.
TASTE	• Pumpkin seed meal as a nutty flavour. Note: Pumpkin seed butter is a great replacement for peanut butter when looking for peanut flavour. • Pumpkin seed protein powder has a more neutral flavour and can be incorporated into more baked items without impacting the flavour of the final product.
USE	• Pumpkin seed meal can be added to a gluten-free flour mix at the time of baking to increase the protein content and add flavour. Due to the short shelf-life, pumpkin seed meal should not be added to flour mixes in advance. This is not true for pumpkin seed protein powder which can be added to gluten-free flour mixes in advance.

- Pumpkin seed meal/protein powder can be used in granola cereals, cookies, pastries, pancakes, waffles, muffins, and cakes.

- Pumpkin seed meal adds weight to baked products. Muffins, cakes, pancakes, and waffles rise better and have a lighter crumb when smaller amounts of pumpkin seed meals are used.

- Pumpkin seed meals tend to do well in mixtures where the main ingredients are egg white-based foam mixed with sugar and a small amount of flour. When this is baked into a thin sheet cake or biscuit, it can be used to create layer cakes including torte or even jelly roll. With these items, some lighter seed meals can be used exclusively with great success.

- Pumpkin seed meals add flavour and tenderness to pastries and cookies.

- Pumpkin seed protein powder is partially-defatted pumpkin seed flour; it is finer and can be added to baked goods like partially-defatted nut flours. Pumpkin seed protein powder tends to make items less heavy because of the lower fat content.

- Partially-defatted pumpkin seed flour can be more easily substituted into recipes for a portion of the flour mix and can be added to gluten-free flour mixes.

FLAVOUR PAIRING

- Pumpkin seed meal/protein powder pairs well with many savoury or sweet items. It does have a nutty flavour that blends well with other flavours.

- Pumpkin seed meal/protein powder pairs well with rice flour, corn flour, oat* flour/flakes/bran, sorghum flour, fonio flour, teff flour, millet flour, quinoa flour/flakes, white bean flour, lentil flour, chickpea flour, garfava bean flour, whole bean flour, and amaranth flour.

- Pumpkin seed meal/protein powder pairs well with and is complimentary to sweet or savoury flavours much like peanuts do with chocolate, vanilla, toffee, caramel, honey, apples, bananas and many other fruits, curry, heat spices, garlic, onions, bacon, and cheese.

STORAGE

- Buy or make pumpkin seed meal in small amounts and store in an airtight glass container for up to 3 months in the refrigerator or up to 6 months in the freezer. Glass canning jars with plastic screw-top lids work well.

NOTES

RAW SEED MEAL: Wash seeds thoroughly under running water. Drain seeds and place on a clean tea towel to remove excess water. Dehydrate the nuts in a 170°F oven for about 2 hours. Remove from oven and let cool completely. Place washed/dried seeds into a food processor and process until desired consistency. Be careful not to over-process as seeds turn to butter.

TOASTED SEED MEAL: Put a single layer of dehydrated seeds on a baking sheet and toast at 350°F for 6-8 minutes. Stir frequently. Seeds should be fragrant and light brown when done. Remove from oven and let cool completely. Place into a food processor and process until desired consistency is reached.

- 1 cup of seeds makes about 1 cup of meal.
- To make finely ground pumpkin seed meal requires a high quality grinder. Regular household grinders generally make coarser pumpkin seed meal.

- **PUMPKIN SEED PROTEIN POWDER:** Can be purchased commercially.

FLOUR GROUP 8
FLOUR GROUP 9

PINE NUT MEAL
DEFATTED PINE NUT FLOUR

CHARACTERISTICS

- Pine nuts are actually a seed and not a nut. Siberian pine nut flour is made after the oil has been expelled, hence, making it partially-defatted seed flour. Pine nut meal is ground raw or roasted pine nut seeds.

- Pine nuts are seeds which makes them a replacement for people with nut allergies.

- Pine nut meal is low in carbohydrate content and higher in protein, fat and fibre and does not absorb as much liquid or thicken like grain or bean flours. Pine nut meal is heavier due to the protein and fat content and weighs down the flour mixture. Pine nut meal adds texture, flavour, and mouth-feel to baked goods. It assists in reducing the carbohydrate content of a baked good as well as in lowering the glycemic index of the flour mix by increasing the protein, fat, and fibre content.

- Pine nut flour is defatted pine nuts.

- Pine nut flour is high in protein and low in fat making it versatile. It can assist in adding protein needed for adding structure and strength to baked goods.

TASTE

- Pine nut flour/meal is mild, nutty, and fairly neutral in flavour.

USE

- Pine nut meal can be added to a gluten-free flour mix at the time of baking to increase the protein content and add flavour. Due to the short shelf-life, pine nut meal should not be added to flour mixes in advance. Defatted pine nut flour can be added in advance.

- Pine nut meal/defatted pine nut flour can be used in granola cereals, cookies, pastries, pancakes, waffles, muffins, and cakes.

- Pine nut meal adds weight to baked products. Muffins, cakes, pancakes, and waffles rise better and have a lighter crumb when a smaller volume of pine nut meal is used.

- Partially-defatted pine nut flour can be more easily substituted into recipes for a portion of the flour mix and can be added to gluten-free flour mixes.

- Pine nut meal adds flavour and shortness to pastries and cookies.

FLAVOUR PAIRING

- Due to its more neutral flavour, pine nut meal/defatted pine nut flour pairs with all flours and flavours.

STORAGE

- Buy or make pine nut meal in small amounts and store in an airtight glass container for up to 3 months in the refrigerator or up to 6 months in the freezer. Glass canning jars with plastic screw-top lids work well.

NOTES

RAW SEED MEAL: Wash seeds thoroughly under running water. Drain seeds and place on a clean tea towel to remove excess water. Dehydrate the nuts in a 170°F oven for about 2 hours. Remove from oven and let cool completely. Place washed/dried seeds into a food processor and process until desired consistency is reached. Be careful not to over process as pine nuts turn to butter.

TOASTED SEED MEAL: Put a single layer of dehydrated seeds on a baking sheet and toast at 350°F for 6-8 minutes. Stir frequently. Seeds should be fragrant and light brown when done. Remove from oven and let cool completely. Place into a food processor and process until desired consistency is reached.

- 1 cup of nuts makes about 1 cup of meal.
- To make finely ground pine nut meal takes a high quality grinder. Regular household grinders generally make coarse pine nut meal.
- **DEFATTED PINE NUT FLOUR:** Can be purchased commercially.

FLOUR GROUP 8	**PEANUT MEAL**
FLOUR GROUP 9	**PARTIALLY-DEFATTED PEANUT FLOUR**

CHARACTERISTICS

- Peanuts are not a true nut. Peanuts belong to the legume family. Peanut flour is made from partially-defatted peanuts whereas ground full fat peanuts make peanut meal. In the manufacturing of both peanut flour and peanut meal the peanuts are ground. To make partially-defatted peanut flour, the ground mixture is pressed to remove the oil and then processed further into flour.

- Peanut meal is low in carbohydrate content and higher in protein, fat and fibre and does not absorb as much liquid or thicken like grain or bean flours. However it does thicken better than other nut and seed meals. Peanut meal is heavier due to the protein and fat content and weighs down the flour mixture. Peanut meal adds texture, flavour, and mouth-feel to baked goods. It assists in reducing the carbohydrate content of a baked good as well as in lowering the glycemic index of the flour mix by increasing the protein, fat, and fibre content.

- Defatted peanut flour is high in protein and low in fat making it versatile. It can be added to baked goods to increase protein content and assists in adding structure and strength to baked goods.

- When placed in water-based liquid, partially-defatted peanut flour absorbs moisture and thickens the liquid. This action can be enhanced by cooking and will continue to thicken over time. Peanut flour absorbs liquid and responds much like cocoa powder because they are not nuts but instead are part of the bean and legume families.

- As with tree nuts, many people have allergies or sensitivities to peanuts.

TASTE

- There is light and dark peanut flour. Light peanut flour is roasted less and has less flavour and aroma than darkly roasted flour which has a stronger flavour and aroma. Partially-defatted peanut flour has a milder flavour.

USE

- Peanut meal can be added to a gluten-free flour mix at the time of baking to increase the protein content and add flavour. Due to the short shelf-life, peanut meal should not be added to flour mixes in advance. Defatted peanut flour can be added to flour mixes in advance.

- Unlike nut and seed flours, defatted peanut flour absorbs moisture. It is not a "sponge" like coconut flour; instead it absorbs liquid similarly to cocoa powder. Defatted peanut flour needs to be counted as part of the flour mix that will absorb liquid. If adding additional defatted peanut flour to recipe (over and above the flour mix), compensate for this addition by increasing the recipe's liquid content slightly.

- Peanut meal/defatted peanut flour can be used in granola cereals, cookies, pastries, pancakes, waffles, muffins, and cakes.

- Peanut meal adds weight to baked items. Muffins, cakes, pancakes, and waffles rise better and have a lighter crumb when smaller amounts of nut/seed meals are used.

- Peanut meals tend to do well in mixtures where the main ingredients are egg white-based foam mixed with sugar and a small amount of flour. When this is baked into a thin sheet cake or biscuit, it can be used to create layer cakes including torte or even jelly roll.

- Peanut meal adds flavour and shortness to pastries and cookies.

- Defatted peanut flour can be generally substituted 1-for-1 with cocoa powder to create new and delicious baked goods.

- Partially-defatted peanut flour can easily be substituted into recipes for a portion of the flour mix and can be added to gluten-free flour mixes.

FLAVOUR PAIRING

- Peanut meal/defatted peanut flour pairs well with rice flour, corn flour, oat* flour/flakes/bran, sorghum flour, fonio flour, teff flour, millet flour, quinoa flour/flakes, white bean flour, lentil flour, chickpea flour, garfava bean flour, whole bean flour, and amaranth flour.

- Peanut meal/defatted peanut flour pairs well with and is complementary to sweet and savoury flavours such as chocolate, vanilla, toffee, caramel, honey, apple, banana and many other fruits, curry, heat spices, garlic, onions, bacon, and cheese.

- Defatted peanut flour has a more neutral flavour lending itself to increased pairing options.

STORAGE

- Buy or make peanut meal in small amounts and store in an airtight glass container for up to 3 months in the refrigerator or up to 6 months in the freezer. Glass canning jars with plastic screw-top lids work well.

NOTES

RAW NUT MEAL: Wash nuts thoroughly under running water. Drain nuts and place on a clean tea towel to remove excess water. Dehydrate the nuts in a 170°F oven for about 2 hours. Remove from oven and let cool completely. Place raw nuts into a food processor and process until desired consistency is reached.

TOASTED NUT MEAL: Put a single layer of dehydrated nuts on a baking sheet and toast at 350°F for 6-8 minutes. Stir frequently. Nuts should be fragrant and light brown when done. Remove from oven and let cool completely. Place into a food processor and process until desired consistency is reached.

- To make finely ground peanut meal takes a high quality grinder. Regular household grinders generally make coarser peanut meal.

- Making peanut flour is impossible to do due to its higher fat content. It is easier to make peanut meal in your home grinder. It is important not to over-process as peanuts turn to peanut butter quickly.

DEFATTED PEANUT FLOUR: Can be purchase commercially.

POWDERED PEANUT BUTTER: Can be purchased commercially.

NOTE: Powdered peanut butter contains added sugar.

FLOUR GROUP 9 | COCOA POWDER

CHARACTERISTICS

- Cocoa powder is partially-defatted bean flour. To make cocoa powder, 80-90% of the cocoa butter fat is removed from the chocolate liquor, producing a cocoa cake which is then processed further into cocoa powder.

- There are two types of cocoa powder: alkalized and non-alkalized. Both are available commercially. Alkalized cocoa powder must be labelled as processed with alkali. Non-alkalized cocoa is simply labelled cocoa or unsweetened cocoa without mention of alkalization.

- Alkalized cocoa powder is known as Dutch Cocoa or European Cocoa. During processing, the crushed cocoa cake is treated with potassium carbonate which increases the pH to neutral/slightly alkaline (pH 7-8), increasing solubility in liquids, enhances the dark colour and smooths the flavour making it less bitter. The dark charcoal colour is characteristic of highly alkalized cocoa powder (think: Oreo® cookies.) The alkalization process reduces antioxidant content of the cocoa powder by approximately one-half. That being said, even alkalized cocoa powder contains a decent amount of antioxidants (more than a glass of red wine.) If using alkalized cocoa powder in baking, you will need to add baking powder, baking soda and an acid back to maximize leavening.

- Non-alkalized cocoa powder is known as Natural or Unsweetened Cocoa and is dark reddish-brown (not charcoal) in colour. Non-alkalized cocoa is acidic (pH 5), bitter and has an intense flavour, does not mixed easily into liquid but thickens liquids. When natural cocoa is combined with baking soda it creates a leavening action during cooking.

- Cocoa powder, like other bean flours, absorbs and thicken liquid. To enhance cocoa flavour, mix cocoa powder with a small amount of boiling water to create a chocolate paste.

TASTE

- Alkalized cocoa has a chocolate-like flavour without being bitter.
- Non-alkalized cocoa is bitter with an intense flavour.

USE

- Cocoa powder can be added to a gluten-free flour mix at the time of baking to increase the protein content and add flavour. Cocoa powder can also be added to flour mixes in advance.

- Cocoa powder can be used in granola cereals, cookies, pastries, pancakes, waffles, muffins, and cakes.

USE	- Unlike nut and seed flours, cocoa powder absorbs moisture. It is not a "sponge" like coconut flour; instead it absorbs liquid similarly to defatted peanut flour. Cocoa powder needs to be counted as part of the flour mix that will absorb liquid. If adding additional cocoa powder to recipe (over and above the flour mix), compensate for this addition by increasing the recipe's liquid content slightly. - Cocoa powder is higher in protein therefore adding strength and structure to baked goods. Cakes made with cocoa powder often have higher fat content to soften crumb. - Cocoa powder can be generally substituted 1-for-1 with defatted peanut flour to create new and delicious baked goods.
FLAVOUR PAIRING	- Cocoa powder pairs well with rice flour, corn flour, oat* flour/flakes/bran, sorghum flour, fonio flour, teff flour, millet flour, quinoa flour/flakes, white bean flour, lentil flour, chickpea flour, garfava bean flour, whole bean flour, and amaranth flour. - Cocoa powder pairs well with and is complementary to sweet and savoury flavours such as vanilla, toffee, caramel, honey, apple, banana, berries and many other fruits, nuts and seeds, heat spices, ginger, cinnamon, cardamom, cloves, nutmeg, and sweet root vegetables and squashes such as pumpkin.
STORAGE	Buy commercially prepared cocoa powder and store as directed.
NOTES	We recommend using high quality, non-alkalized cocoa powder.

SUMMARY TABLE:
CHAPTER 1:

GLUTEN-FREE FLOURS
BY FLOUR GROUP

If you are like us, seeing all of those flours made our heads spin. So, in order to summarize their functions and make sense of the information, we have grouped all of the flours into one of nine groups based on their function in baked goods. All ingredients within a group can be substituted one-for-one.

SUMMARY TABLE:
GLUTEN-FREE FLOURS BY FLOUR GROUP

	FLOUR GROUP 1	FLOUR GROUP 2	FLOUR GROUP 3	FLOUR GROUP 4	FLOUR GROUP 5	FLOUR GROUP 6	FLOUR GROUP 7	FLOUR GROUP 8	FLOUR GROUP 9
FLOURS, MEALS AND BRAN	Brown or white rice flour	Teff flour	Millet flour	Quinoa flour	Amaranth flour	Coconut flour	Rice bran	Almond flour	Cocoa powder
	Corn flour	Sorghum flour		White bean flour				Walnut meal	Defatted peanut flour
	Pure oat* flour	Fonio flour		Black bean flour				Pecan meal	Defatted pumpkin seed flour
	Buckwheat flour	Pure oat-meal*		Garfava bean flour				Macadamia nut meal	Defatted nut and seed flours
		Cornmeal		Chickpea flour				Pumpkin seed meal	
		Teff grain		Lentil flour				Sunflower seed meal	
				Whole bean flour				Pine Nut (seed) meal	
				Pure oat* bran				Hemp seed/hearts	
CONSISTENCY AND THICKNESS WHEN COOKED	Firm pudding	Thick pudding	Pudding	Soft pudding	Runny pudding	Grainy, pablum-like consistency	Thicker liquid	Stays in suspension	Runny pudding
	Thick and sticky	Thick and "smooshy"	Custard-like	Soft "smooshy"	Gravy-like	Soft and "smooshy"	Runny	Does not thicken	Honey-like thickened liquid

FLOUR GROUP 1
(BUCKWHEAT FLOUR, BROWN RICE FLOUR, CORN FLOUR, AND PURE OAT* FLOUR):

- Flour Group 1 is comprised of grain-based flours from the Grain Products group of *Eating Well with Canada's Food Guide* (the Food Guide). Flour Group 1 is a group of flours which are higher in carbohydrate and lower in protein and fat than other flour groups. The fibre content varies within this group.

- Flours from Flour Group 1 are the most absorbent of the flours and have the greatest thickening power when cooked.

- Flours from Flour Group 1 are important when making recipes that are higher in water-based liquids to assist in providing stronger structures and absorbing moisture. This group on its own produces drier products and is best used in combination with flours from other Flour Groups such as Flours Groups 2 and/or 3, and/or 4, with the inclusion of flours from Flour Groups 7, and/or 8, and/or 9.

- Flours from Flour Group 1 are a great addition to any gluten-free flour mix. The volume included depends on what baked good is being produced. Dough that requires more stretch and stronger structures such as those with yeast breads and pizza dough require higher volumes of flours from Flour Group 1. To create flour mixes for muffins, cakes, pancakes, and snack ball batters, consider using a combination of flours to achieve the best result. Include less flour from Flour Group 1 and more from Flour Groups 2 and/or 3 and/or 4. Include flours from Groups 7, 8 and 9 individually or combined to obtain desired crumb and texture. Fat-based dough or batters for cookies, biscuits and pastry need very little, if any, flour from Flour Group 1 and more of Flour Groups 4 and/or 5, with inclusion of flours from Flour Group 6 and/or 7 and/or 8 and/or 9.

- Flours from Flour Group 1 work well with all hydrophilic binders. When making stretchy and strong structured dough as when making yeast breads and pizza dough, concentrated hydrophilic binders that require agitation such as xanthan gum and methylcellulose will create a stronger, chewier end product. Batters for muffins, cakes, and pancakes, work best when flours from Flour Group 1 work in combination with hydrophilic binders (those that require agitation and those that require time – see section on hydrophilic binders).

- Having the right proportion of gluten-free flour mix, fat, liquid and hydrophilic binders is important. Adjusting flour volumes to add thickness and structure, particularly with flours from Flour Group 1, eventually takes away from product quality and will leaves the baked product heavy, dry, and crumbly.

FLOUR GROUP 2
(TEFF FLOUR, SORGHUM FLOUR, FONIO FLOUR, PURE OATMEAL*, AND CORNMEAL) AND TEFF GRAIN:

- Flour Group 2 is comprised of grain-based flours from the Grain Products of the Food Guide. Flour Group 2 is a group of flours which are higher in carbohydrate and lower in protein and fat than flours found in other Flour Groups. The fibre content varies within this group.

- Flours in Flour Group 2 are slightly less absorbent and have slightly less thickening power when cooked than those from Flour Group 1.

- Flours from Flour Group 2 work well in combination with flours from other Flour Groups. Flour Group 2 flours are important when making recipes that are higher in water-based liquids to assist in providing stronger structures and absorbing moisture. This group on its own produces drier products and is best used in combination with other flour groups such as Flour Group 1 and/or 3 and/or 4, with the inclusion of flours from Flour Groups 7 and/or 8 and/or 9.

- Flours from Flour Group 2 are great additions to any gluten-free flour mix. Flour Group 2 flours are in muffins, cakes, pancakes, waffles, scones, snack balls, cookies, bars, and brownie batters. The volume included in the flour mix depends on what baked good is being produced. Dough that requires more stretch and stronger structures as with yeast breads and pizza dough requires higher volumes of Group 1 flours and may include flours from Flour Group 2. If you use Flour Group 2 alone or even in combination with other flours (other than Flour Group 1), it does not produce a yeast bread or pizza dough. Flours from Flour Group 1 are needed to create strength in the structure. Flour Group 2 flours are better designed for the "quick bread" category of baking and works well with flours from Flour Groups 1 and/or 3 and/or 4, with the inclusion of flours from Flour Groups 7 and/or 8 and/or 9. Fat-based dough or batters for biscuits, cookies, and pastry, can have some flour from Flour Group 2 but they require more of Flour Groups 4 and/or 5, with inclusion of flours from Flour Groups 6 and/or 7 and/or 8 and/or 9. Flour Group 1 flours may or may not be included in fat-based batters.

- Flour Group 2 flours work well with all hydrophilic binders. Because Flour Group 2 flours work best when making baked goods from the "quick bread" category, using hydrophilic binders in combination tend to work best (e.g. smaller amounts of those hydrophilic binders that require agitation used in combination with hydrophilic binders that require time to work. See section on hydrophilic binders for more information).

- Having the right proportion of gluten-free flour mix, fat, liquid, and hydrophilic binders is important. Adjusting flour volumes to add thickness and structure eventually takes away from product quality and leaves the final product heavy, dry, and crumbly.

FLOUR GROUP 3
(MILLET FLOUR):

- Currently Flour Group 3 is comprised only of millet flour. Flour Group 3 is grain-based flour from the Grain Products group of the Food Guide. Flour Group 3 is higher in carbohydrate and lower in protein and fat than other flour groups. The fibre content of millet flour is greater than most of the other high-carbohydrate grain flours.

- Of the flours that we have tried, millet flour is in a group of its own. Millet flour is less absorbent than the flours in Flour Groups 1 and 2 and when cooked thickens to a custard-like consistency versus a pudding-like consistency. When the volume of flour to liquid is increased and then cooked to a thickened consistency, millet becomes more "gluey" in nature. This gluey consistency adds stretch and chew factor to a baked product. This attribute makes millet a good flour to add to baked goods when chew and stretch factor is important as with yeast breads, pizza dough, flat breads, and pasta.

Recipes, Ingredients, Tools, & Techniques

- Use flour from Flour Group 3 in baked goods that contain higher amounts of water-based liquid such as with muffins, cakes, and pancakes to add moisture and produce a softer crumb. Millet is a good addition to all gluten-free flour mixes and the volume added depends on the baked product being created. Millet is best used in combination with other flours and not used on its own. Flour Group 3 flour is great to add to Flour Group 1 flours for yeast breads and pizza dough. For muffin, loaf, cake, pancake, waffle, and snack ball batters, Flour Group 3 works well with other flours from Flour Groups 1 and/or 2 and/or 4, with inclusion of flours from Flour Groups 7 and/or 8 and/or 9. Fat-based dough or batters for biscuits, cookies, and pastry can have some flour from Flour Group 3 but needs more flour from Flour Groups 2 and/or 4 and/or 5, with the inclusion of 6 and /or 7 and/or 8 and/or 9. Flour Group 1 flours may or may not be included in fat-based batters.

- Flour Group 3 works well with all hydrophilic binders. Because Flour Group 3 can be added to flour mixes from yeast breads to pastries, it is important to choose the hydrophilic binder that best fits the baked item being created. See section on hydrophilic binders for more information.

- Having the right proportion of gluten-free flour mix, fat, liquid, and hydrophilic binders is important. Adjusting flour volumes to add thickness and structure eventually takes away from product quality and leaves the final product heavy, dry, and crumbly.

FLOUR GROUP 4
(QUINOA FLOUR, WHITE BEAN FLOUR, BLACK BEAN FLOUR, GARFAVA BEAN FLOUR, CHICKPEA FLOUR, LENTIL FLOUR, WHOLE BEAN FLOUR, AND PURE OAT* BRAN):

- Flour Group 4 is made up of some flours from the Meats and Alternatives group of the Food Guide and are lower in carbohydrate and higher in protein. Fat and fibre content varies in this group. Other flours from Flour Group 4 are found in the Grain Products group of the Food Guide. Quinoa is considered a pseudo-cereal as it does not come from the grass family but is generally accepted as part of the Grain Products group. Oat* bran is also part of the Grain Products group.

- Quinoa flour acts more like bean flour than it does grain flour. This makes quinoa useful for people who have intolerance to bean and bean flour or who wish to slowly increase the volume of bean flour in their diet.

- Bean flours are high in fibre which is recommended as part of a healthy diet. However, adding too much fibre, too quickly, can result in abdominal discomfort, gas, bloating, and frequent, soft bowel movements. If gluten-free flour mixes or products contain a significant amount of bean flour, multiple servings of these breads and/or baked products daily may cause discomfort and inconvenient negative side effects which although are not harmful, they are unpleasant. Mixing bean flours with quinoa flour can be the perfect solution when increasing fibre and maintaining gut happiness.

- Flour Group 4 is a group of flours that are even less absorbent and have less thickening power than the first three Flour Groups.

- Flour Group 4 flours are excellent for holding moisture in a product and work best when part of a gluten-free flour mix. Because this group holds moisture, if the ratio of flour to water-based liquid is incorrect, a baked product can become too moist, pasty or pudding-like in consistency when chewed. This creates a mouth-feel and effect that the product is not sufficiently baked even though the product is completely baked. The greater the volume of liquid in the recipe, the greater volume of flours from Flour Group 4 is required to reduce overly wet products. Increasing the volume of flour can lead to heavier, drier and more crumbly end products. The best way to avoid this is to use flours from Flour Group 4 in combination with other Flour Groups in the gluten-free flour mix. Reducing the amount of Group 4 flours and increasing the amount of flours from Flour Groups 1 and/or 2 in combination with Flour Groups 3 and/or 7 and/or 8 and/or 9 produces better results.

- Flour Group 4 works well in dough or batters where the liquid is predominantly fat- and/or egg- (or alternate protein-) based batter. Biscuit, cookie and pastry dough can have some flour from Flour Group 4 but requires more of Flour Groups 2 and/or 3 and/or 5, with inclusion of Flour Groups 6 and/or 7 and/or 8 and/or 9. Flour Group 1 flours may or may not be included in fat-based batters.

- Flour Group 4 flours work well with all hydrophilic binders. When using bean flours, it is helpful to include psyllium husk as part of the hydrophilic binder mix as it is a complementary fibre to the fibre in bean flour when being processed by the gastrointestinal tract. Because Flour Group 4 can be added to flour mixes for everything from yeast breads to pastries, it is important to choose the hydrophilic binder that best fits the baked item being created. See the section on hydrophilic binders for more information.

- Having the right volume of gluten-free flour mix, fat, liquid, and hydrophilic binders is important. Adjusting the flour volumes to add thickness and structure eventually takes away from product quality and leaves the baked product heavy, dry, and crumbly.

FLOUR GROUP 5
(AMARANTH FLOUR):

- Flour Group 5 is made up of only amaranth flour. Amaranth falls in the Grain Products group of the Food Guide. Amaranth is lower in carbohydrate and higher in protein and fat. The fibre content is consistent with other whole grain flours.

- Amaranth is not a grain but is in the same family as spinach, Swiss chard and beets. It is in the category of pseudo-cereals and it can be ground into flour.

- Amaranth flour has a very low absorbency and poor thickening power when cooked, less so than the first four Flour Groups.

- It is not recommended that Flour Group 5 be added to gluten-free flour mixes that are to be used for higher volume water-based liquid batters and dough for yeast breads, muffins, loaves, pancakes, waffles, cakes, and snack balls as it can create an uncooked "gluey" consistency and undesirable crumb. If adding amaranth to baked goods such as those listed above, the volume must be small. For best results, keep the quantity of amaranth flour to 10 % or less by volume. For example, in 100 ml of flour mix, up to 10 ml can be comprised of amaranth flour.

- Amaranth performs superbly as the base for fat-based or egg-based dough or batters such as those used in cookies, pastries, torte, jelly roll, biscuit, and angel food-style cakes. This group also works well for pasta where a wet, chewy texture is desired. In fat-based and/or egg-based dough and batter, amaranth flour can be used exclusively or as part of a flour mix with any other flour from any Flour Group. Using Flour Group 5 as the main base for the gluten-free flour mix leads to desirable end products - cooked pastries turn out golden-brown, short, crisp, and flakey and cookies flatten nicely and turn out golden-brown and crispy. In granola, amaranth bakes golden-brown and crunchy and adds to the quality of granola by clumping into cookie-like pieces when mixed. Note: all of these desirable effects disintegrate when water-based liquids are added in any great volume to Flour Group 5.

- Because Flour Group 5 works best in a fat-based environment, the need for hydrophilic (water-loving) binders is small. Only small amounts of hydrophilic binders are needed in fat-based goods to work with the small amounts of water-based liquid present.

- Having the right proportion of gluten-free flour mix, fat, liquid and hydrophilic binders is important. Adjusting flour volumes to add thickness and structure eventually takes away from the quality of the end product and leaves the baked product heavy, dry and crumbly.

FLOUR GROUP 6
(COCONUT FLOUR):

- Flour Group 6 is comprised of coconut flour. Coconut has been classified as a fruit, nut, and seed but it is most closely matched to the Meats and Alternatives group of the Food Guide in terms of nutrient content. Coconut flour is lower in carbohydrate than grain flours, but it is has the highest level of carbohydrate of all the nut and seed flours. Coconut flour is high in protein and fibre.

- Coconut flour acts like a sponge when combined with water-based liquid. When water is added to coconut flour, the flour soaks up the liquid completely. Coconut flour does not need to be cooked to absorb flour or to thicken.

- It is not recommended that Flour Group 6 be added to gluten-free flour mixes that are to be used for higher volume water-based liquid batters and dough for yeast breads, muffins, loaves, pancakes, waffles, cakes, and snack balls as it creates an uncooked "pablum-like" consistency and undesirable crumb. No matter how long the item is baked or cooked, it does not create a "cooked" consistency crumb.

- If adding coconut flour to baked goods such as those listed above, the volume must be small. For best results, keep the quantity of coconut flour to 10 % or less by volume. For example, in 100 ml of flour mix, up to 10 ml could be comprised of coconut flour.

- Flour Group 6 shines as part of a flour mix used for dough or batters that are fat-based and/or egg-based such as those required for cookies, pastries, tortes, jelly roll, biscuit and angel food-style cakes. In fat and egg-based dough or batters, coconut flour can be used as part of a flour mix with any flour from any other Flour Group. Coconut flour adds flavour, richness, and fibre.

- Because Flour Group 6 works best in a fat-based environment, the need for hydrophilic binders is small. Hydrophilic means works with water. Smaller amounts of hydrophilic binders are needed in fat-based baked goods to work with the small amounts of water-based liquid that is present.

- Having the right proportion of gluten-free flour mix, fat, liquid, and hydrophilic binders is important. Adjusting flour volumes to add thickness and structure eventually takes away from product quality and leaves the baked product heavy, dry, and crumbly.

FLOUR GROUP 7
(RICE BRAN):

- Flour Group 7 is composed of rice bran which is a component of brown rice flour. It is included as Flour Group 7 because when it is added to recipes, it does have an effect on the end product. It can be considered a part of the Grain Products group of Canada's Food Guide and is predominantly composed of fibre.

- Rice bran is a wonderful add-in to all baked goods (yeast bread, quick breads, cookies, biscuits and more) to increase the fibre content of the baked good. Rice bran absorbs liquid, but it is slow and not like other hydrophilic fibres. Rice bran cannot be used as a binding ingredient.

- Rice bran can be added to any gluten-free baked product with minimal texture change. If no texture change is desired, place rice bran in liquid ingredients and let sit until dissolved prior to adding to batter.

FLOUR GROUP 8:
NUT AND SEED MEALS AND "FLOURS" AND HEMP SEEDS/HEARTS. THIS GROUP DOES NOT INCLUDE DEFATTED NUT OR SEED FLOURS.

- Flour Group 8 is comprised of flours that are found in the Meat and Alternatives group of the Food Guide. This group is low in carbohydrate and higher in protein and fat than other flours. The fibre content varies within this group.

- Meals and "flours" in Flour Group 8 do not absorb water and do not thicken when cooked in liquid; instead the liquid becomes cloudy and the nut/seed flour or meal sinks to the bottom of the liquid.

- Meals and "flours" from Flour Group 8 are heavy and add weight to flour mixes with fat, protein, carbohydrate, and fibre. Flour Group 8 is not best used in dough that requires strength and stretch such as yeast breads as they weigh the dough down, reduce rising and weaken the stretch and strength of the dough.

- Increasing protein content is desirable to create stronger dough and batters; however, nut meals contain high fat which weighs down the product. Use defatted nut flour from Flour Group 9 instead.

- Adding nuts and seeds to yeast bread and other dough and batters in whole or chopped form is often the better way to incorporate nuts and seeds into baked goods that are water-based and where rise is desired as is the case with yeast breads, loaves, muffins, and cakes.

- Flour Group 8 flours and meals can be added to flour mixes just before use for items such as loaves, muffins, pancakes, waffles, and snack balls if the quantity is kept in small volumes so as to not compromise leavening and crumb consistency.

- Flour Group 8 flours really shine as part of a flour mix when used for dough or batters that are fat-based and/or egg-based in cookies, pastries, tortes, jelly roll, biscuit and cake. In fat-based and/or egg-based dough or batters, Flour Group 8 can be used exclusively or as part of a flour mix with any of the other flour groups. Flour Group 8 flours add flavour, richness, protein, fat, and fibre.

FLOUR GROUP 9
(UNSWEETENED COCOA POWDER AND PARTIALLY-DEFATTED NUT AND SEED FLOURS):

- Flour Group 9 flours come from the Meats and Alternative group of the Food Guide and are composed primarily of protein.

- Flour Group 9 flours include cocoa powder which comes from the cocoa bean. Cocoa powder is partially-defatted cocoa seed powder. Partially-defatted nut and seed powders/flours act or respond similarly in baked goods. Cocoa powder is higher in carbohydrate and lower in protein than other defatted nut or seed powders/flours. Like coconut flour, cocoa powder is high in fibre.

- Flour Group 9 flours do not require heating to thicken and thicken to a honey-like consistency. This group continues to absorb fluid and thicken over time.

- Flour Group 9 flours make great additions to all baked goods. The added protein benefits the structure of all baked goods and does not interfere with other ingredients such as binders. Flour Group 9 flours add protein to the flour mix and enhance the strength of batters; especially those of yeast bread and quick bread which helps the other ingredients (binders and leaveners) work more effectively. Flour Group 9 flours enhance the nutrient profile of the end product.

- Flour Group 9 flours do add flavour to the end product; however, because the flour has been partially-defatted, the flavour of the nut or seed is reduced, making it less prominent and better able to take on the flavour of the recipe's other ingredients.

- Flour Group 9 flours have a long shelf life and can be added to any flour mixture in advance. The proportion of Flour Group 9 flours used depends on the item being produced. In small quantities all defatted nut and seed powders/flours can be exchanged one-for-one.

NOTE: You may be tempted to exchange defatted nut or seed protein powders with whey protein powder. Whey protein powders do not react the same as Flour Group 9 flours, most notably it dissolves in liquid. If using whey protein powder you will need to add additional gluten-free flours from Flour Groups 4 or 5 in approximately equal quantity.

CHAPTER 2:
STARCHES BY STARCH GROUP

UNDERSTANDING STARCHES

Starches are predominantly carbohydrate, refined carbohydrate. This is generally not a selling feature from a nutrition standpoint.

Starches have some functional benefit in gluten-free baking. When thickened, most gluten-free flours create a pudding-like substance. When wheat flour is thickened it has a "gluey" consistency. This gluey consistency is desirable for creating a chew-factor in the baked goods. This gluey texture is missing from most gluten-free flours and gluten-free bakers look for ingredients to aid in the creation of a gluey texture. Two starches are able to produce a gluey stretch when thickened: tapioca starch and arrowroot starch. These starches assist in creating a gluey texture in gluten-free baking.

Starches start to thicken very quickly in the presence of heat which is a disadvantage when trying to thicken a hot liquid. By diluting the starch in cold liquid first and then stirring it into the hot liquid, lumps and frustration can be avoided. It also can be an advantage. By pouring boiling liquid into dough during beating activates the characteristics of the starch and assists in creating the desired effect in the dough. For example, adding tapioca starch to dough and then pouring boiling water into the dough while beating enhances the stretch factor in the dough; this increases the ease or ability to roll the dough out. This is useful when making pasta, ravioli or tortilla rounds.

When starches are cooked to a thickened state the end product is clear. This is desirable when thickening clear liquids such as fruit juices in fruit sauces.

Another characteristic and functional benefit of starch is that it is very finely ground and can sift in-between the individual grains of flours, making the crumb of the gluten-free baked product less granular and reducing the "sandpaper" mouth-feel of the baked item.

Understanding the characteristics of starches when cooked helps to provide a clear picture of how the starch is going to respond in baking. Despite the functional benefits of starches, more is not better. Knowing the desired effect and then choosing the most powerful starch in the smallest quantity to achieve that effect is preferred.

SUMMARY TABLE:
STARCH AND STARCH-LIKE FLOURS

	GLUEY OR STRETCHY STARCH		PUDDING OR SMOOTH STARCH		
	STARCH GROUP 1	STARCH GROUP 2	STARCH GROUP 3	STARCH GROUP 4	STARCH GROUP 5
STARCH	Tapioca	Arrowroot	Potato	Corn	Sweet rice flour
THICKNESS	Very thick	Thick	Very thick	Thick	Thick
"GLUE FACTOR"	Very gluey	Gluey	"Smooshy" pudding	"Smooshy" pudding	"Smooshy" pudding
TRANSLUCENCY WHEN COOKED	Clear	Clear	Clear	Clear	Cloudy

STARCH GROUP 1: Tapioca starch produces a stronger and gluier consistency than arrowroot starch when mixed in the same volume of liquid and then cooked until thickened. This means that to get the same stretch and "chew" factor for a baked item, less tapioca starch is required. Or if a baked item requires more chew or stretch as is the case with pizza dough or tortilla shells, using slightly more tapioca starch *may* assist in obtaining the desired texture. The addition of tapioca starch is only one component of developing stretch. See Binders and Fats for more details. Since starch is very high in carbohydrate and low in nutrition, using less starch is desirable. This is where tapioca starch shines over arrowroot starch as it can be used in smaller amounts to achieve the desired end result.

STARCH GROUP 2: Arrowroot starch creates a softer stretch and less "chew" factor in baked products. Arrowroot starch may be more desirable in cakes where a soft crumb and low chew is desired and where the addition of starch adds to the lightness or airiness of the end product. Arrowroot starch also thickens before the boiling point. It is good to use this starch if the item being created is not to be heated to boiling.

STARCH GROUP 3: Potato starch is the most concentrated of the clear pudding-like starches. Adding potato starch helps to thicken and add a pudding-like texture to baked goods. Since most flours add a pudding-like consistency, this is not a starch that is needed in most baked goods. Starch is high in carbohydrate and low in nutrition. It is better to add additional flour than to add starch to achieve a pudding-like consistency. That being said, if a lighter flour mix is desired, the use of starch may be suitable. Potato starch may be useful as part of a starch mix if needing a lighter flour mix for feathery-light cakes, or on its own if the gluten-free flour mix is more gluey than pudding-like in character.

STARCH GROUP 4: Cornstarch creates a softer, pudding-like substance than the other starches. Adding cornstarch helps to thicken and add a pudding-like texture to baked goods. Since most flours add pudding-like consistency, cornstarch is not a starch that is needed in most baked goods. Starch is high in carbohydrate and low in nutrition. It is better to add additional flour than to add starch to achieve a pudding-like consistency. Cornstarch may be more desirable in cakes where a soft crumb and low chew is desired and where the addition of starch adds to the lightness or airiness of the end product. When a lighter flour mix is desired, the use of starch may be suitable. Cornstarch may be useful as part of a starch mix if needing a lighter flour mix for feathery-light cakes, or on its own if the gluten-free flour mix is more gluey than pudding-like in character.

STARCH GROUP 5: Sweet rice flour is part of the rice flour family; however, it acts, and can be used, like a starch. As flour, it is lower in nutrition than other gluten-free flours. For these reasons I do not use sweet rice flour as flour. However, it has functional and nutritional benefits as a starch and adds thickness to a batter that is slightly too thin or can be used for rolling out biscuits, cookies, pizza dough, flat breads or pie dough. It adds more texture than a starch but does not dry out the dough like other gluten-free flours. Sweet rice flour thickens to a pudding-like consistency similar to potato starch and cornstarch. When thickened, sweet rice flour remains *trans*lucent. When thickening clear fluids, this may not be desirable. The one benefit of sweet rice flour is that it withstands freezing well. True starches break down when frozen and the liquid runs out of the thickened mass. Sweet rice flour is more stable so thickened fruit and/or sauces can be frozen and defrosted successfully, making sweet rice flour a good thickener in fruit pies. Like all starches, it is best to use sweet rice flour in small amounts.

CHAPTER 3:
NUTRIENT ANALYSIS OF GLUTEN-FREE FLOURS AND STARCHES

CATEGORY 1:
NUTRIENT ANALYSIS GRAPHS

All flours have been analyzed for nutrients, vitamins, and minerals and results have been presented using bar graphs.

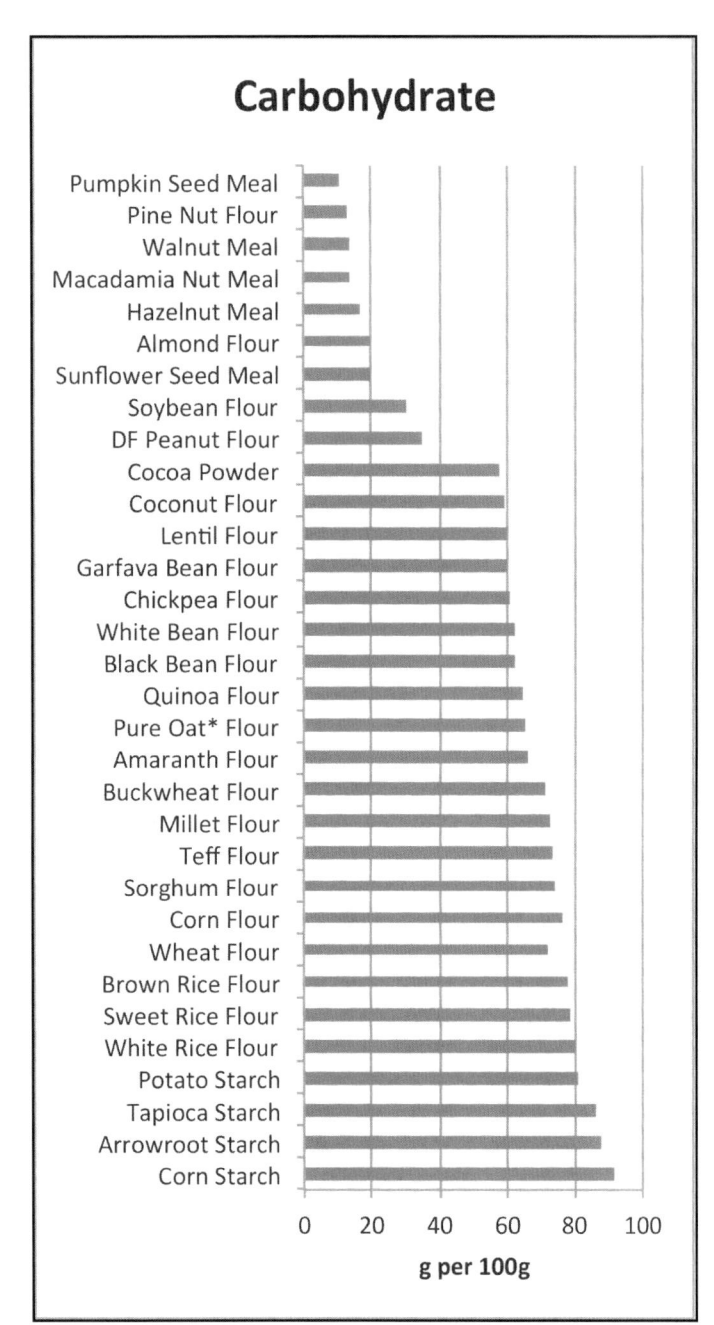

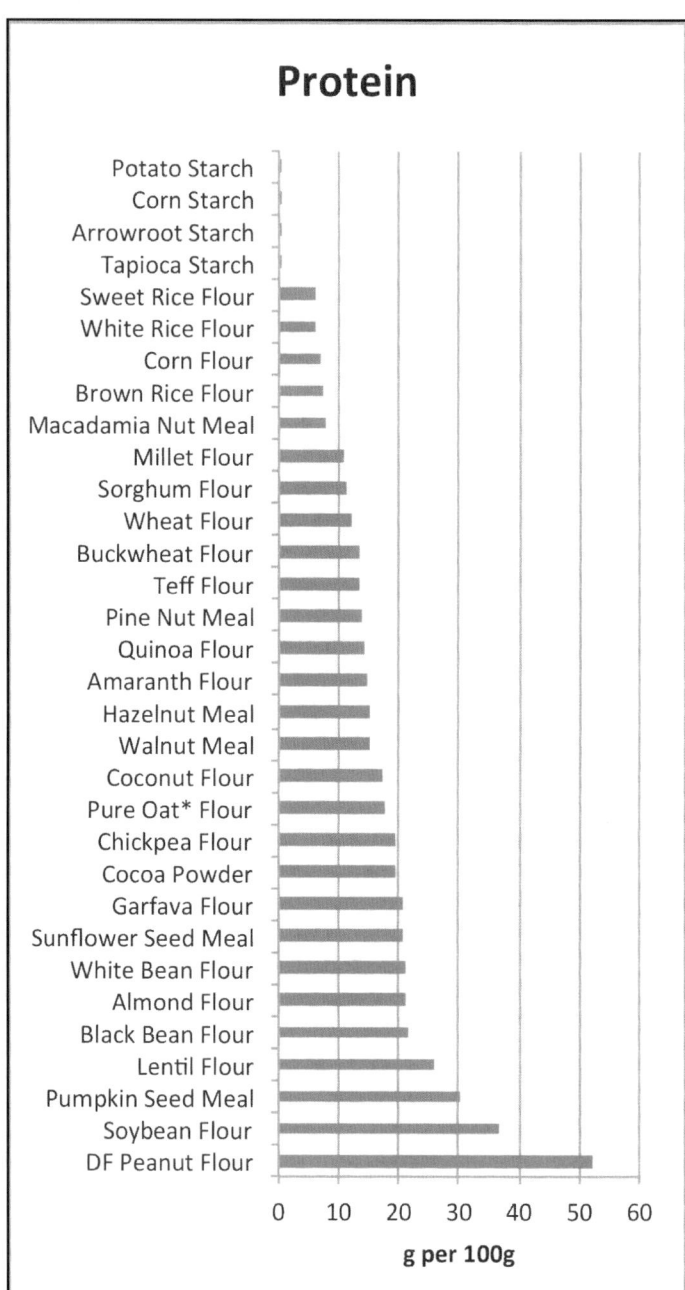

Carbohydrate

Flour/Meal	g per 100g
Pumpkin Seed Meal	
Pine Nut Flour	
Walnut Meal	
Macadamia Nut Meal	
Hazelnut Meal	
Almond Flour	
Sunflower Seed Meal	
Soybean Flour	
DF Peanut Flour	
Cocoa Powder	
Coconut Flour	
Lentil Flour	
Garfava Bean Flour	
Chickpea Flour	
White Bean Flour	
Black Bean Flour	
Quinoa Flour	
Pure Oat* Flour	
Amaranth Flour	
Buckwheat Flour	
Millet Flour	
Teff Flour	
Sorghum Flour	
Corn Flour	
Wheat Flour	
Brown Rice Flour	
Sweet Rice Flour	
White Rice Flour	
Potato Starch	
Tapioca Starch	
Arrowroot Starch	
Corn Starch	

Protein

Flour/Meal	g per 100g
Potato Starch	
Corn Starch	
Arrowroot Starch	
Tapioca Starch	
Sweet Rice Flour	
White Rice Flour	
Corn Flour	
Brown Rice Flour	
Macadamia Nut Meal	
Millet Flour	
Sorghum Flour	
Wheat Flour	
Buckwheat Flour	
Teff Flour	
Pine Nut Meal	
Quinoa Flour	
Amaranth Flour	
Hazelnut Meal	
Walnut Meal	
Coconut Flour	
Pure Oat* Flour	
Chickpea Flour	
Cocoa Powder	
Garfava Flour	
Sunflower Seed Meal	
White Bean Flour	
Almond Flour	
Black Bean Flour	
Lentil Flour	
Pumpkin Seed Meal	
Soybean Flour	
DF Peanut Flour	

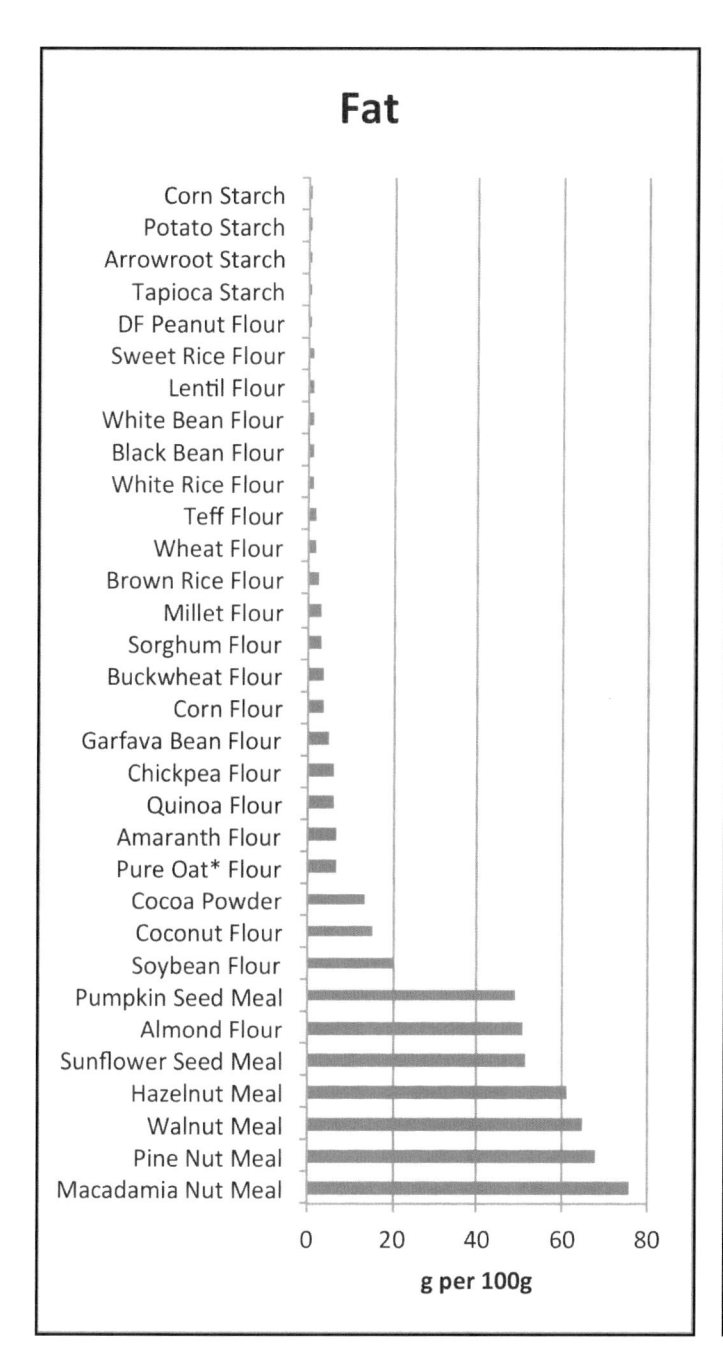

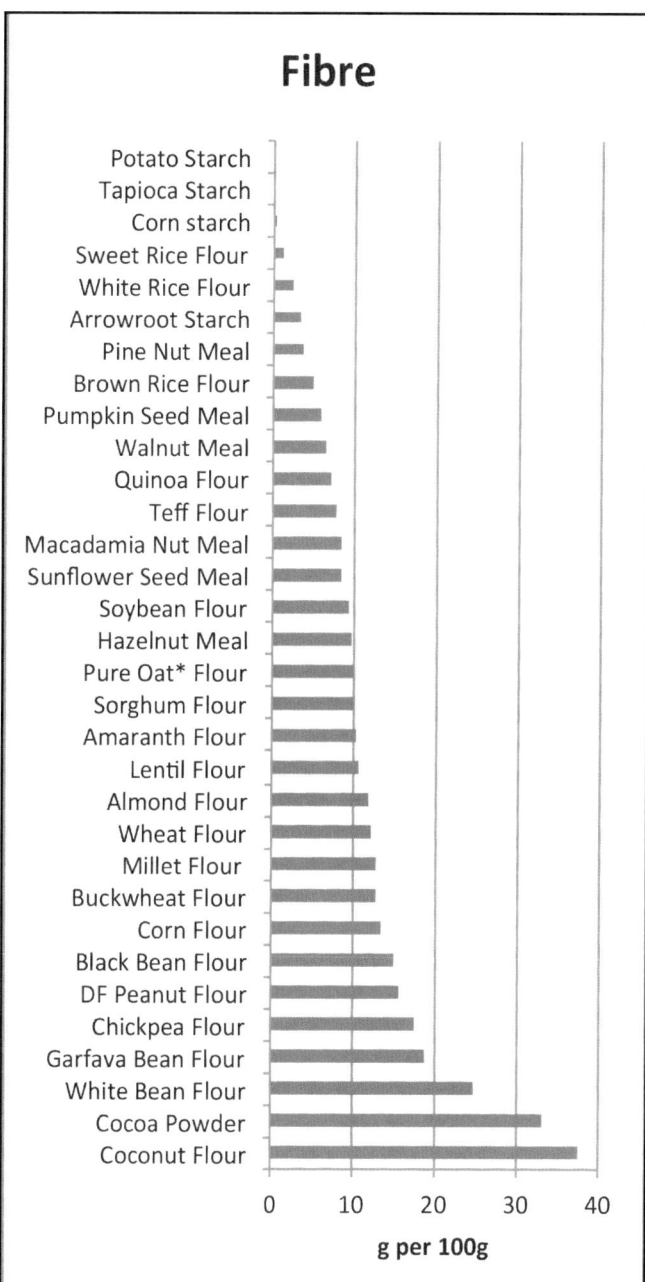

Fat

Flour	g per 100g
Corn Starch	
Potato Starch	
Arrowroot Starch	
Tapioca Starch	
DF Peanut Flour	
Sweet Rice Flour	
Lentil Flour	
White Bean Flour	
Black Bean Flour	
White Rice Flour	
Teff Flour	
Wheat Flour	
Brown Rice Flour	
Millet Flour	
Sorghum Flour	
Buckwheat Flour	
Corn Flour	
Garfava Bean Flour	
Chickpea Flour	
Quinoa Flour	
Amaranth Flour	
Pure Oat* Flour	
Cocoa Powder	
Coconut Flour	
Soybean Flour	
Pumpkin Seed Meal	
Almond Flour	
Sunflower Seed Meal	
Hazelnut Meal	
Walnut Meal	
Pine Nut Meal	
Macadamia Nut Meal	

Fibre

Flour	g per 100g
Potato Starch	
Tapioca Starch	
Corn starch	
Sweet Rice Flour	
White Rice Flour	
Arrowroot Starch	
Pine Nut Meal	
Brown Rice Flour	
Pumpkin Seed Meal	
Walnut Meal	
Quinoa Flour	
Teff Flour	
Macadamia Nut Meal	
Sunflower Seed Meal	
Soybean Flour	
Hazelnut Meal	
Pure Oat* Flour	
Sorghum Flour	
Amaranth Flour	
Lentil Flour	
Almond Flour	
Wheat Flour	
Millet Flour	
Buckwheat Flour	
Corn Flour	
Black Bean Flour	
DF Peanut Flour	
Chickpea Flour	
Garfava Bean Flour	
White Bean Flour	
Cocoa Powder	
Coconut Flour	

Calcium

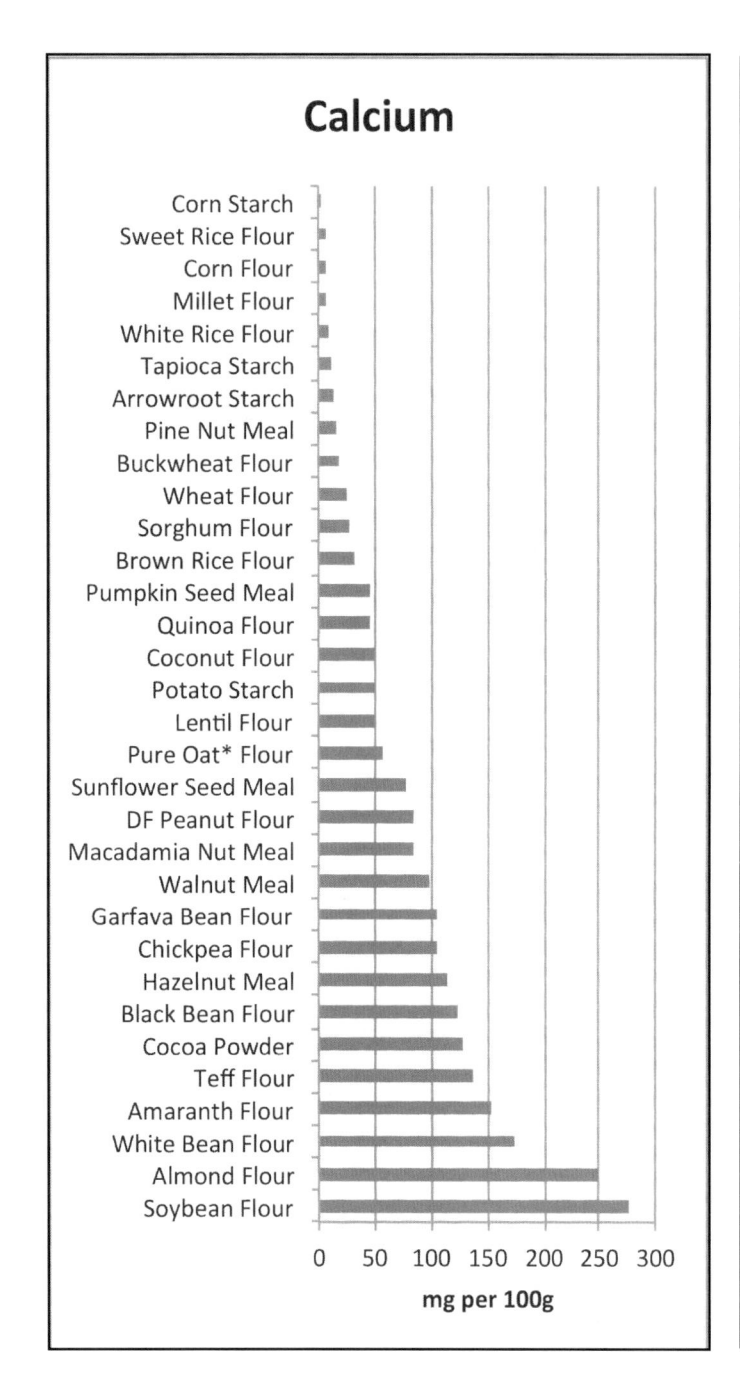

Flour	mg per 100g
Corn Starch	
Sweet Rice Flour	
Corn Flour	
Millet Flour	
White Rice Flour	
Tapioca Starch	
Arrowroot Starch	
Pine Nut Meal	
Buckwheat Flour	
Wheat Flour	
Sorghum Flour	
Brown Rice Flour	
Pumpkin Seed Meal	
Quinoa Flour	
Coconut Flour	
Potato Starch	
Lentil Flour	
Pure Oat* Flour	
Sunflower Seed Meal	
DF Peanut Flour	
Macadamia Nut Meal	
Walnut Meal	
Garfava Bean Flour	
Chickpea Flour	
Hazelnut Meal	
Black Bean Flour	
Cocoa Powder	
Teff Flour	
Amaranth Flour	
White Bean Flour	
Almond Flour	
Soybean Flour	

Chloride

Flour	mg per 100g
White Rice Flour	
White Bean Flour	
Wheat Flour	
Teff Flour	
Tapioca Flour	
Sweet Rice Flour	
Soybean Flour	
Sorghum Flour	
Potato Starch	
Millet Flour	
Lentil Flour	
Garfava Bean Flour	
Corn Flour	
Corn Starch	
Coconut Flour	
Chickpea Flour	
Brown Rice Flour	
Black Bean Flour	
Arrowroot Starch	
Amaranth Flour	
Buckwheat Flour	
Hazelnut Meal	~18
Almond Flour	~18

Copper

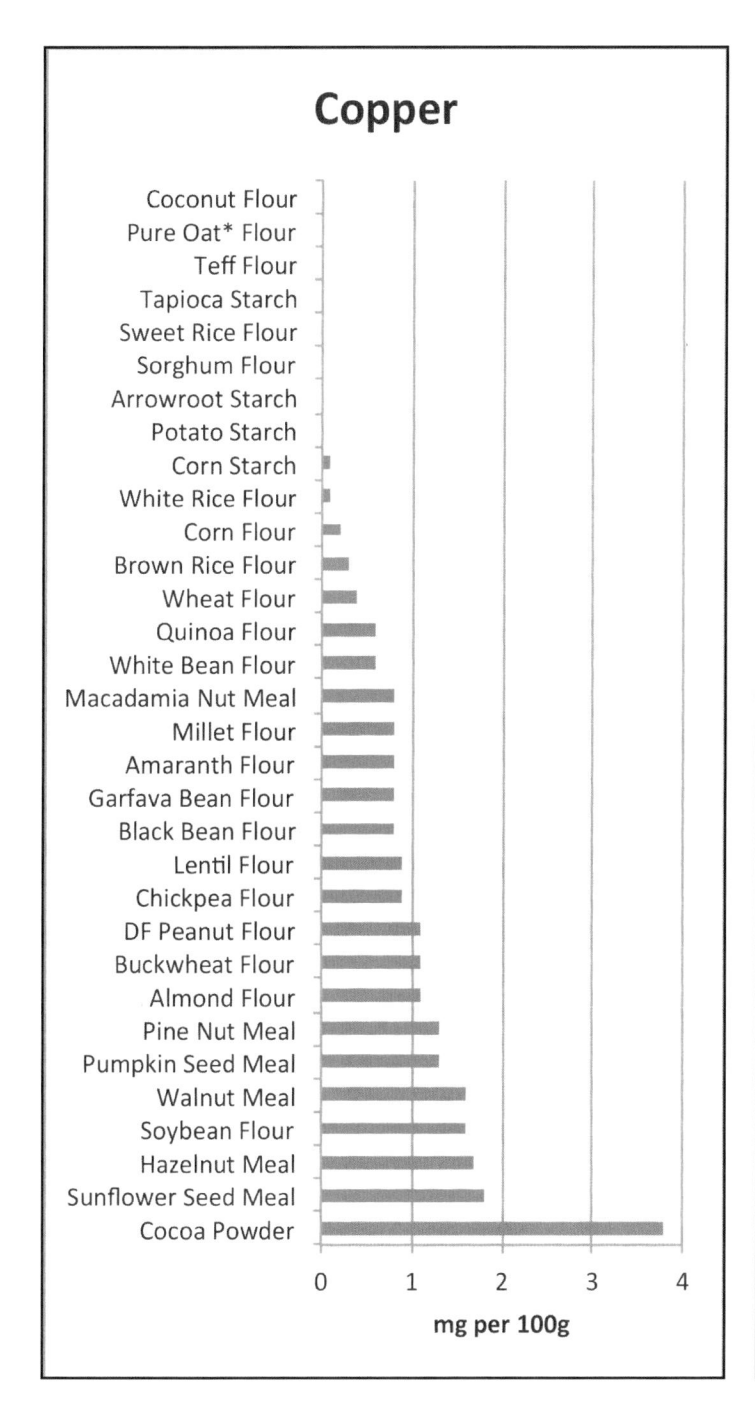

Food	mg per 100g
Coconut Flour	
Pure Oat* Flour	
Teff Flour	
Tapioca Starch	
Sweet Rice Flour	
Sorghum Flour	
Arrowroot Starch	
Potato Starch	
Corn Starch	
White Rice Flour	
Corn Flour	
Brown Rice Flour	
Wheat Flour	
Quinoa Flour	
White Bean Flour	
Macadamia Nut Meal	
Millet Flour	
Amaranth Flour	
Garfava Bean Flour	
Black Bean Flour	
Lentil Flour	
Chickpea Flour	
DF Peanut Flour	
Buckwheat Flour	
Almond Flour	
Pine Nut Meal	
Pumpkin Seed Meal	
Walnut Meal	
Soybean Flour	
Hazelnut Meal	
Sunflower Seed Meal	
Cocoa Powder	

Iodine

Food	mcg per 100g
Coconut Flour	
Soybean Flour	
Wheat Flour	
White Bean Flour	
Teff Flour	
Sweet Rice Flour	
Sorghum Flour	
Potato Starch	
Lentil Flour	
Garfava Bean Flour	
Corn Flour	
Corn Starch	
Chickpea Flour	
Buckwheat Flour	
Brown Rice Flour	
Black Bean Flour	
Arrowroot Starch	
Amaranth Flour	
Pure Oat* Flour	
Tapioca Starch	
White Rice Flour	
Almond Flour	
Millet Flour	
Hazelnut Meal	

Iron

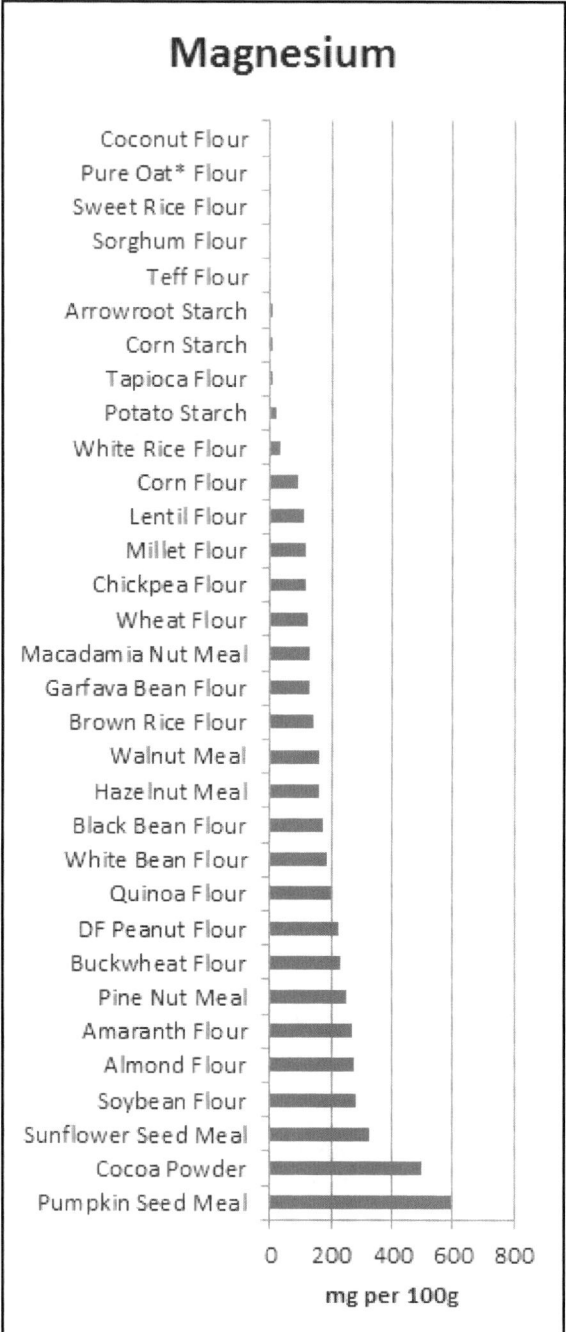

Flour	mg per 100g
Arrowroot Starch	
Sweet Rice Flour	
Potato Starch	
White Rice Flour	
Corn Starch	
Tapioca Starch	
DF Peanut Flour	
Brown Rice Flour	
Buckwheat Flour	
Corn Flour	
Walnut Meal	
Millet Flour	
Wheat Flour	
Macadamia Nut Meal	
Almond Flour	
Sorghum Flour	
Quinoa Flour	
Pure Oat* Flour	
Hazelnut Meal	
Black Bean Flour	
Sunflower Seed Meal	
Pine Nut Meal	
Pumpkin Seed Meal	
Chickpea Flour	
Garfava Bean Flour	
Amaranth Flour	
White Bean Flour	
Lentil Flour	
Coconut Flour	
Cocoa Powder	
Soybean Flour	
Teff Flour	~55

Magnesium

Flour	mg per 100g
Coconut Flour	
Pure Oat* Flour	
Sweet Rice Flour	
Sorghum Flour	
Teff Flour	
Arrowroot Starch	
Corn Starch	
Tapioca Flour	
Potato Starch	
White Rice Flour	
Corn Flour	
Lentil Flour	
Millet Flour	
Chickpea Flour	
Wheat Flour	
Macadamia Nut Meal	
Garfava Bean Flour	
Brown Rice Flour	
Walnut Meal	
Hazelnut Meal	
Black Bean Flour	
White Bean Flour	
Quinoa Flour	
DF Peanut Flour	
Buckwheat Flour	
Pine Nut Meal	
Amaranth Flour	
Almond Flour	
Soybean Flour	
Sunflower Seed Meal	
Cocoa Powder	
Pumpkin Seed Meal	~600

Manganese

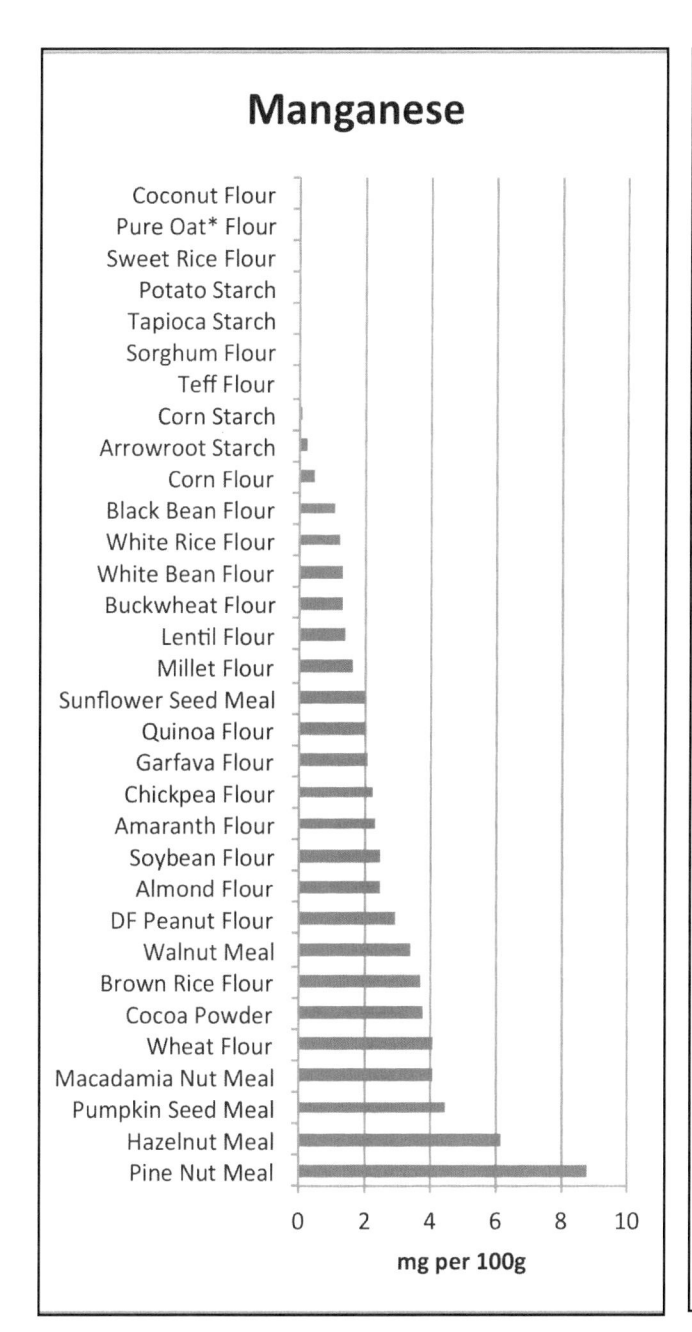

Flour	mg per 100g
Coconut Flour	
Pure Oat* Flour	
Sweet Rice Flour	
Potato Starch	
Tapioca Starch	
Sorghum Flour	
Teff Flour	
Corn Starch	
Arrowroot Starch	
Corn Flour	
Black Bean Flour	
White Rice Flour	
White Bean Flour	
Buckwheat Flour	
Lentil Flour	
Millet Flour	
Sunflower Seed Meal	
Quinoa Flour	
Garfava Flour	
Chickpea Flour	
Amaranth Flour	
Soybean Flour	
Almond Flour	
DF Peanut Flour	
Walnut Meal	
Brown Rice Flour	
Cocoa Powder	
Wheat Flour	
Macadamia Nut Meal	
Pumpkin Seed Meal	
Hazelnut Meal	~6
Pine Nut Meal	~9

Molybdenum

Flour	mcg per 100g
Wheat Flour	
Sweet Rice Flour	
Corn Starch	
Potato Starch	
Arrowroot Starch	
Tapioca Starch	
Amaranth Flour	
Black Bean Flour	
White Bean Flour	
Lentil Flour	
Chickpea Flour	
Garfava Bean Flour	
Millet Flour	
Teff Flour	
Corn Flour	
White Rice Flour	
Brown Rice Flour	
Buckwheat Flour	
Pure Oat* Flour	
Coconut Flour	
Hazelnut Meal	
Sorghum Flour	
Almond Flour	~30
Soybean Flour	~75

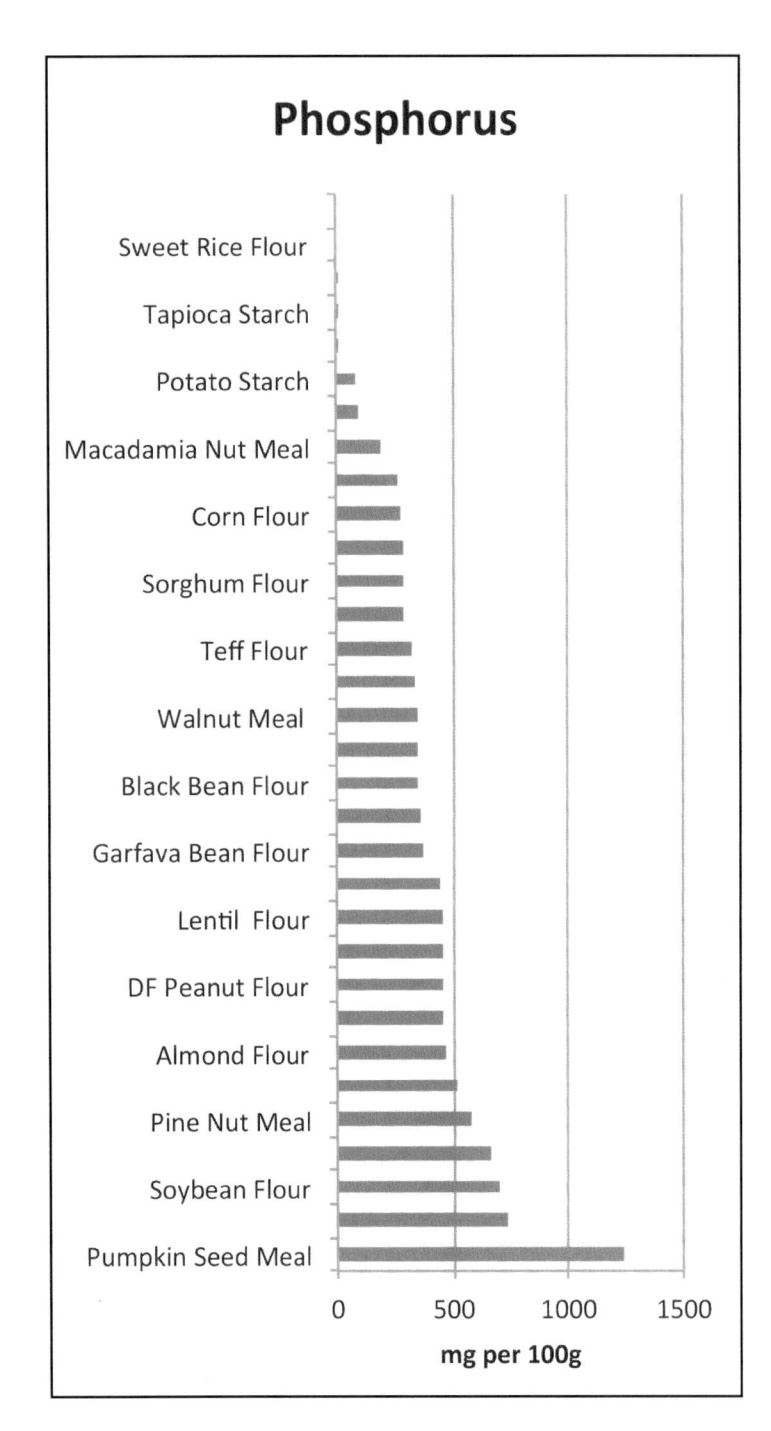

Phosphorus

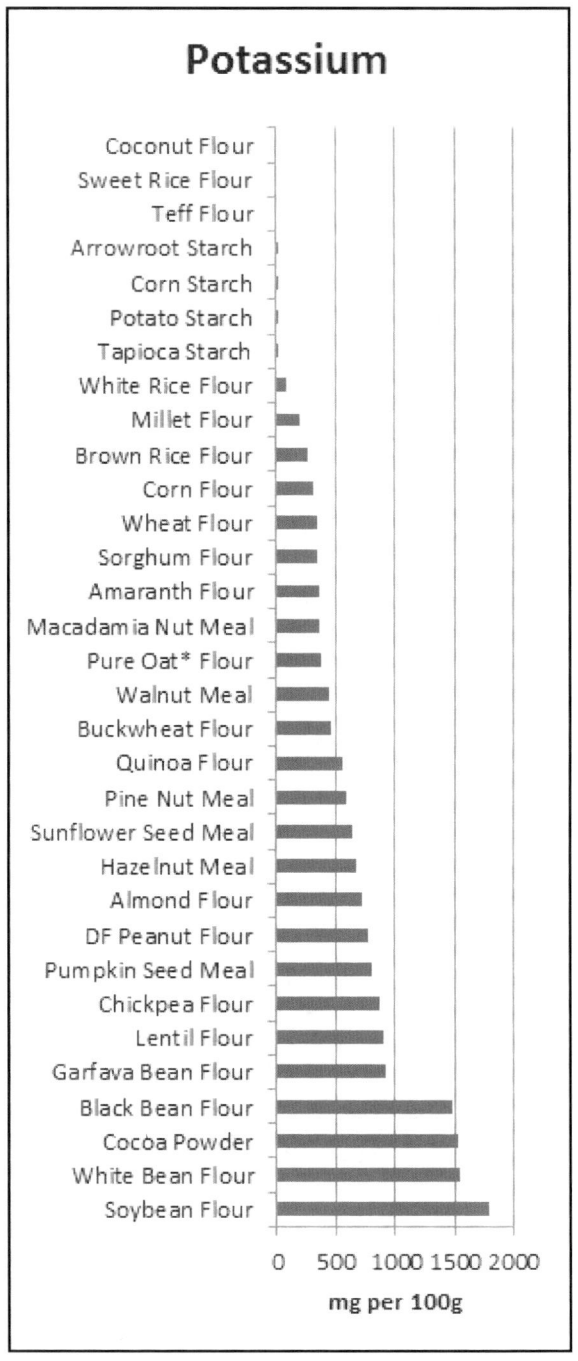

Flour	mg per 100g
Sweet Rice Flour	
Tapioca Starch	
Potato Starch	
Macadamia Nut Meal	
Corn Flour	
Sorghum Flour	
Teff Flour	
Walnut Meal	
Black Bean Flour	
Garfava Bean Flour	
Lentil Flour	
DF Peanut Flour	
Almond Flour	
Pine Nut Meal	
Soybean Flour	
Pumpkin Seed Meal	

Potassium

Flour	mg per 100g
Coconut Flour	
Sweet Rice Flour	
Teff Flour	
Arrowroot Starch	
Corn Starch	
Potato Starch	
Tapioca Starch	
White Rice Flour	
Millet Flour	
Brown Rice Flour	
Corn Flour	
Wheat Flour	
Sorghum Flour	
Amaranth Flour	
Macadamia Nut Meal	
Pure Oat* Flour	
Walnut Meal	
Buckwheat Flour	
Quinoa Flour	
Pine Nut Meal	
Sunflower Seed Meal	
Hazelnut Meal	
Almond Flour	
DF Peanut Flour	
Pumpkin Seed Meal	
Chickpea Flour	
Lentil Flour	
Garfava Bean Flour	
Black Bean Flour	
Cocoa Powder	
White Bean Flour	
Soybean Flour	

Sodium

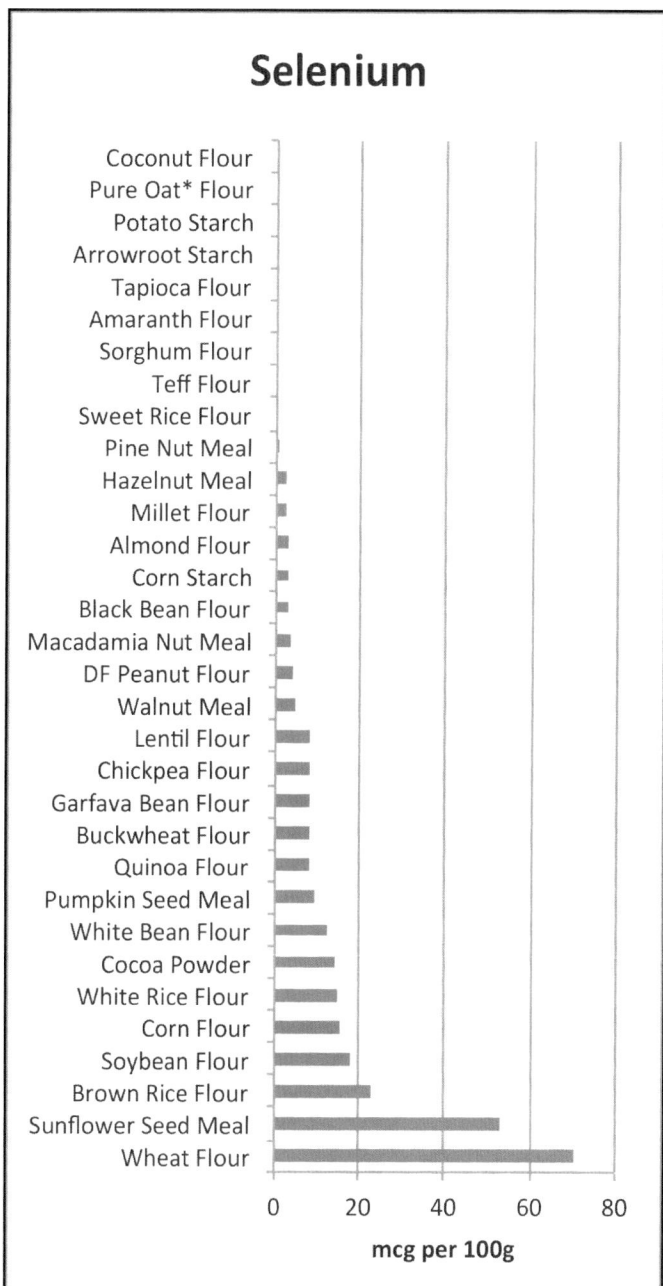

Flour	mg per 100g
Hazelnut Meal	
White Rice Flour	
Almond Flour	
Buckwheat Flour	
Pine Nut Meal	
Soybean Flour	
Arrowroot Starch	
Sweet Rice Flour	
Walnut Meal	
Wheat Flour	
Quinoa Flour	
Tapioca Starch	
Pure Oat* Flour	
Macadamia Nut Meal	
Black Bean Flour	
Sorghum Flour	
Lentil Flour	
Corn Flour	
Pumpkin Seed Meal	
Millet Flour	
Potato Starch	
Sunflower Seed Meal	
Corn Starch	
White Bean Flour	
Brown Rice Flour	
Teff Flour	
Cocoa Powder	
Amaranth Flour	
Garfava Flour	
Chickpea Flour	
DF Peanut Flour	~105
Coconut Flour	~200

Selenium

Flour	mcg per 100g
Coconut Flour	
Pure Oat* Flour	
Potato Starch	
Arrowroot Starch	
Tapioca Flour	
Amaranth Flour	
Sorghum Flour	
Teff Flour	
Sweet Rice Flour	
Pine Nut Meal	
Hazelnut Meal	
Millet Flour	
Almond Flour	
Corn Starch	
Black Bean Flour	
Macadamia Nut Meal	
DF Peanut Flour	
Walnut Meal	
Lentil Flour	
Chickpea Flour	
Garfava Bean Flour	
Buckwheat Flour	
Quinoa Flour	
Pumpkin Seed Meal	
White Bean Flour	
Cocoa Powder	
White Rice Flour	
Corn Flour	
Soybean Flour	
Brown Rice Flour	
Sunflower Seed Meal	~53
Wheat Flour	~70

Zinc

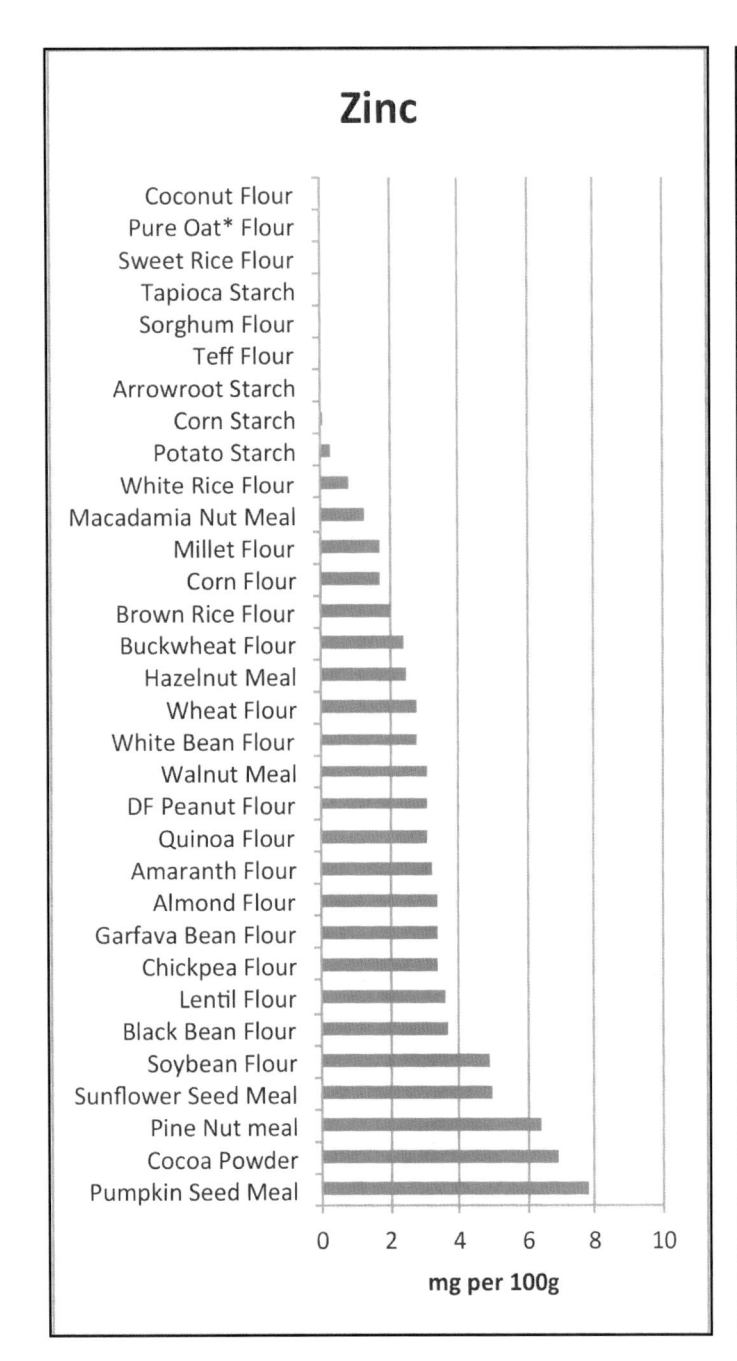

Flour	mg per 100g
Coconut Flour	0
Pure Oat* Flour	0
Sweet Rice Flour	0
Tapioca Starch	0
Sorghum Flour	0
Teff Flour	0
Arrowroot Starch	0
Corn Starch	~0
Potato Starch	~0.2
White Rice Flour	~0.8
Macadamia Nut Meal	~1.2
Millet Flour	~1.5
Corn Flour	~1.7
Brown Rice Flour	~2
Buckwheat Flour	~2.4
Hazelnut Meal	~2.5
Wheat Flour	~2.8
White Bean Flour	~2.8
Walnut Meal	~3
DF Peanut Flour	~3
Quinoa Flour	~3
Amaranth Flour	~3.2
Almond Flour	~3.3
Garfava Bean Flour	~3.4
Chickpea Flour	~3.4
Lentil Flour	~3.6
Black Bean Flour	~3.7
Soybean Flour	~4.8
Sunflower Seed Meal	~5
Pine Nut meal	~6.5
Cocoa Powder	~6.8
Pumpkin Seed Meal	~7.8

Vitamin A

Flour	IU per 100g
Cocoa Powder	0
DF Peanut Flour	0
Coconut Flour	0
Soybean Flour	0
Pure Oat* Flour	0
Sweet Rice Flour	0
Corn Starch	0
Potato Starch	0
Arrowroot Starch	0
Tapioca Starch	0
Amaranth Flour	0
Black Bean Flour	0
White Bean Flour	0
Millet Flour	0
Sorghum Flour	0
Teff Flour	0
White Rice Flour	0
Brown Rice Flour	0
Buckwheat Flour	0
Macadamia Nut Meal	0
Almond Flour	~2
Wheat Flour	~10
Quinoa Flour	~14
Pumpkin Seed Meal	~16
Walnut Meal	~20
Hazelnut Meal	~20
Pine Nut Meal	~29
Lentil Flour	~39
Sunflower Seed Meal	~50
Garfava Bean Flour	~67
Chickpea Flour	~67
Corn Flour	~240

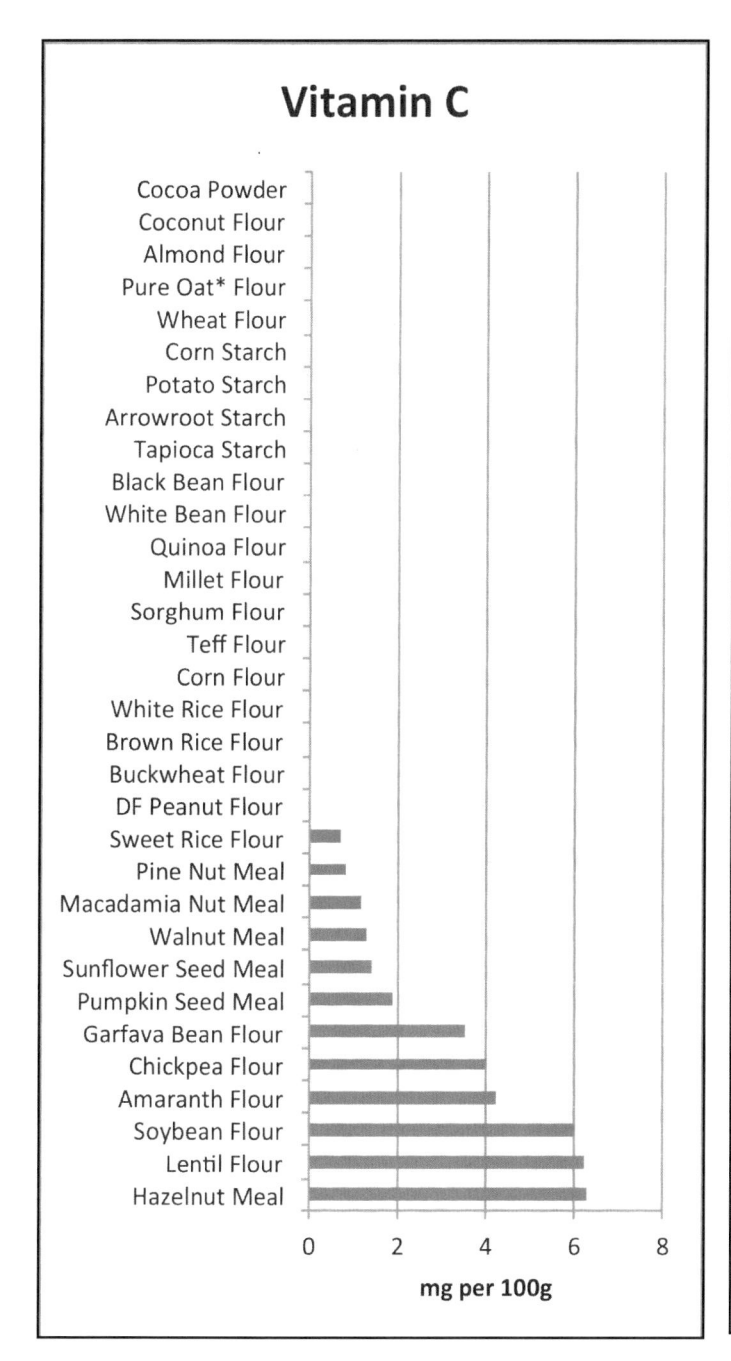

Vitamin C

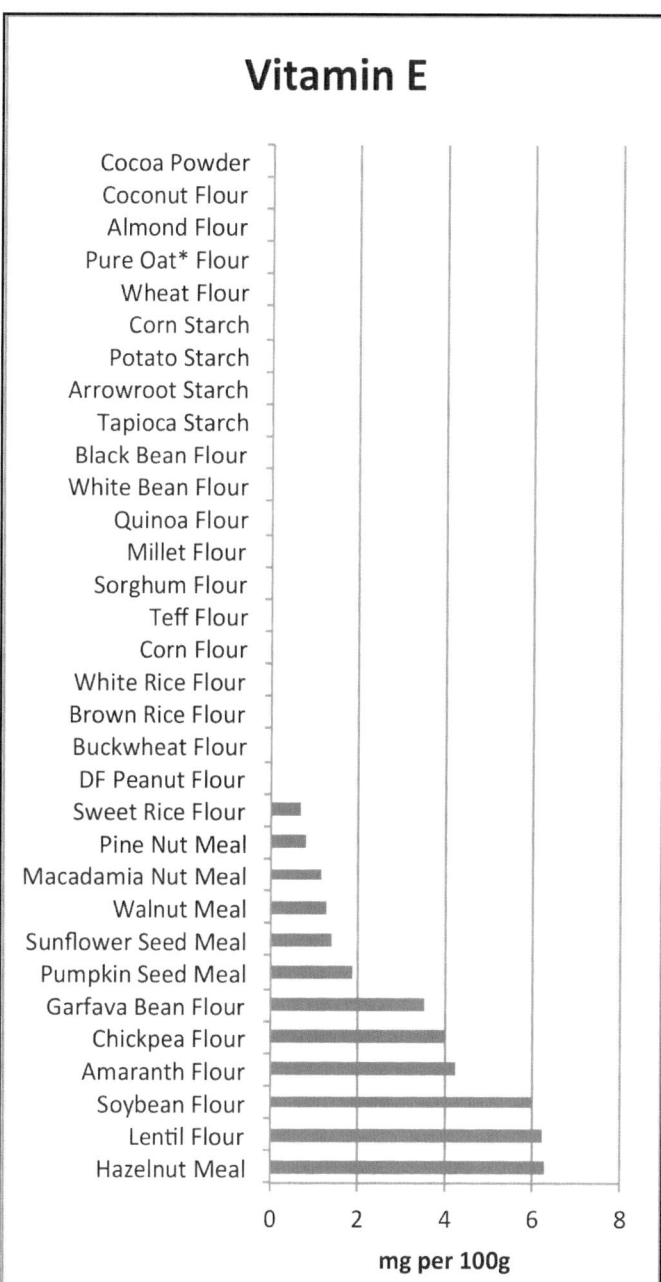

Food	mg per 100g
Cocoa Powder	0
Coconut Flour	0
Almond Flour	0
Pure Oat* Flour	0
Wheat Flour	0
Corn Starch	0
Potato Starch	0
Arrowroot Starch	0
Tapioca Starch	0
Black Bean Flour	0
White Bean Flour	0
Quinoa Flour	0
Millet Flour	0
Sorghum Flour	0
Teff Flour	0
Corn Flour	0
White Rice Flour	0
Brown Rice Flour	0
Buckwheat Flour	0
DF Peanut Flour	0
Sweet Rice Flour	~0.7
Pine Nut Meal	~0.8
Macadamia Nut Meal	~1.2
Walnut Meal	~1.3
Sunflower Seed Meal	~1.4
Pumpkin Seed Meal	~1.9
Garfava Bean Flour	~3.5
Chickpea Flour	~4
Amaranth Flour	~4.2
Soybean Flour	~6
Lentil Flour	~6.3
Hazelnut Meal	~6.3

Vitamin E

Food	mg per 100g
Cocoa Powder	0
Coconut Flour	0
Almond Flour	0
Pure Oat* Flour	0
Wheat Flour	0
Corn Starch	0
Potato Starch	0
Arrowroot Starch	0
Tapioca Starch	0
Black Bean Flour	0
White Bean Flour	0
Quinoa Flour	0
Millet Flour	0
Sorghum Flour	0
Teff Flour	0
Corn Flour	0
White Rice Flour	0
Brown Rice Flour	0
Buckwheat Flour	0
DF Peanut Flour	0
Sweet Rice Flour	~0.7
Pine Nut Meal	~0.8
Macadamia Nut Meal	~1.2
Walnut Meal	~1.3
Sunflower Seed Meal	~1.4
Pumpkin Seed Meal	~1.9
Garfava Bean Flour	~3.5
Chickpea Flour	~4
Amaranth Flour	~4.2
Soybean Flour	~6
Lentil Flour	~6.3
Hazelnut Meal	~6.3

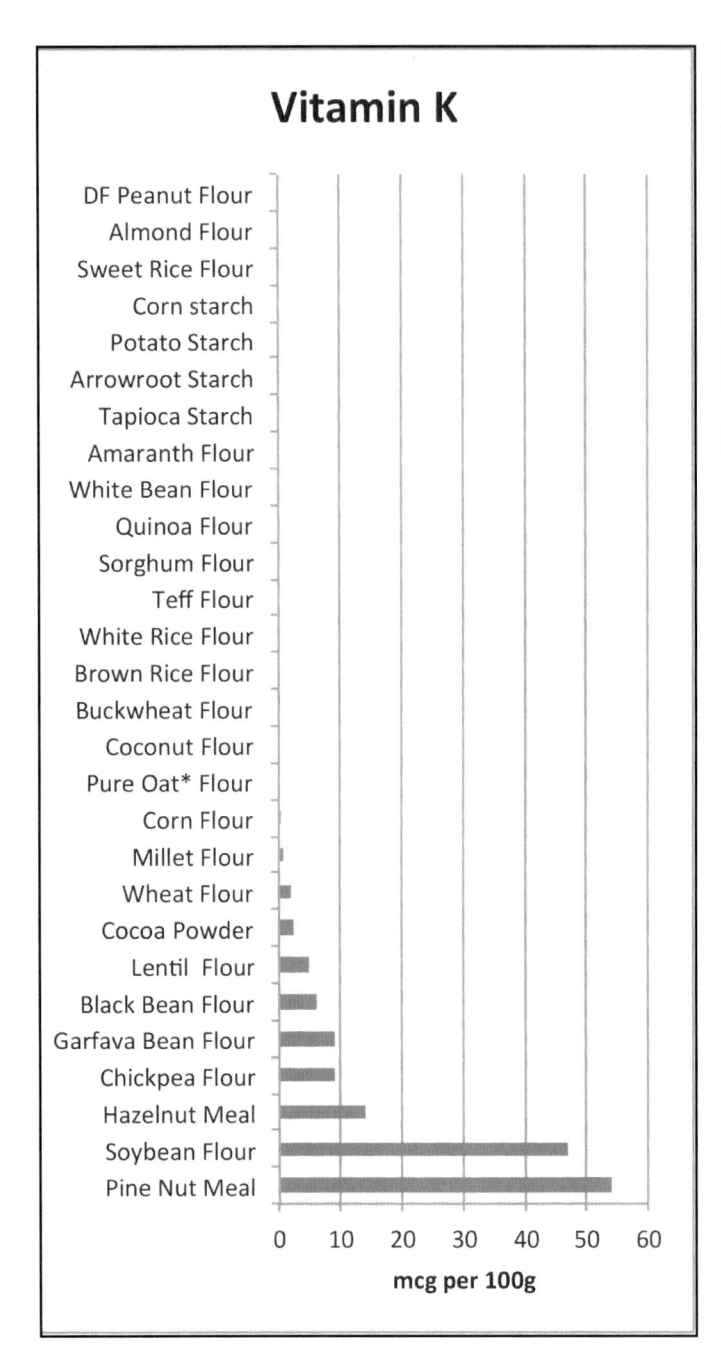

Vitamin K

Flour	mcg per 100g
DF Peanut Flour	
Almond Flour	
Sweet Rice Flour	
Corn starch	
Potato Starch	
Arrowroot Starch	
Tapioca Starch	
Amaranth Flour	
White Bean Flour	
Quinoa Flour	
Sorghum Flour	
Teff Flour	
White Rice Flour	
Brown Rice Flour	
Buckwheat Flour	
Coconut Flour	
Pure Oat* Flour	
Corn Flour	
Millet Flour	
Wheat Flour	
Cocoa Powder	
Lentil Flour	
Black Bean Flour	
Garfava Bean Flour	
Chickpea Flour	
Hazelnut Meal	
Soybean Flour	~47
Pine Nut Meal	~54

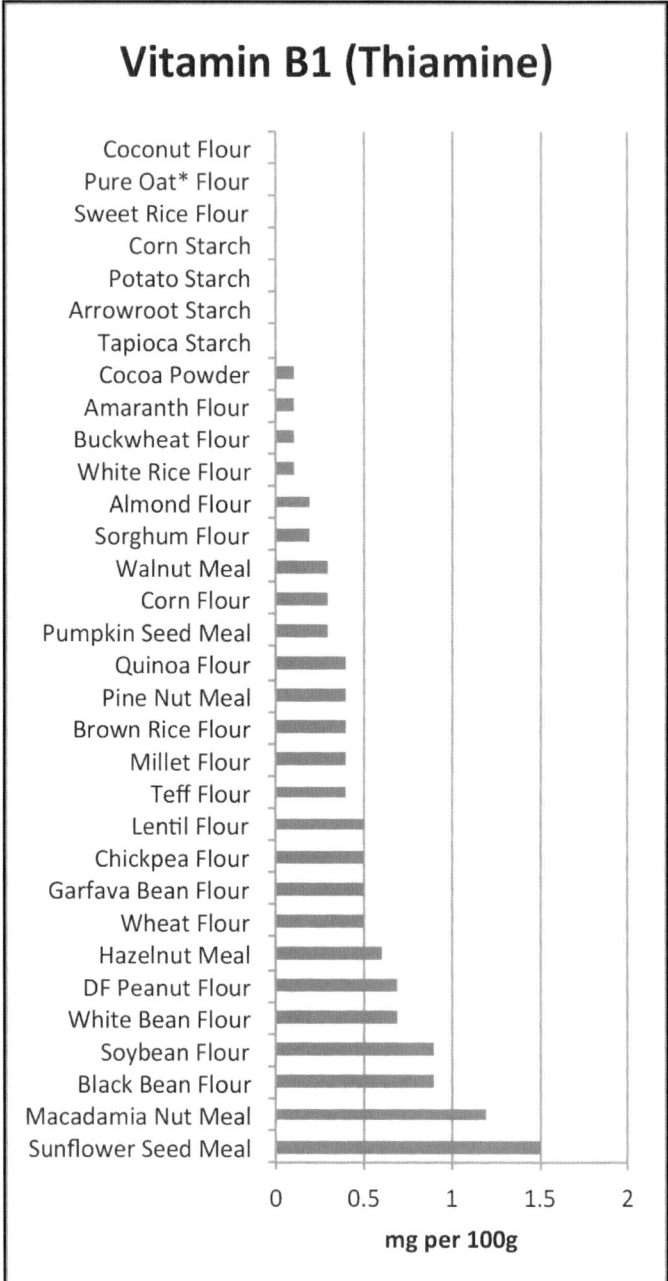

Vitamin B1 (Thiamine)

Flour	mg per 100g
Coconut Flour	
Pure Oat* Flour	
Sweet Rice Flour	
Corn Starch	
Potato Starch	
Arrowroot Starch	
Tapioca Starch	
Cocoa Powder	
Amaranth Flour	
Buckwheat Flour	
White Rice Flour	
Almond Flour	
Sorghum Flour	
Walnut Meal	
Corn Flour	
Pumpkin Seed Meal	
Quinoa Flour	
Pine Nut Meal	
Brown Rice Flour	
Millet Flour	
Teff Flour	
Lentil Flour	
Chickpea Flour	
Garfava Bean Flour	
Wheat Flour	
Hazelnut Meal	
DF Peanut Flour	
White Bean Flour	
Soybean Flour	
Black Bean Flour	
Macadamia Nut Meal	~1.2
Sunflower Seed Meal	~1.5

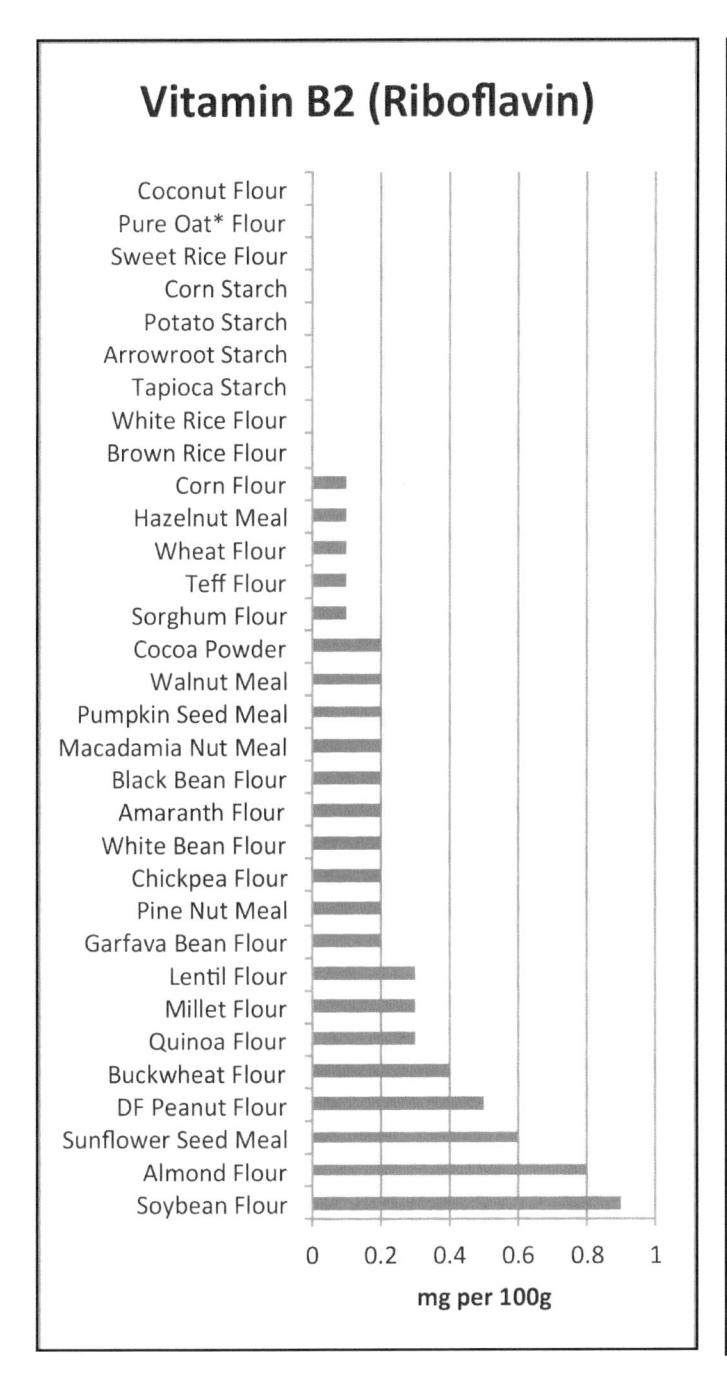

Vitamin B2 (Riboflavin)

Flour	mg per 100g
Coconut Flour	
Pure Oat* Flour	
Sweet Rice Flour	
Corn Starch	
Potato Starch	
Arrowroot Starch	
Tapioca Starch	
White Rice Flour	
Brown Rice Flour	
Corn Flour	~0.1
Hazelnut Meal	~0.1
Wheat Flour	~0.1
Teff Flour	~0.1
Sorghum Flour	~0.1
Cocoa Powder	~0.2
Walnut Meal	~0.2
Pumpkin Seed Meal	~0.2
Macadamia Nut Meal	~0.2
Black Bean Flour	~0.2
Amaranth Flour	~0.2
White Bean Flour	~0.2
Chickpea Flour	~0.2
Pine Nut Meal	~0.2
Garfava Bean Flour	~0.2
Lentil Flour	~0.3
Millet Flour	~0.3
Quinoa Flour	~0.3
Buckwheat Flour	~0.4
DF Peanut Flour	~0.5
Sunflower Seed Meal	~0.6
Almond Flour	~0.8
Soybean Flour	~0.9

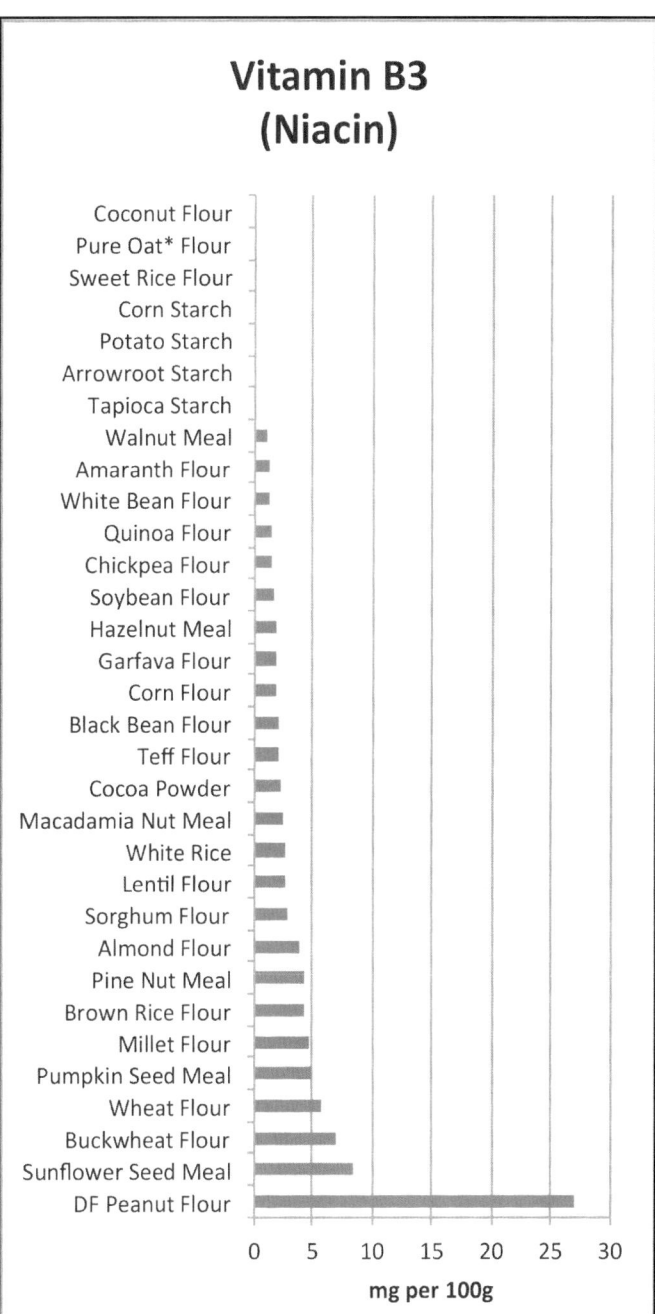

Vitamin B3 (Niacin)

Flour	mg per 100g
Coconut Flour	
Pure Oat* Flour	
Sweet Rice Flour	
Corn Starch	
Potato Starch	
Arrowroot Starch	
Tapioca Starch	
Walnut Meal	~1
Amaranth Flour	~1
White Bean Flour	~1
Quinoa Flour	~1
Chickpea Flour	~1
Soybean Flour	~2
Hazelnut Meal	~2
Garfava Flour	~2
Corn Flour	~2
Black Bean Flour	~2
Teff Flour	~2
Cocoa Powder	~2
Macadamia Nut Meal	~2
White Rice	~3
Lentil Flour	~3
Sorghum Flour	~3
Almond Flour	~4
Pine Nut Meal	~4
Brown Rice Flour	~4
Millet Flour	~5
Pumpkin Seed Meal	~5
Wheat Flour	~6
Buckwheat Flour	~7
Sunflower Seed Meal	~8
DF Peanut Flour	~27

Vitamin B6 (Pyridoxine)

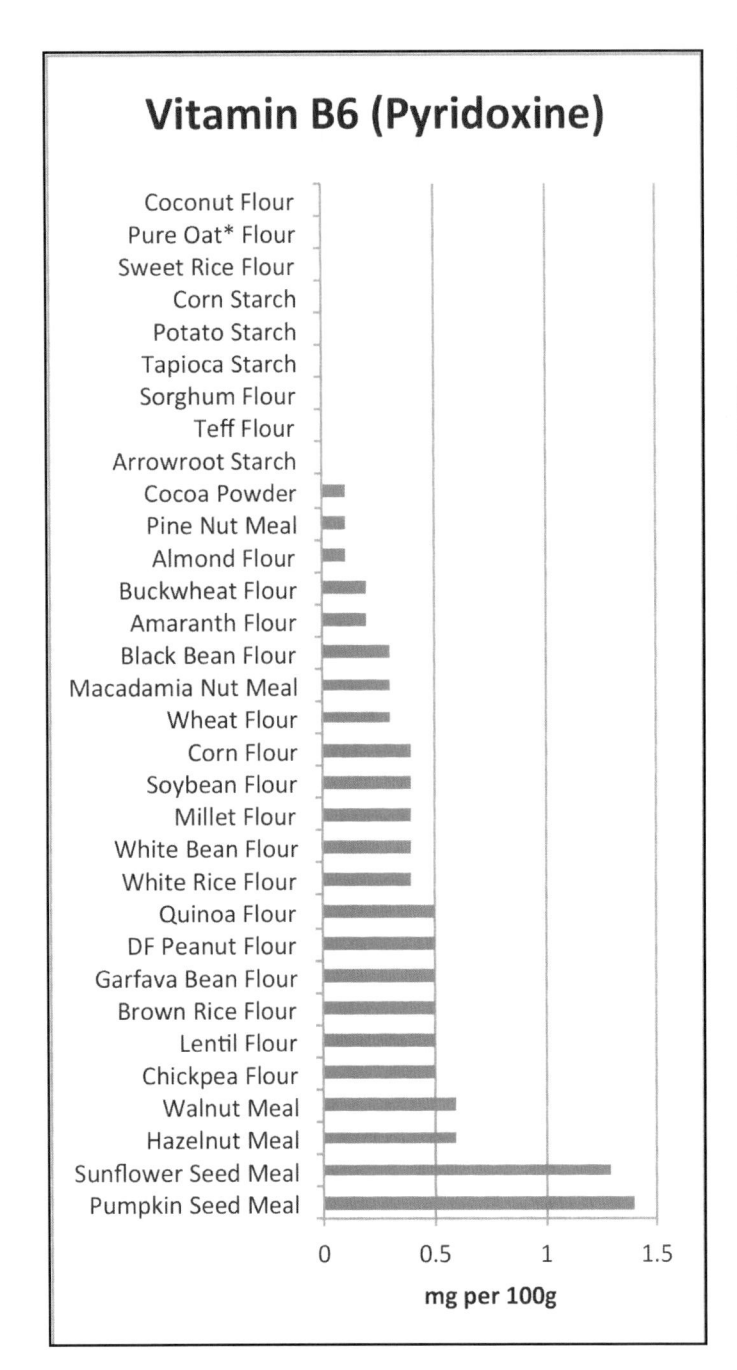

Flour	mg per 100g
Coconut Flour	
Pure Oat* Flour	
Sweet Rice Flour	
Corn Starch	
Potato Starch	
Tapioca Starch	
Sorghum Flour	
Teff Flour	
Arrowroot Starch	
Cocoa Powder	~0.1
Pine Nut Meal	~0.1
Almond Flour	~0.1
Buckwheat Flour	~0.2
Amaranth Flour	~0.2
Black Bean Flour	~0.3
Macadamia Nut Meal	~0.3
Wheat Flour	~0.3
Corn Flour	~0.4
Soybean Flour	~0.4
Millet Flour	~0.4
White Bean Flour	~0.4
White Rice Flour	~0.4
Quinoa Flour	~0.5
DF Peanut Flour	~0.5
Garfava Bean Flour	~0.5
Brown Rice Flour	~0.5
Lentil Flour	~0.5
Chickpea Flour	~0.5
Walnut Meal	~0.6
Hazelnut Meal	~0.6
Sunflower Seed Meal	~1.3
Pumpkin Seed Meal	~1.4

Biotin

Flour	mcg per 100g
Coconut Flour	
Soybean Flour	
Pure Oat* Flour	
Wheat Flour	
Sweet Rice Flour	
Corn Starch	
Potato Starch	
Arrowroot Starch	
Tapioca Starch	
Amaranth Flour	
Black Bean Flour	
White Bean Flour	
Lentil Flour	
Chickpea Flour	
Garfava Bean Flour	
Millet Flour	
Sorghum Flour	
Teff Flour	
White Rice Flour	
Buckwheat Flour	
Brown Rice Flour	~1
Corn Flour	~2
Almond Flour	~64
Hazelnut Meal	~76

80

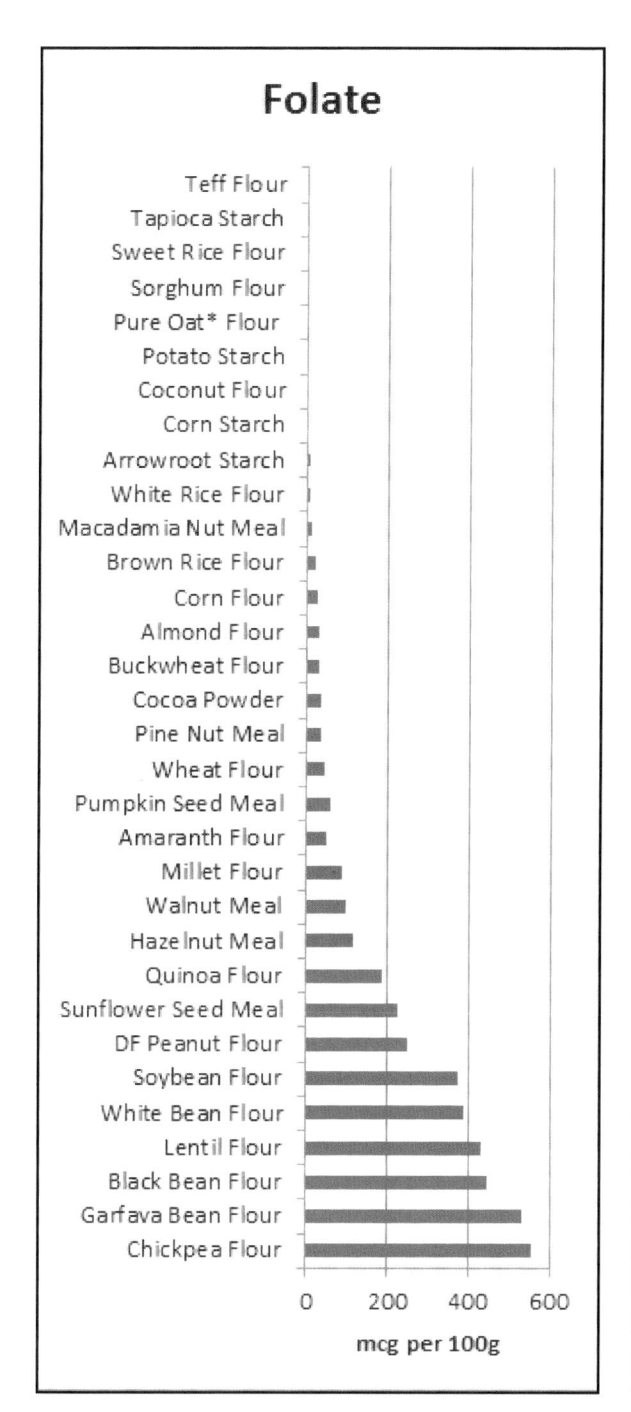

Folate

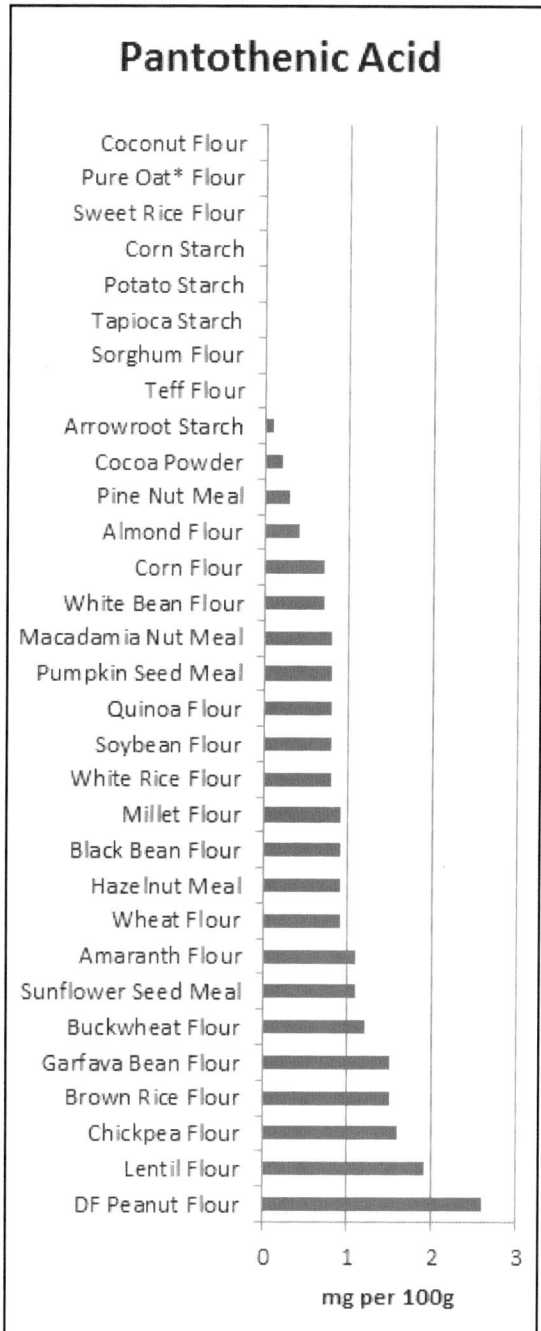

Flour	mcg per 100g
Teff Flour	0
Tapioca Starch	0
Sweet Rice Flour	0
Sorghum Flour	0
Pure Oat* Flour	0
Potato Starch	0
Coconut Flour	0
Corn Starch	0
Arrowroot Starch	~5
White Rice Flour	~5
Macadamia Nut Meal	~10
Brown Rice Flour	~20
Corn Flour	~25
Almond Flour	~30
Buckwheat Flour	~30
Cocoa Powder	~32
Pine Nut Meal	~35
Wheat Flour	~40
Pumpkin Seed Meal	~55
Amaranth Flour	~60
Millet Flour	~85
Walnut Meal	~100
Hazelnut Meal	~110
Quinoa Flour	~185
Sunflower Seed Meal	~225
DF Peanut Flour	~245
Soybean Flour	~375
White Bean Flour	~390
Lentil Flour	~435
Black Bean Flour	~445
Garfava Bean Flour	~525
Chickpea Flour	~555

Pantothenic Acid

Flour	mg per 100g
Coconut Flour	0
Pure Oat* Flour	0
Sweet Rice Flour	0
Corn Starch	0
Potato Starch	0
Tapioca Starch	0
Sorghum Flour	0
Teff Flour	0
Arrowroot Starch	~0.1
Cocoa Powder	~0.25
Pine Nut Meal	~0.3
Almond Flour	~0.45
Corn Flour	~0.65
White Bean Flour	~0.7
Macadamia Nut Meal	~0.75
Pumpkin Seed Meal	~0.75
Quinoa Flour	~0.8
Soybean Flour	~0.8
White Rice Flour	~0.8
Millet Flour	~0.85
Black Bean Flour	~0.9
Hazelnut Meal	~0.9
Wheat Flour	~0.95
Amaranth Flour	~1.05
Sunflower Seed Meal	~1.1
Buckwheat Flour	~1.2
Garfava Bean Flour	~1.45
Brown Rice Flour	~1.5
Chickpea Flour	~1.6
Lentil Flour	~1.9
DF Peanut Flour	~2.6

CATEGORY 2:
NUTRIENT ANALYSIS: FREQUENCY OF FLOUR IN TOP 3 FOR VITAMIN AND MINERAL CONTENT

Gluten-free baking has opened up the world of alternate flours. No longer are baked goods made from just grain flours. Flours from beans, legumes, nuts, and seeds are flooding the market. Available flours are now found in two different food groups as outlined in the Food Guide: Grain Products and Meats and Alternatives. Depending on the type and volume of flour(s) in the recipe determines the food group(s) that baked products fall in to. These alternate flours and meals tend to be more concentrated in nutrients, vitamins, and minerals when compared to their grain counterparts. This can assist in the creation of more desirable baked goods from both a sensory and nutritional standpoint. When flours from Meat and Alternatives are included in a gluten-free flour mix, the added protein, fat, and fibre reduces the overall carbohydrate content of the flour mix thereby reducing the glycemic load of the baked good. The following graphs reflect the number of times each flour ranks in the top 3 for vitamin and mineral content. These graphs have been included to demonstrate the nutritional benefit of gluten-free flours and reinforce the reasoning behind mixing gluten-free flours.

FLOURS FROM
THE GRAIN PRODUCTS GROUP

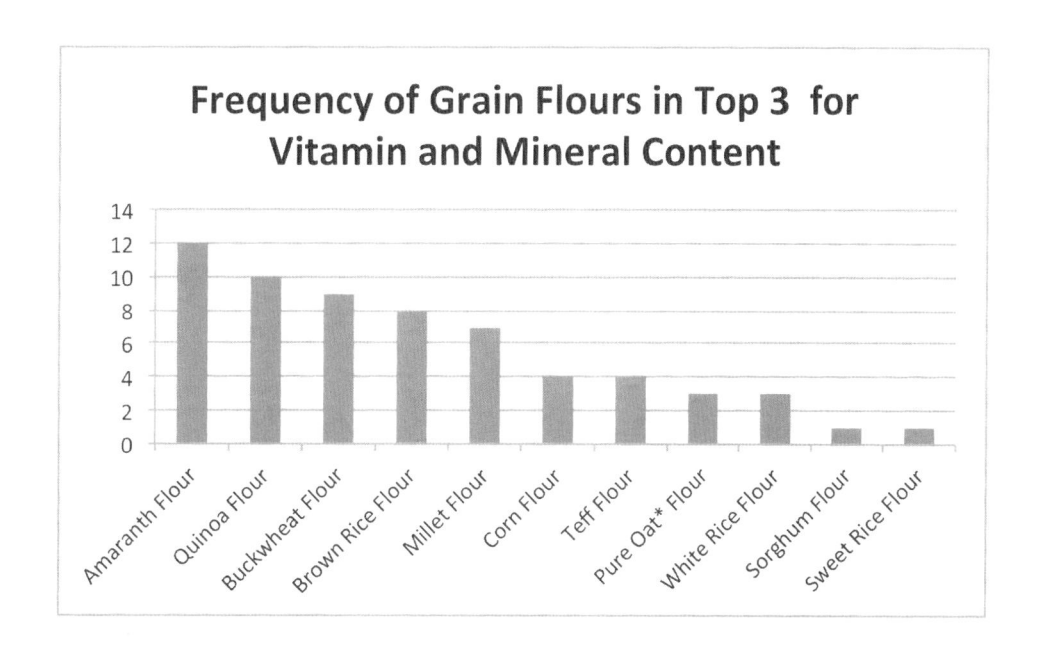

Frequency of Grain Flours in Top 3 for Vitamin and Mineral Content

Flour	Frequency
Amaranth Flour	12
Quinoa Flour	10
Buckwheat Flour	9
Brown Rice Flour	8
Millet Flour	7
Corn Flour	4
Teff Flour	4
Pure Oat* Flour	3
White Rice Flour	3
Sorghum Flour	1
Sweet Rice Flour	1

Looking at flours in this way made us realize the benefits of mixing up the flours we use in baking based on their nutrition and functional benefits. Like vegetables and fruit, eating a variety of flours is truly a benefit. Some of these flours are higher in vitamins and some of them are higher in minerals. Buckwheat flour, brown rice flour, and millet flour are higher in vitamin content where the others *tend* to be higher in mineral content. Quinoa is balanced in its vitamin and mineral content.

FLOURS FROM
THE MEAT & ALTERNATIVES GROUP

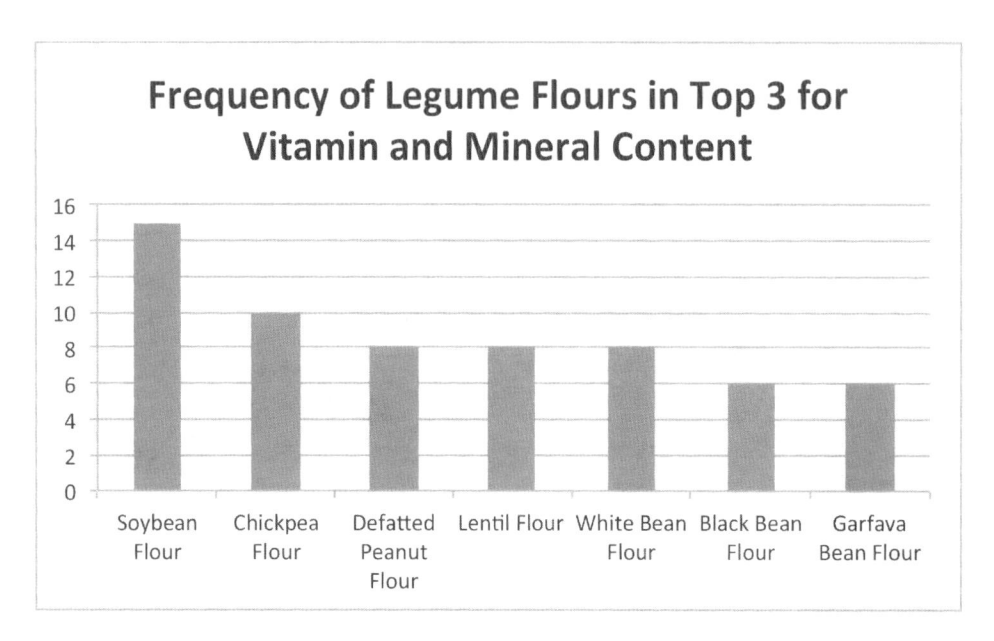

Frequency of Legume Flours in Top 3 for Vitamin and Mineral Content

Flour	Frequency
Soybean Flour	15
Chickpea Flour	10
Defatted Peanut Flour	8
Lentil Flour	8
White Bean Flour	8
Black Bean Flour	6
Garfava Bean Flour	6

Soybean is the powerhouse of the legume family. However, soybean can be harder to incorporate into baking due to its high fat content and heavy weight. Also, there tends to be a greater number of people with concerns about and/or sensitivities to soybean. The other legume flours have plenty to offer as far as functional benefit to baking and nutritional benefit for health.

Frequency of Nut & Seed Flours in Top 3 for Vitamin and Mineral Content

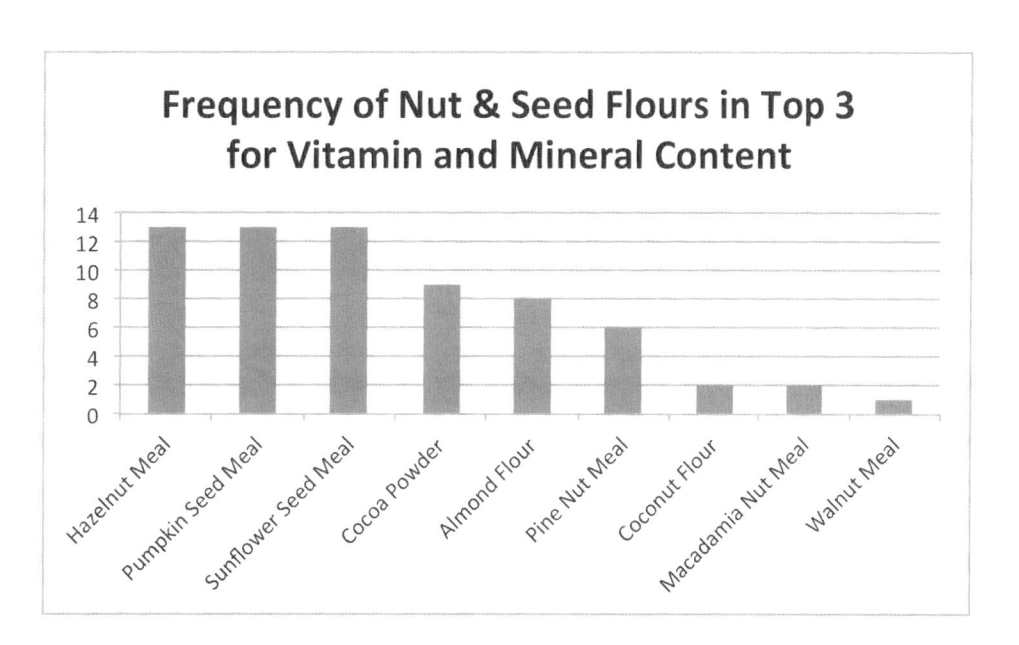

Flour	Frequency
Hazelnut Meal	13
Pumpkin Seed Meal	13
Sunflower Seed Meal	13
Cocoa Powder	9
Almond Flour	8
Pine Nut Meal	6
Coconut Flour	2
Macadamia Nut Meal	2
Walnut Meal	1

It is interesting to note that sunflower seed and pumpkin seed frequent the Top 3 list for nutritional diversity which is good news for people with nut allergies.

Cocoa powder is not generally thought of as nut/seed flour but it has high nutritional benefit as well as great flavour. Be sure to buy cocoa powder with a high percentage of cocoa. The incorporation of seed flours into gluten-free baking assists in widening the audience to include nut-free individuals as well. Like grain flours, some nut and seed flours are higher in vitamins, some are higher in minerals, while others are more balanced in their vitamin and mineral content. Partially-defatted nut and seed flours are more easily incorporated into a wider variety of baked items; their use in gluten-free flour mixes is a benefit in increasing protein content while keeping the fat and carbohydrate content low. Partially-defatted nut/seed flours are more stable and have a longer shelf-life than their full fat counterparts. We encourage you to create your own flour mixes with partially-defatted nut or seed flours to incorporate the nutritional benefits on a routine basis. The fats derived from nuts and seeds are beneficial as well, and the oils can be purchased separately and added back in volumes desired at the time of baking. Baked goods generally turn out more successful and delicious with this approach.

SUMMARY

So far we have touched on carbohydrate, protein, fat, fibre, minerals, and vitamins. Phytonutrients and phytochemicals are also important for heath and prevention of disease. These are components of plants that help them protect themselves from the hazards around them - sun, inclement weather, bugs, disease, etc. There are thousands of phytonutrients and phytochemicals known to science and all plants contain their own cocktail. Many studies have shown that phytonutrients and phytochemicals react similarly in the human body as well and assist in protection and disease prevention. While they may not be considered by all to be as essential to the same degree for life like nutrients, vitamins, and minerals, we feel that they are very beneficial to consume - particularly in natural form (think real food). Whole grains like corn, brown rice and pure oats*, nuts, seeds and legumes all contain phytonutrients and phytochemicals. Eating whole grain products has been shown to improve health. By adding these flours and nut and seed meals/flours to your baking, you will also be adding phytonutrients and phytochemicals.

Flours have different properties that contribute to baking. Brown rice flour, buckwheat flour and corn flour assist in producing stronger structures, while amaranth flour, quinoa flour, bean flours, nut and seed meals/flours are best used when a softer crumb is called for or where the moisture base is derived from fat. Utilizing a variety of flours to maximize each of their strengths creates more delicious products and diversifies the nutrients, vitamins, and minerals that you eat.

As demonstrated in the composition tables, starches provide essentially no nutritional benefit. Starches should be eliminated if their function is not needed or at the very least used in limited amounts when required to produce a superior end product.

Reflecting on this it is easy to see that no one flour is the perfect flour and that the real benefits come from mixing a variety of flours in baking.

SECTION 2

About Liquids, Binders, Foams, Leavening Agents and Sweeteners

CHAPTER 1:
INTRODUCTION TO LIQUIDS

Liquids play an important role in gluten-free baked goods. Liquids add moisture, water for hydrophilic binders to work, and potentially flavour, protein, fat, and sugar. It is good to understand the composition of the liquid in the recipe, especially when replacing it with another liquid because not all liquids are created equal.

In the following table liquids have been divided into those that contain protein and those that do not. Some liquids contain fat and others do not. The amount of protein in a liquid seems to play more of a role than the amount of fat, unless the fat content is exceptionally high as is the case with canned coconut milk or whipping cream. There are other ingredients, like yogurt, that are seen as solid or partially-solid that have higher amounts of liquid or water in them and need to be counted as part of the liquid volume. In order to make substitutions for liquids properly, the substitute liquid needs to supply similar amounts of protein, fat, acid and water. If it does not, then additions such as lemon juice, added protein, water or oil may need to be added to the liquid volume. For example, 1 cup of buttermilk can be replaced with 2 tsp lemon juice, 1 tbsp protein powder and ½ tsp oil topped up with grain-based "milk" to the 1 cup mark.

SUMMARY TABLE:
LIQUIDS

NON-PROTEIN-CONTAINING LIQUIDS (WITH OR WITHOUT FAT)								PROTEIN-CONTAINING LIQUIDS (WITH OR WITHOUT FAT)			
LIQUID GROUP 1	LIQUID GROUP 2	LIQUID GROUP 3	LIQUID GROUP 4	LIQUID GROUP 5	LIQUID GROUP 6	LIQUID GROUP 7	LIQUID GROUP 8	LIQUID GROUP 9	LIQUID GROUP 10	LIQUID GROUP 11
Water	Juice	Grain "milk"	Nut "milk"	Seed "milk"	Mashed fruit/ veg	Cream	Legume "milks"	Dairy milk	Partially- solid dairy	Partially- solid, dairy-free
Tap water	Fruit	Rice milk	Almond milk	Coconut milk	Banana	Whipping cream	Soy milk	Cows milk	Yogurt	Yogurt
Bottled water	Vegetable	Quinoa milk		Hemp milk	Pumpkin	Coffee cream		Goat milk	Sour cream	
Carbonated water		Oat* milk			Apple sauce	Half and half		Butter-milk	Cottage cheese	
Coconut water					Grated vegetable			Kefir		

LIQUID GROUP 1: Water adds liquid and acts to moisten the baked item. It does not add carbohydrate, protein or fat. If carbonated water is added the carbon gas will assist in leavening. Water can be substituted 1-for-1 for other liquids. However, if using water to replace a protein-containing liquid, addition of a concentrated protein powder such as pumpkin seed protein powder, gelatin, agar or egg white powder is necessary to maintain strength in the crumb structure.

LIQUID GROUP 2: Juice can come from vegetables or fruit and adds liquid as well as acid and carbohydrate or "sugar" to your baked item. When juice is combined with baking soda, the acid in the juice reacts with the baking soda to create a gas which will assist in leavening (see leavening). It is best to use 100% fruit or vegetable juice instead of a fruit beverage, punch or drink to keep the sugar content down. Vegetable and fruit juices add flavour to the baked product. It is important to choose a fruit or vegetable juice that complements the baked item. Juice can be substituted 1-for-1 for other liquids. Review the liquid being replaced and ensure that the liquid's components such as protein and/or fat are also included in the replacement liquid. If using juice to replace a protein-containing liquid, addition of a concentrated protein powder such as, pumpkin seed protein powder, gelatin, agar or egg white powder is necessary to maintain strength in the crumb structure.

LIQUID GROUP 3: Grain beverages add liquid and act to moisten the baked item. Grain beverages also add to the carbohydrate content of the baked good. It is best to use an unflavoured, unsweetened version of grain beverages to keep the flavour neutral and the sugar content down. Grain beverages can be substituted 1-for-1 with other liquids. If using grain beverage to replace a protein-containing liquid, addition of a concentrated protein powder such as, pumpkin seed protein powder, gelatin, agar or egg white powder is necessary to maintain strength in the crumb structure.

LIQUID GROUP 4: Nut beverages add liquid and act to moisten baked items. Nut beverages also add to the carbohydrate content of the baked good. It is best to use the unflavoured, unsweetened versions of nut beverages to keep the flavour neutral and the sugar content down. Nut beverages can be substituted 1-for-1 with other liquids. If using a nut beverage to replace a protein-containing liquid, add a concentrated protein powder such as, pumpkin seed protein powder, gelatin, agar or egg white powder is necessary to maintain strength in the crumb structure.

LIQUID GROUP 5: Coconut milk beverages add liquid and act to moisten baked items. There are two styles of coconut milk: full fat, canned coconut milk, intended for baking and cooking, and reduced fat, coconut beverage, intended for drinking. Coconut milk adds significantly to fat content and requires an adjustment in the amount of fat used in the recipe. Coconut beverages also add to the carbohydrate content of the baked good. It is best to use the unflavoured, unsweetened versions of coconut beverages to keep the flavour neutral and the sugar content down. Coconut milk beverages can be substituted 1-for-1 with other liquids. If using coconut milk to replace a protein-containing liquid, the addition of a concentrated protein powder such as, pumpkin seed protein powder, gelatin, agar or egg white powder is necessary to maintain strength in the crumb structure.

Hemp milk adds liquid and acts to moisten the baked item. Hemp milk also adds to the carbohydrate, protein, and fat content. It is best to use the unflavoured, unsweetened versions of hemp milk to keep the flavour neutral and the sugar content down. This milk can be substituted for other protein-containing liquids with the addition of added protein. Hemp milk can be used to replace non-protein, non-fat liquids 1-for-1. Hemp milk has a flavour that can be detected when used in higher quantities. Consideration of flavour pairings for hemp milk may be desirable for some palates.

LIQUID GROUP 6: Mashed or grated vegetables and fruit add to the volume of fluid in the recipe. This volume needs to be accounted for in the fluid content. Generally count about 75% fluid for mashed or grated vegetables and fruit into your recipe. For example, a regular pancake recipe may have 2 cups of milk or liquid in the recipe. To create a banana pancake recipe, the recipe would use 1 cup mashed banana and 1 ¼ cup milk to create similar moisture content in the pancake batter.

LIQUID GROUP 7: Cream is a non-protein containing liquid which predominately adds fat and moisture. There are differing percentages of fat in cream and it is best to use the type of cream that is called for in the recipe. Whipping cream is the only cream that will create a stable airy foam.

LIQUID GROUP 8: Soy milk adds liquid and acts to moisten the baked item. Soy milk adds to the carbohydrate, protein, and fat content. It is best to use the unflavoured, unsweetened versions of soy milk to keep the flavour neutral and the sugar content down. This milk can be substituted for other protein liquids 1-for-1. This will result in a slightly softer crumb. This is generally not noticeable, except in items like French bread. Soy milk has a flavour that can be detected in higher quantities. Consideration of flavour pairings for soy milk may be desirable for some palates.

LIQUID GROUP 9: Dairy milks add liquid and act to moisten baked items. Many recipes in North America and Europe use dairy milk as the main liquid in baking. Dairy milks provide a source of carbohydrate, protein, and fat. It is best to use the unflavoured, unsweetened versions of dairy milk to keep the flavour neutral and the carbohydrate content down. Diary milk also comes in fermented form such as buttermilk and kefir. Fermented dairy milks assist in leavening when used in combination with baking soda. Dairy milk can be substituted for other protein liquids 1-for-1. It can also be used to replace non-protein-containing liquids 1-for-1. When substituted in items normally made with non-protein-containing liquids, a slightly softer crumb may result. This is generally not noticeable, except in items like French bread. Plain milk has a neutral flavour and is not noticeable in most baked goods.

LIQUID GROUPS 10 AND 11: Semi-solid liquids made from dairy and non-dairy ingredients add liquid to the baked good and need to be considered as part of the liquid content of the dough or batter. They also add carbohydrate, protein, and fat to the baked item. Semi-solid dairy and non-dairy liquids tend to be higher in protein and fat than full liquid milks/beverages and benefit the structure and mouth-feel of the product. When using semi-solid liquids, consider the liquid portion to make up 75% of the total volume. For example, 100mL of yogurt contains approximately 75mL of liquid. Semi-solid liquids can generally be used to substitute for full liquids in most recipes, if needed, by "thinning" them down. For example, for 1 cup of milk use ⅔ cup semi-solid liquid and ½ cup full liquid. Semi-solid liquids are generally always fermented and assist in leavening when used in combination with baking soda.

CHAPTER 2:
INTRODUCTION TO BINDERS - INGREDIENTS THAT "STICK" OR "BIND"

There are two types of binders: hydrophilic (water-loving) binders and protein binders. Both play a very important role in creating delicious desirable gluten-free baked goods. Gluten-free recipes should be designed to include both types of binders for greatest success. Hydrophilic binders work with the water-based liquid ingredients in the baked good to absorb the moisture and form a "glue" that keeps the baked good together reducing the risk of it crumbling or completely falling apart when cut. The second is protein binders. Protein binders hold gluten-free items together when baked because when protein is cooked, it changes form and creates a strong and solid structure (think of an egg, when you crack it into a hot frying pan, the liquid egg coagulates and forms a solid structure).

CATEGORY 1:
HYDROPHILIC BINDERS

Hydrophilic means "water-loving". Hydrophilic binders work with the water-based liquids in the baked product to gel or glue the baked good together. There are two different types of hydrophilic binders: those that work best when agitated or beaten, and those that require time for absorption. It has been our experience that those that require agitation are more concentrated and thus produce a stronger binding effect. We have also found that hydrophilic binders that require agitation also provide more "chew" in the baked good than those that require time. This is useful to note when choosing which binders to use. Yeast breads and pizza dough need higher quantities of hydrophilic binders that require agitation but cake requires much less of this type of binder and has to be used in combination with those hydrophilic binders that require time. I have also found that hydrophilic binders that require time for maximum effect are less chewy and produce a softer crumb.

Xanthan gum is an example of a hydrophilic binder that requires agitation or beating. It does not stir or mix into water well. It needs to be beaten into liquid using a stick beater or it needs to be added to the dry ingredients first. After combining the wet and dry ingredients, the dough or batter needs to be beaten for at least 1 minute for maximum effect.

Psyllium is a hydrophilic binder that requires time to work. You can beat psyllium all you like, but it will not change the thickness of the liquid. If you mix psyllium with water-based liquid it will swirl around in the liquid and settle to the bottom; however, if you let it sit, it will start to form a gel. You can stir the gel and the psyllium will stay in suspension. The gel will continue to thicken until maximum absorbency is reached.

When using hydrophilic binders in your baked goods, it is important to know if the hydrophilic binder needs agitation or time to ensure you apply the right technique. So if you add xanthan gum, you need to beat the dough or batter for at least 1 minute. If you add psyllium, you need to place the batter into the baking containers and let it sit for about 10-20 minutes prior to baking to maximize effect. If you have added both, then you need to beat batter or dough and let it sit. The following table lists some of the hydrophilic binders assigned by category (agitation versus time and strength of bind - strong versus soft).

SUMMARY TABLE:
HYDROPHILIC BINDERS

STRENGTH OF BIND	STRONG		SOFT		
	REQUIRES AGITATION FOR MAXIMUM EFFECT		REQUIRES TIME FOR MAXIMUM EFFECT		
GROUP	HB GROUP 1	HB GROUP 2	HB GROUP 3	HB GROUP 4	HB GROUP 5
HYDROPHILIC BINDERS	Xanthan gum	Methylcellulose	Psyllium husk	Ground chia seeds	Ground flax seeds
	Guar gum			Whole chia seeds	Whole flax seeds
FORM	Concentrated powder	Concentrated powder	Fibre	Seed	Seed
STRENGTH	Very strong	Very strong	Strong	Moderate strength	Very weak
BINDER TO WATER RATIO	1/2 tsp: 1/2 cup water	1 tsp: 1/2 cup water	1 tbsp: 1/2 cup water	3 tbsp: 1/2 cup water	8 tbsp: 1/2 cup water

HB GROUP 1: Gums work with water-based liquids to enhance strength and stretch in the structure of the baked item. Gums add to the "chew" factor in the texture. The amount of gum that is used is based on the amount of water-based liquid present in the recipe and the amount of stretch and "chew" desired in the final product. The higher the ratio of gum to water-based liquid in the recipe the greater the "chew" factor in the final product. To fully activate the gum's strength and stretch, gums need to be beaten at high speed for approximately 1-2 minutes. The amount of gum used in the recipe is specific to the desired outcome. For example, we use 4+ tsp xanthan gum in one loaf of bread, but only ½ tsp in a batch of 12 muffins, an adjustment either way can affect the final result.

Gums do not stir in or mix well with liquid so it is best to mix them in first with other dry ingredients. Because they are concentrated hydrophilic agents, as soon as the gum connects with water it will get gummy and be difficult to mix. However, if you wish to combine a gum with liquid, it must be beaten with a stick beater until thoroughly combined and thickened. Gums are used in yeast breads, flat breads, tortilla, pasta, crêpes and benefit muffins, coffee cake, quick breads, snack balls, pancakes, and other products.

Gums can be used on their own or in combination with other hydrophilic binders. When a softer crumb is desired, a combination of hydrophilic binders, those needing agitation and those needing time is more desirable than one or the other alone.

It is important to note that fat interferes with the function and strength of gums. Oils have a greater impact on the function of hydrophilic binders. To imagine this, think of participating in a tug o' war while wearing greased gloves. Fats and/or oils coat the binder and flour particles, notably reducing binder function. If you desire a cake-like texture or you need to reduce the gluey consistency of your dough, a little oil does the trick.

HB GROUP 2: Methylcellulose works with water-based liquids to enhance the strength and stretch of the final project. Methylcellulose adds to the "chew" factor in texture. The amount of methylcellulose used is based on the amount of water-based liquid present in the recipe and the amount of stretch and "chew" desired in the final product. The higher the ratio of methylcellulose to water-based liquid incorporated into the baked item, the greater the "chew" factor. To fully activate methylcellulose's strength and stretch, it needs to be beaten at high speed for approximately 1-2 minutes. Methylcellulose does not like to mix directly with a liquid. It is best to mix it in with the dry ingredients. To combine methylcellulose with liquid, it must be beaten with a stick hand beater until thoroughly combined and foamy. When beaten, methylcellulose produces foam which is a very useful characteristic for adding volume and structure (see Foams for more information).

Methylcellulose can be used on its own or in combination with other hydrophilic binders. Methylcellulose is excellent for use in yeast bread, pizza dough, flat breads, tortilla, and other products.

Methylcellulose is impacted by oil-type fats to a lesser extent than gums - particularly when incorporated into the batter as foam.

HB GROUP 3: Psyllium husk is a hydrophilic fibre that works with water-based liquids to enhance the strength of the final product. Psyllium is not as concentrated as the hydrophilic binders that require agitation from Groups 1 and 2 nor does it create as strong a structure or stretch, making it a good choice for items such as pancakes, muffins, cakes, and cookies. Psyllium is often used in combination with the binders found in Groups 1 and 2 in order to create the best texture for the baked item. Although psyllium is a fibre, it dissolves so it is not noticeable in the crumb structure. Of all the Binder Groups, psyllium's effectiveness is least impacted by oil-type fats.

HB GROUP 4: Chia seeds work with water-based liquid to enhance the strength and stretch of the baked structure. Chia seeds work best when ground. This maximizes the hydrophilic binding effect and reduces any impact on visual appearance of seeds in the crumb or added texture from the seed structure. When left whole chia seeds provide a slight crunch and have a slightly slimy mouth-feel. This effect results in a desire to continue to chew longer than is usual in an effort to clear the little bits of seed from your mouth. Even when ground they can be visible in the baked item if the crumb is light and fine. Ground chia seed is not as concentrated as the hydrophilic binders that require agitation from Groups 1 and 2 nor does it create as strong a structure or stretch. This makes chia seeds a good choice for pancakes, muffins, cakes, and cookies. Ground chia seed is often used in combination with the binders found in Group 1 and 2 in order to create the best texture for the baked item. If you cannot find ground chia seeds, you can make them yourself using a coffee grinder. Grind the seeds as needed. The effectiveness of chia seeds, ground or whole, is impacted by oil-type fats.

HB GROUP 5: In terms of function, flax seeds are best when ground. Grinding also reduces the seeds' impact on texture. Ground flax seeds are the weakest of the hydrophilic binders and the volume required to achieve the effect is often too great and starts to take away from product quality.

Flax seeds, ground or whole, provide nutritional benefit and, in limited quantities, may be added without negative impact on the final product. If using flax seeds as a hydrophilic binder, they must be used in combination with other hydrophilic binders to provide the binding power required to hold the item together.

CATEGORY 2:
PROTEIN BINDERS

You will see two protein binders under the section on foams, namely gelatin and egg white. These ingredients have multiple benefits due to their characteristics. Protein Binders assist in binding or "sticking" baked goods together by increasing the strength of the structure and adding the "glue" that keeps the ingredients together.

PROTEIN BINDERS

	PB GROUP 1	**PB GROUP 2**	**PB GROUP 3**
INGREDIENT	Egg white	Gelatin	Agar
	Egg white powder		
SOURCE	Animal	Animal	Vegetable
FORM	Liquid / Powder	Powder	Powder

PB GROUP 1
(EGG WHITE, EGG WHITE POWDER):

- Binders in PB Group 1 contain protein that provides strength and structure to gluten-free products and enhances leavening. Egg whites change in structure when heated to create a binding effect. Powdered egg whites are an excellent way to enhance the recipe's protein content and add strength to gluten-free products.

- Egg whites are neutral in flavour, add liquid to recipes, work well with all flours, can be used alone or in combination with other binders and can be beaten into foam to assist in leavening. All of this makes egg white the most versatile of the protein binders.

PB GROUP 2
(GELATIN):

- Gelatin is a concentrated protein powder that can be added to batters to enhance strength and structure. Gelatin can be used in combination with other protein binders to enhance structure and binding and it can be used in place of other protein binders.

- Gelatin can be used with all flours and in most forms of baking. Fat-based items do not tend to turn out well when gelatin is used.

- Gelatin, in the right quantity and volume, is very effective. It is easy to overdo gelatin and when it is used in higher quantities, it can take away from the texture and flavour of the final product. For example, for one loaf of bread we use 3 packages of gelatin dissolved in 1 cup of water, beaten into stiff foam. A similar concentration of gelatin in a cake would make the cake too firm and the taste of gelatin would be noticeable.

PB GROUP 3
(AGAR):

- Agar is a concentrated protein powder that can be added to batters to enhance strength and structure.

- Agar is an excellent option for vegan baking.

- Agar can be used in combination with other protein binders to enhance structure and binding or can be used in place of other protein binders.

- Agar will not beat into foam.

- It is best to dissolve agar into the liquid portion of the recipe prior to incorporating into the baked good. This enhances its binding effect.

- Agar enhances the saltiness of the baked good so it is necessary to reduce the amount of salt called for in the recipe.

- Like other binders, the volume used in the recipe depends on what is being created. Yeast breads require greater quantities where muffins require less. Generally speaking, if you are going to gel 2 cups of liquid you need about 1½ tsp agar powder or about 1 tbsp agar flakes. When making 1 loaf of yeast bread, we dissolve about 2½ - 3 tsp agar in the liquid required for the recipe and when making a batch of muffins, we only use about ½ - ¾ tsp agar.

CHAPTER 3:
LEAVENING AGENTS AND FOAMS – INGREDIENTS THAT MAKE "GAS" AND "AIR"

There are two groups of ingredients that help to add "air" or "gas" to a baked good, to create a lighter, more desirable crumb and an end product that leaves us saying "yum". The first is leavening agents; the second is foams.

CATEGORY 1:
LEAVENING AGENTS

Leavening agents are very important in creating delicious baked products – gluten-free or otherwise! The chemistry of baking is apparent with leavening agents. We have talked about flour mixes and ingredients that assist in creating stronger structure and the goal in leavening is to produce gas during preparation and cooking that will push up on the cellular structure causing it to rise. To achieve and maintain the rise, a baked good's structure needs to be elastic enough to be stretched by the gas, and strong enough to contain the gas and sustain the rise. However, gas is only so strong, so if the batter structure is too heavy, the product won't rise. In other words, the greater the weight of the batter, the harder it is for the gas to lift the structure up.

BAKING POWDER

CHARACTERISTICS
- Baking powder is a fine white powder. It is a chemical leavener containing alkali (baking soda) and acid (cream of tartar) which, when mixed with liquid, produces carbon dioxide gas. Double-acting baking powder contains a fast-release and a slow-release acid: one that works at room temperature and one that is activated with heat. Baking powder is either aluminum-containing or aluminum-free.

USE
- Used to produce gas in baked products to assist leavening. Double-acting baking powder is best in gluten-free baking because it allows for two opportunities to produce gas and subsequently to allow for rise. When creating a baked good with double-acting baking powder, allow the baked good to sit in the pan for 10-15 minutes prior to baking to allow the first release of gas to occur. The second release will work when the product is placed in the heat of the oven.
- Baking powder is used in flat beads, quick breads, muffins, cakes, biscuits, scones, cookies, pancakes, waffles, and crêpes.

STORAGE
- Baking powder has a long shelf life. Store in an airtight container.

BAKING SODA

CHARACTERISTICS
- Baking soda is a fine white powder made from sodium bicarbonate.. It is a chemical leavener that gives off carbon dioxide gas in the presence of moisture, particularly acidic liquids such as lemon juice, fruit juice, vinegar, and fermented dairy products.

USE
- Used to produce gas in baked goods to assist in leavening. If an acidic ingredient is called for in a recipe, even a small amount of baking soda can significantly increase the amount of air produced.
- Baking soda is used in flat breads, quick breads, muffins, cakes, biscuits, scones, cookies, pancakes, waffles, and crêpes.
- Baking soda has a metallic taste and is detectable if too much is added to a recipe. Use the smallest amount required to achieve the desired result.

STORAGE
- Baking soda has a long shelf life. Store in an airtight container.

CREAM OF TARTAR

CHARACTERISTICS
- Cream of tartar is a white, fine crystalline powder that naturally forms on the inside walls of wine barrels during the fermentation process of grape juice.

USE
- Cream of tartar is a component of baking powder and it can be added on its own to provide additional acid. Cream of tartar assists in the production of gas and is used for leavening.
- Cream of tartar adds stability and volume to beaten egg whites and other foams.

STORAGE
- Cream of tartar has a long shelf life. Store in an airtight container.

EGG REPLACER

CHARACTERISTICS
- Egg replacer is a white powder that is often used to replace eggs when eggs are not an option (e.g. allergy to eggs or vegan diets). Egg replacer assists in leavening. It is comprised of starch (potato starch, tapioca starch), leaveners (calcium lactate, calcium carbonate, and cream of tartar) and gums (cellulose gum and modified cellulose).
- When mixed with water the resulting liquid assists in gas production, thickening, and binding.

USE
- Use to assist in leavening and lightening gluten-free products. For best results mix first with water and beat with a stick beater (hand beater) and then add the mixture to batter. Egg replacer can be added to dry ingredients as a powder to assist in leavening even when eggs are included in the batter.
- Egg replacer can be used in all baked goods. In the case of yeast bread, other binders and "gas" producing ingredients are needed as well for best results.

STORAGE
- Egg replacer has a long shelf life. Store in an airtight container.

YEAST

CHARACTERISTICS
- Yeast comes in different forms. Generally, yeast is sold as beige granules. Yeast feeds off sugars in the baked item and produces gas as a result (known as fermentation). When soaked in water and small amounts of sugar, yeast activates and foams. It is the gas production that results as a byproduct of fermentation that assists leavening.

USE
- Yeast is added to assist leavening in products such as breads, buns, some biscuits, pizza dough, bread sticks, some "Italian style" flat breads, and more.
- Yeast adds flavour to baked products: the more yeast, the greater the flavour and the greater the rise.

STORAGE
- Store in the refrigerator once opened. Follow expiration dates.

VINEGAR, LEMON AND LIME JUICE

CHARACTERISTICS
- Vinegar, lemon and lime juice are concentrated acidic liquids that react with baking soda to produce gas and assist leavening. Small amounts can make a large volume of gas without affecting the flavour of the baked item.

USE
- Acidic liquids are used to enhance acid content of a baked item and assist leavening when baking soda is present. Acidic liquids are used in items such as pancakes, waffles, muffins, loaves, non-yeast breads, biscuits, scones, and cookies.

STORAGE
- Store as directed on the label.

CARBONATED LIQUIDS

CHARACTERISTICS
- Liquid with gas! The carbonation process forces gas in to liquids, creating bubbles.

USE
- Carbonated liquids are used in gluten-free baking to assist leavening by adding pre-formed "gas" into the batter.
- Many carbonated liquids (e.g. soda and colas) are acidic. When combined with baking soda, carbonated liquids create and add gas to the baked product.
- Carbonated beverages can add to flavour of the baked good. Be sure to pair the flavour of the beverage to your baking.

STORAGE
- Store as directed on the label.

CATEGORY 2:
FOAMS

All foams add "air" to a baked item but they also add moisture. There are two different types of foam: those that add structural stability, binding and "air" and those that just add "air". The incorporation of air into gluten-free baked goods is very important and can change a good product into a great product. For example, adding eggs to muffins assists in binding and rising, but adding beaten egg whites and beaten egg yolks lifts, lightens, and strengthens the muffins to be beautifully delicious.

FOAM GROUP 6 - AIRY FOAM: Coconut cream creates unstable or fragile airy foam. Coconut cream foam can be made more stable if the cream is refrigerated for several hours prior to being whipped. Adding a small amount of acid, such as cream of tartar, and a small amount of sugar, such as corn syrup, assists in strengthening the foam. Whipped coconut cream is useful in such items as cakes, muffins, or other delicate batters where maximizing the leavening is desirable.

FOAM GROUP 7 - AIRY FOAM: Evaporated milk can be beaten into airy foam. Evaporated milk has less water volume than other milks and thus will create weak foam. To increase the stability of evaporated milk foam, add an acid such as cream of tartar or lemon juice, and a liquid sugar, such as corn syrup. The advantage of evaporated milk is that it is lower in fat. Evaporated milk foam does have a slightly stronger flavour than other foams, which many palates consider enriches the rich taste of the product.

CHAPTER 4:
INTRODUCTION TO SWEETENERS

Most sweeteners are carbohydrates, commonly called sugars. Sugars have many important roles in baking. Sugars add moisture and binding, and they tenderize product crumb. Sugar melts in baked products helping the product spread out and crisp up. Sugar caramelizes at high temperatures and enhances flavours and, of course, adds sweetness. Sugars also extend the shelf life of baked goods. There are different forms of sweeteners – liquid, crystal or powder. There are also white sugars and dark sugars. Not all sweeteners are equally substituted one-for-one. The quality and desirability of the baked product can be enhanced or diminished by the type and volume of the sweetener used. See the following charts to learn more about sweeteners.

CATEGORY 1:
LIQUID SWEETENERS

SWEETENER	HONEY
CHARACTERISTIC	• Sweet, thick liquid sweetener. It is sweeter than sugar in flavour. Honey hardens when heated to high temperature and cooled can be used as "glue" in baked goods such as granola bars. Honey contains moisture so if adding to baked goods, you may need to reduce the liquid content slightly.
COMPOSITION	• Composed mainly of fructose and glucose. Honey is similar in composition to synthetically produced syrup. • 82.5% Carbohydrate, 17% water, 0.5% protein.
TASTE	• Mild flavour that changes with area and type of flowers.

Recipes, Ingredients, Tools, & Techniques

USE	• For every cup of sugar use ¾ cup of honey. Reduce liquid by 2-3 tbsp or increase flour by 3 tbsp. Add a pinch of baking soda to neutralize the acidity unless the recipe calls for fermented dairy (yogurt, sour cream, or buttermilk).
STORAGE	• Store in sealed container at room temperature.
NOTES	• Honey is made by bees and is not considered a plant-based sweetener, but an animal based sweetener. For this reason honey is not part of vegan diets.

SWEETENER	**MAPLE SYRUP**
CHARACTERISTIC	• Thin brown syrup with a distinct maple flavour. Can be cooked down to thicken.
COMPOSITION	• Composed mainly of sucrose and water. Sucrose is a sugar which Is made up of glucose and fructose combined together. • 67% Carbohydrate, 33% water.
TASTE	• Distinct maple flavour.
USE	• For every cup of sugar use ⅔ cup of maple syrup. Reduce liquid by 3 tbsp or increase flour by 4 tbsp.
STORAGE	Refrigerate after opening.

SWEETENER	**AGAVE SYRUP**
CHARACTERISTIC	• Thin light or darker golden syrup. Sweeter than sugar. Can be cooked down to concentrate. Does not form strong "glue" in baked goods such as granola bars. Bars will be softer and not crunchy due to the increased moisture content.
COMPOSITION	• Composed mainly of fructose and glucose. It can be as high as 92% fructose.
TASTE	• Sweet liquid with a slight flowery flavour.
USE	• For every cup of sugar use ⅔ cup of agave syrup, reduce liquid by ¼ cup or increase flour by 4 tbsp.

STORAGE	• Store in sealed container at room temperature.

SWEETENER	**BROWN RICE SYRUP**
CHARACTERISTIC	• Light golden syrup. Does not taste as sweet as sugar.
COMPOSITION	• Composed mainly of glucose, maltose, and maltotriose.
TASTE	• Nutty, sweet liquid.
USE	• For every cup of sugar use 1 cup of brown rice syrup. Reduce liquid by 3-5 tbsp or increase flour by 4 tbsp.
STORAGE	• Store in sealed container at room temperature.
NOTES	• Make sure brown rice syrup is labeled gluten-free. If it does not state gluten-free, it may contain gluten.

SWEETENER	**MOLASSES**
CHARACTERISTIC	• Molasses can either come from sugarcane or beet plants and is incorporated as part of animal feeds. Cane sugar molasses is used to make black strap molasses. Thick syrup that is not as sweet as some syrups. There is light and dark molasses.
COMPOSITION	• Composed mainly of sucrose. Sucrose is a sugar which is made up of glucose and fructose combined together. • Beet molasses = 16.5% water, 53% carb, 19% non-sugar materials, 11.5% inorganic materials (ash). • Cane molasses 20% water, 62% carb, 10% non-sugar materials, 8% inorganic materials (ash).
TASTE	• Distinct flavour. Dark, full bodied, almost burnt caramel flavour. The darker the molasses, the stronger the "burnt" flavour.
USE	• For every cup of sugar use 1⅓ c of molasses and reduce the liquid by ½ c. Since molasses is more acidic than sugar, add ½ tsp baking soda for every cup of molasses.
STORAGE	• Store in a sealed container at room temperature.

Recipes, Ingredients, Tools, & Techniques

NOTES	• Black strap molasses is a source of iron, potassium, calcium, and magnesium.

SWEETENER	**CORN SYRUP**
CHARACTERISTIC	• Also known as glucose syrup. Comes in white or dark and is a thick sticky liquid.
COMPOSITION	• Composed of 93-96% glucose.
TASTE	• Corn syrup has a mild flavour and is sweet.
USE	• Corn syrup is useful in baking as it tends to harden when heated. This can be a useful tool if you want to create harder crunch items such as granola bars. It can also help to hold structure in items such as whipping cream if you are adding whipped cream to your recipe. When using, you may have to reduce the sugar in your recipe.
STORAGE	• Store in sealed container at room temperature.

SWEETENER	**FRUIT JUICE CONCENTRATE**
CHARACTERISTIC	• Thin fruity syrup with high moisture content.
COMPOSITION	• Composition will vary among juice concentrates from 37% to 43% carbohydrate.
TASTE	• Flavour depends on the type of fruit juice concentrate used. Very similar to natural fruit flavour.
USE	• A wonderful substitute for sugar. Use ¾ c of fruit juice concentrate for every 1 c of sugar and reduce the liquid by 3 tbsp, or add ¼ c of flour.
STORAGE	Refrigerate after opening.

CATEGORY 2:
CRYSTAL SWEETENERS

All crystal sugars have had most of the moisture removed to form the crystal. Sugars are used to sweeten, to assist in creating desired texture, and to assist in creating a golden colour. Sweeteners also assist in preserving. From our experience crystal sugars have the same sticking or binding power.

SWEETENER	MAPLE SUGAR
CHARACTERISTIC	• A golden coloured sweetener that comes from the maple tree.
COMPOSITION	• Maple sugar is composed of roughly 90% sucrose, the remainder consists of variable amounts of glucose and fructose.
TASTE	• Has a distinct maple flavour.
USE	• Can be used in place of cane sugar. Is noted to be about twice as sweet as cane sugar.
STORAGE	• Store in air tight container in pantry.
NOTES	• If sugar hardens into a hard lump, place a small drip of maple syrup onto the top of the hard lump and leave overnight to assist in adding moisture and breaking up the harder lumps.

SWEETENER	COCONUT PALM SUGAR
CHARACTERISTIC	• Is a dark brown sweetener that has a distinct molasses-like flavour.
COMPOSITION	• Coconut palm sugar is approximately 70-79% sucrose. Sucrose is a sugar which is made of up glucose and fructose combined together. Glucose and fructose are also present individually – each of these sugars is present in less than 10%.
TASTE	• Has a brown sugar-like taste that is closer to caramel than molasses.
USE	• Best used in place of brown sugar. Can be substituted one-for-one with sugar.
STORAGE	• Store in an air tight container in a dark and dry, cool place.

NOTES	• Studies on coconut sugar indicate that it is lower in glycemic index than other sugars and is thought to be a healthier sweetener than sugar. It is also contains potassium, magnesium, and iron in greater quantities than brown sugar.
SWEETENER	**WHITE SUGAR**
CHARACTERISTIC	• A white sugar that is sweet and is what most people think of when we talk about "sugar". The two main sources of "sugar" are sugarcane and sugar beets.
COMPOSITION	• White sugar is sucrose (glucose and fructose combined.)
TASTE	• Has a sweet flavour that picks up the predominant flavour of what it is combined with.
USE	• Can be used in anything to increase sweetness. • Comes in granular (white sugar) and powder (icing sugar) forms.
STORAGE	• Store in an airtight container in the pantry.

SWEETENER	**BROWN SUGAR**
CHARACTERISTIC	• Brown sugar is white granular sugar with the presence of molasses. It can be created in two ways, either by processing sucrose pods or by adding molasses back to refined sugar. The second option is more cost effective and provides a consistent level of molasses in brown sugar. Light brown sugar has 3.5% molasses content, and dark brown sugar has 6.5 %molasses content
COMPOSITION	• A product produced from sugarcane mixed with molasses, brown sugar contains more moisture than white sugar due to the molasses content.
TASTE	• Light brown sugars have a milder flavour than dark brown sugars. The darker the colour the more the flavour increases from caramel to molasses.
USE	• Can be used in anything to increase sweetness.
STORAGE	• Store in an airtight container in the pantry.
NOTES	• If sugar hardens into a lump, place a small amount of molasses onto the top of the hard lump and leave overnight to assist in adding moisture and breaking up the harder lump.

SWEETENER	**DATE SUGAR**
CHARACTERISTIC	• Date sugar is simply powdered dried dates.
COMPOSITION	• Made from powdered dried dates.
TASTE	• Tastes like dates.
USE	• Cannot be used to replace sugar 1-for-1. Can be added as a flavour and sweetener but will not replace stick factor or moisture of sugar.
STORAGE	• Store in an airtight container.
NOTES	• Is a source of calcium, magnesium, phosphorus, and potassium.

SWEETENER	XYLITOL
CHARACTERISTIC	• Is a white crystal created by extracting xylitol from fruits and vegetables and processing it to be a sugar-like crystal. Most Xylitol comes from China and is corn based. Canadian xylitol comes from hardwood trees.
COMPOSITION	• Xylitol is a "tooth-friendly" non-fermentable sugar alcohol.
TASTE	• Has a sweet flavour that picks up the predominant flavour of the ingredients with which it is combined.
USE	• Xylitol has the same sweetness as sugar and can be substituted one-for-one for sugar in all recipes. • If you want brown sugar, add a small amount (1-2 tbsp) of molasses to xylitol. • Xylitol is a sugar alcohol so it does not provide food for yeast to grow. If you are creating yeast bread products, you have to add some other sweetener such as sugar or honey to allow the yeast to grow and produce gas for leavening. • Xylitol does not brown well and does not melt like other sweeteners do. Baked goods can be drier because of this. Adding moisture containing foods such as apple sauce, mashed banana or pumpkin or yogurt that pairs well with what you are making assists in reducing dryness. Liquid can also be added. For every cup of xylitol add about ¼ cup of added moisture. Xylitol also does not have the sticking or binding power of sugar. Adding a small amount (scant ⅛ tsp) of xanthan gum to the xylitol can assist in binding.
STORAGE	• Store in an airtight container in a dark, dry and cool place.
NOTES	• Xylitol is noted to assist in decreasing dental caries (cavities or tooth decay). There are many other health claims connected to xylitol. Xylitol was first created by German and French chemists as a safe sugar for people with diabetes to consume. • Xylitol in larger quantities may have a laxative effect. • Like chocolate, xylitol is life-threatening to dogs.

SWEETENER	**STEVIA**
CHARACTERISTIC	• Stevia rebaudiana, commonly known as sweet leaf or sugar leaf.
TASTE	• Has a sweet taste that is slower to develop, but has a longer and sweeter licorice aftertaste that some people find to be a bit bitter.
USE	• Comes in liquid and powder form and is much sweeter than sugar. Below is a conversion chart for using stevia.
	• Stevia Conversion Chart

1 tsp stevia (powered) = 1 cup sugar
1 tsp stevia (liquid) = 1 cup sugar
1 individually-sized packet (for coffee or tea) = 1 tsp stevia = 1 tbsp sugar
6 drops liquid stevia = 1 tbsp sugar
A pinch of stevia= 1 tsp sugar
2 drops liquid stevia= 1 tsp sugar

- Because stevia is not a sugar, it does not melt or provide added moisture. To adjust for this deficit you have to add ¼ to ½ cup (per cup of sugar in the recipe) of a moisture-containing food that pairs well with what you are making such as apple sauce, yogurt, mashed banana or pumpkin, etc. You can even add liquid such as water, fruit or vegetable juice, dairy or alternate milk. It is also beneficial to add a small amount (scant ⅛ tsp) of xanthan gum as stevia has no binding power.

- Stevia does not feed yeast for growth. If you are creating yeast bread products, you have to add some other sweetener such as honey or sugar to allow the yeast to grow and produce gas for leavening.

STORAGE
- Store in an airtight container or closed bottle in your pantry.

NOTES
- Stevia has been used for centuries around the world. There has been some concern raised in recent years about the use of stevia and the possible negative side-effects. Today stevia is sold as a dietary supplement. Stevia has a rating on the glycemic index of zero thus is very popular in low carbohydrate diets.

- Brand-to-brand the same volume of stevia does not produce the same sweetness. Experiment to taste.

There has been much discussion about carbohydrate intake and health. The glycemic index of foods has been researched and used in research studies. Foods containing carbohydrates have a glycemic index rating. The glycemic index is the measurement of how quickly blood sugar levels rise after eating or drinking a food or fluid. The higher the glycemic index the greater the capacity the food or fluid has in raising blood sugars. However, glycemic index does not take into account the amount of carbohydrate in the serving being consumed. "Glycemic Load" is the measurement that looks at both of these factors. For instance you could have a food that has a high glycemic index, but has low volume per serving resulting in a lower glycemic load. Research is showing that it is important to include low glycemic index foods in the diet and even one per meal, but not all foods consumed need to be low in glycemic index. There are other factors that impact rise in blood sugars. For example, the presence of protein, fat, and soluble fibres slows down the rate of carbohydrate breakdown in the gut – another reason to eat a mixed diet of lean meat and meat alternatives, including flours from, nuts and seeds along with healthy fats and soluble fibres from legumes, grains, and nuts and seeds.

For health and function, use the sweetener you need, in the smallest volumes required, to get the best result.

SUMMARY TABLE:
SWEETENERS

LIQUID SWEETENERS | **CRYSTAL OR POWDER SWEETENERS**

CARBOHYDRATE CONTAINING		NON-CARBOHYDRATE CONTAINING	CARBOHYDRATE CONTAINING			NON-CARBOHYDRATE CONTAINING
SWEETENER GROUP 1	SWEETENER GROUP 2	SWEETENER GROUP 6	SWEETENER GROUP 3	SWEETENER GROUP 4	SWEETENER GROUP 5	SWEETENER GROUP 6
Corn syrup	Maple syrup	Stevia	White sugar	Brown sugar	Date sugar	Xylitol
Cane syrup	Agave syrup			Raw sugar		Stevia
Honey				Demerara sugar		
Molasses				Coconut sugar		
Brown rice syrup						

SWEETENERS GROUP 1
(CORN SYRUP, CANE SYRUP, HONEY*, MOLASSES, BROWN RICE SYRUP)

Sweeteners in Sweeteners Group 1 are sweet syrups that have multiple uses in baked goods. These syrups are carbohydrate-containing sweeteners and provide sweetness, browning, moisture to crumb, and binding capacity. Many recipes have been designed specifically for these liquid sweeteners taking advantage of their strong "stick" or binding capacity. If substituting these syrups into an existing recipe, then the conversions listed in the chart will assist in maintaining moisture content and sweetness of the recipe. Honey is marked with a symbol as this sweetener is produced by bees and thus is not considered plant based, but animal based. Honey is not part of vegan diets.

SWEETENERS GROUP 2
(MAPLE AND AGAVE SYRUP)

Sweeteners in Sweeteners Group 2 are sweet syrups that have multiple uses in baked goods. Maple and agave syrups are carbohydrate-containing sweeteners and provide sweetness, browning, moisture to crumb, and some binding capacity. Many recipes have been designed specifically for these liquid sweeteners.

If substituting these syrups into an existing recipe, then the conversions listed in the chart will assist in maintaining moisture content and sweetness of the recipe. Because maple syrup and agave syrup are higher in moisture their "stick" factor is reduced. If syrups are reduced through heating prior to adding to recipe, the stick factor will increase and the moisture adjustment will change to one more similar to that of honey. The sweetness will also intensify. For simplicity it is often better to use maple or agave syrup in recipes like muffins, or cakes versus crunchy granola bars.

SWEETENERS GROUP 3
(WHITE SUGAR)

White sugar is a carbohydrate-containing sweetener used in multiple ways and is commonly referred to as "sugar". White sugar is the standard that we generally compare other sweeteners to for sweetness, browning, flavour, moisture, and binding capacity. If exchanging a liquid sweetener for white sugar, you need to add moisture to maintain the moisture content of the recipe. A general substitution is as follows – for every cup of liquid sweetener use 1¼ cup of sugar plus 3-4 tbsp of liquid such as water.

SWEETENERS GROUP 4
(BROWN SUGAR, RAW SUGAR, DEMERARA SUGAR, COCONUT SUGAR)

Sweeteners in Sweeteners Group 4 are carbohydrate-containing sweeteners and provide sweetness, browning, flavour, moisture to crumb and binding capacity. This group tends to provide more moisture than sweeteners in Sweeteners Group 3 due to the molasses or sap content. Generally this group can be substituted one-for-one with Sweeteners Group 3 and the rules for substitution between crystal sweetener and liquid sweetener generally apply. The sweeteners in this group provide more minerals than those in Sweetener Group 3.

SWEETENERS GROUP 5
(DATE SUGAR)

Date sugar is made from powdered dates. Unlike other sweeteners date sugar does not melt and form a liquid glue thus it does not provide binding or extra moisture like other sweeteners. When adding date sugar to a recipe you generally need to increase the amount of sugar called for in the recipe by 3-4 tbsp of date sugar per cup, add 3-4 tbsp water for moisture, and a binder. For example, if the recipe calls for 1 cup of sugar, you need to add 1 cup of date sugar plus 3-4 tbsp extra of date sugar, 1/4 cup water, and 1/8 tsp gum. Do not use date sugar where the function of the sugar in the recipe is for binding, crispness as well as sweetness (for example, granola-type bars such as quinoa bars.)

SWEETENER GROUP 6
(XYLITOL AND STEVIA)

Sweeteners in Group 6 are sweeteners that do not contain carbohydrate. This makes them trickier to substitute for carbohydrate-containing sweeteners. Xylitol and stevia have similarities and differences as well. This group comes in different forms and flavours which can be beneficial in baking depending on what you are creating. For instance liquid stevia is easier to measure for baking purposes. But the three functions that sweeteners in Sweeteners Group 6 do not provide must be kept in mind when incorporating into baked products.

BROWNING: Sweeteners in Sweeteners Group 6 do not brown when baked. They are heat stable and keep their sweetness, but they do not caramelize.

MOISTURE: They do not add or help retain moisture to baked goods like carbohydrate-containing sweeteners which either contain moisture or melt into a liquid during baking. This means that additional liquids will need to be added to your baked good. See the chart at the start of this section for details.

DOES NOT FEED YEAST: neither one is a food source for yeast to grow and ferment; hence, no gas will be produced for leavening. If you wish to make yeast bread, a small amount of carbohydrate-containing sweetener will have to be used to activate the yeast for growth.

SECTION 3
About Solid and Liquid Fats

INTRODUCTION
TO SOLID AND LIQUID FATS

Fats come from different sources and forms: plant versus animal, saturated versus unsaturated, and hydrogenated versus non-hydrogenated.

Similar to carbohydrates and protein, fats play important functions in baking as well as in our health. In baking and cooking, fats assist with mouth-feel, flavour, moisture, crumb texture (tenderness, crispness, shortness), browning, emulsifying ingredients, and creating light airy structures. In our bodies, fats assist in satiety as well as the absorption rate and quantity of nutrients, minerals, and vitamins. Although saturated fats tend to work better in gluten-free baking it is important to be mindful of the amount of saturated fats that you consume. Eliminating hydrogenated fat and *trans* fats while using smaller amounts of natural saturated fats and larger amounts of natural unsaturated fat, is thought to be healthier for the body. Adding small amounts of oil can help to improve moisture and quality of the crumb. The timing and technique used to incorporate the oil are important to maximize the quality of the end result. In the following table, fats have been divided into solid fats, liquid oils, and semi-solid fats and oils. An overview of the function of each follows.

SUMMARY TABLE:
SOLID FAT

SOLID FAT

	FAT GROUP 1	**FAT GROUP 2**	**FAT GROUP 3**	**FAT GROUP 4**
			SOURCE	
TYPE	Animal	Nut	Animal & Vegetable	Animal & Vegetable
SOURCE	Butter	Macadamia nut butter	Lard	Hard margarine
			Shortening	
COMPOSITION	Mainly Saturated fat.	Mainly mono-unsaturated fat. Even though it is nut butter, macadamia nuts are the highest in fat and the most buttery in flavour. It is a heavier fat due to the carbohydrate, protein, and fibre content.	Lard is produced from animal fat – Mainly natural saturated fat. Shortening is plant based. Mainly mono-unsaturated fat. Original shortenings are hydrogenated and contain trans fats. Today you can get palm oil shortening that is not hydrogenated and does not contain trans fats.	Generally mainly mono-unsaturated fats. Hydrogenated and contain trans fats.

FAT GROUP 1
(BUTTER)

Butter is considered the best fat for multi-purpose baking. It tastes great, it browns nicely, it moistens, it whips and it creams. Butter creates perfect textures from soft crumb to flakey, short and crisp. Butter is a natural fat that is really the best solid true fat base of all of the solid fats – both for function and for body health.

Whipping butter helps to lighten and leaven the baked products by incorporating air into the batter.

Butter coats the flour mixture which assists in tenderizing or softening the structure by reducing the binding capacity. However, butter does not coat or weaken the structure to the same degree as liquid oils do. By using butter (rather than liquid oil), your baked good will be moist, and the binders will function better. During the baking process the batter or dough will have more structural strength to assist leavening and lightening while reducing breakage.

Do not allow butter's high saturated fat content scare you off. This naturally-occurring saturated fat contributes to the body's need for saturated fat. The key is to use only what you need and not consume your sweety-treaties in excess.

FAT GROUP 2
(MACADAMIA NUT)

Macadamia nut makes a nut butter that can be incorporated as part or all of the fat in baked items. For baked goods that need to be lighter, like cakes, a portion of the fat content can come from macadamia nut butter. For baked goods such as cookies, loaves, breads, and some flat breads, all of the fat can come from macadamia nut butter. Macadamia nut butter interferes with hydrophilic binders when used in larger quantities. This can have impact in baked products that need stretch and strength for rising or rolling. In smaller quantities macadamia nut butter has limited impact – less than when oil is used on its own. Macadamia nut butter can be whipped to incorporate air and lighten the fat and the final baked product. For people with allergies to milk products, macadamia nut butter makes a nice substitute for butter as it provides a rich and buttery flavour and responds better to higher temperatures when baking than other oil-based fats.

FAT GROUP 3
(LARD AND VEGETABLE SHORTENING)

Lard is a natural saturated fat that comes from rendered animal fats – usually pig fat, but can be derived from other animal fats as well. Historically, lard was commonly used as a source of fat in baking. Home cooks would save the fat after cooking meats and utilize it for baking once hard - a way of using up all that was available. Today we would call this fat recycling! Lard is a natural, dairy-free solid fat that can be made at home and recycled into baked goods. Lard assists in browning, moistening, tenderizing and creating soft, crisp, flake textures.

Vegetable shortenings are made from saturated vegetable fats.

Because lard comes from animal sources it does tend to add flavour to the baked item. Adding lard to pastry for meat pie can create a delicious end product.

Lard/shortenings, like butter, coats the flour mixture which assists in tenderizing or softening the structure by reducing the binding capacity. However, lard does not coat or weaken the structure to the same degree as liquid oils. By using lard/shortening, your baked goods will be moist and the binders will function better. By using lard/shortening the batter or dough has more structural strength to assist leavening and lightening and reduces breaking.

The key is to use only what you need to achieve the desired effect.

FAT GROUP 4
(HARD MARGARINE)

Hard margarines are "man-made", produced when a liquid oil undergoes the process of hydrogenation. Hydrogenated fats contain *trans* fatty acids which are not recommended for consumption. Our recommendation is not to use hard margarines. If a recipe calls for hard margarine, butter can generally be substituted one-for-one. Margarine does not act like butter and results in a substandard end product. For example, baked products such as cookies flatten out and are more likely to burn around the edges when a hard margarine is used.

SUMMARY TABLE:
SEMI-SOLID AND LIQUID FAT

SEMI-SOLID FAT | | | | **LIQUID FAT**

FAT GROUP 5	FAT GROUP 6	FAT GROUP 7	FAT GROUP 8	FAT GROUP 9
Cream cheese	Mashed avocado	Soft margarine	Low fat soft margarine	Oil
				Vegetable oils
				Nut and seed oils and creamed coconut
Mainly saturated fat. Full fat cream cheese is a high fat dairy product that can be used as a natural fat substitute.	Avocado is a high fat fruit that can be used as a natural fat substitute. Avocado is mainly mono-unsaturated fat.	Can be made from a variety of oils. Mainly mono-unsaturated or poly-unsaturated fats. Today, soft margarines are not hydrogenated and do not contain trans fats. Soft margarines are processed oils and not natural fats.	Can be made from a variety of oils. Mainly mono-unsaturated or poly-unsaturated. Today, soft margarines are not hydrogenated and do not contain trans fats. Soft margarines are processed oils and not natural fats.	Mainly unsaturated fats

FAT GROUP 5
(FULL FAT CREAM CHEESE)

Full fat cream cheese can be used as a fat replacement or in combination with other fats. Cream cheese has a fairly neutral flavour and can be used to enhance richness. Sometimes cream cheese is combined half and half with butter in pastries for tarts to create a stronger tart shell and add a rich, creamy taste to the crust. Cream cheese can be whipped into a light and airy fat to assist in lightening the final baked good. Cream cheese interferes minimally with the hydrophilic binder's ability to bind and hence can be used in baked goods where stretch and strength is required and desired.

FAT GROUP 6
(AVOCADO)

Avocado is not a "usual" fat like the others listed in the chart. Avocado is a high fat fruit that is packed with nutritional goodness and is an excellent natural fat substitute in many baked goods. Replacing half the fat called for in a recipe with mashed avocado results in a very similar or not noticeably different end product. Avocado has mass and moisture both of which are emulsified beautifully in avocado's natural fat, making it a perfect substitute for solid fat. Avocado can also be mixed half and half with oil in recipes that call for oil with minimal impact to the end product. We have successfully substituted avocado into yeast breads, muffins, waffles, cakes, cookies, and pastries.

Avocado does have a flavour and thus needs to be used in limited quantities and/or with stronger complementary flavoured ingredients such as chocolate, molasses, herbs, spices, garlic, tomato, cheese, nutritional yeast, ham, bacon, and such.

Since avocados are green, the colour of the dough does get a greenish tinge especially if the dough is light in colour. When baked, this greenish tinge significantly lightens and the golden brown colour of the baked good dominates.

FAT GROUP 7
(SOFT MARGARINES)

Soft margarines are "man-made", highly processed oils. There are many different kinds of soft margarine, all created from a different blend of oils, and other ingredients that add flavour and stability. The highly processed oils in soft margarines do not function the same as solid fats or liquid oils and often produce baked goods of poor quality. We do not recommend using soft margarines in baking.

FAT GROUP 8
(LOW-FAT SOFT MARGARINES)

Low-fat soft margarines are "man-made", highly processed oils. There are many different kinds of soft margarines, all created from a different blend of oils and other ingredients such as water to reduce the fat content that add flavour and stability. Low-fat soft margarines are even less suitable for baking than soft margarines and lead to a low quality end product. We do not recommend using low-fat soft margarines in baking.

FAT GROUP 9
(OILS)

There are many different types of oils to choose from on the market today. Liquid oils and naturally-occurring semi-solid oils (such as coconut oil/creamed coconut) are a healthier way of incorporating oils into your diet.

Plant-based oils behave differently in baking than solid animal fats do. Plant-based oils thoroughly coat the flour mixture which weakens the binding power of the hydrophilic binders. The weakened structure of the batter or dough limits leavening and increases fragility of the baked good. Because of this, products made with oils tend to be heavier, moister, and more cake-like in texture, rise less and break apart more. Oil in combination with solid fat such as butter or lard helps to keep baked goods moist and prevents drying out.

Oils can add flavour to the product or take on flavour of the other ingredients in the recipe. Choose the oil that best suits the baked item you are making. For example, adding sesame oil to naan-style flat bread may enhance its desirability whereas adding canola oil to pancakes may be more desirable.

Oils can be a good source of essential fatty acids and unsaturated fats, fats that are considered healthier. Some oils can withstand high heats while other oils are best used at lower temperature. Strategically incorporating a variety of oils into your baking results in delicious baked goods and increased potential for improved health.

SECTION 4

Summary of Gluten-Free Baking by Baked Goods

SUMMARY OF GLUTEN-FREE BAKING
BY BAKED GOOD GROUPS

We have divided baked goods into two main groups – water-based baked goods and fat-based baked goods. The flours, starches, binders and moisture in these two types of baked goods play a role in the choices that a baker of gluten-free products needs to make. We have included sample flour mixtures and other ideas with each category of baking.

CHAPTER 1:
WATER-BASED BATTERS AND DOUGH

RECIPE GROUP 1

FLOUR AND STARCH

YEAST BREADS

Bread, Pizza Dough, Buns, Cinnamon Buns, Angel Biscuits, and more

Using a combination of flours results in the best end product. Getting the right flour mix is important. For breads, we have found that having about 60 % of the flour mix come from Flour Group 1 (Brown Rice, Corn, Buckwheat, or Pure Oat* Flours) provides the structure that is needed to produce a lofty and airier bread. We also prefer to use Flour Group 3 (Millet Flour) and Group 4 (Quinoa and Bean Flours) to add moisture over Flour Group 2 (Sorghum, Teff and Fonio Flours). Flour Group 3 (Millet Flour) adds a chewier texture which is not present in Flour Group 2 (Sorghum, Teff and Fonio Flours). From our experience yeast breads need added protein but not added fat. Flour Group 9 (Defatted Nut and Seed Flours, Cocoa Powder and Protein Powder) provides protein without the added fat making it ideal for yeast breads. With the added attention to protein content in diets, there are many protein powders and an increasing number of defatted nut/seed flours on the market. Defatted flours contribute to the structure strength of yeast breads. And finally, we have found that yeast bread texture is better if a small amount of Starch Group 1 (Tapioca Starch) is added to the mix.

From our experience, everyone has their own preferences for flours and starches used – either for taste or ability to eat them. Below is "A Place to Start Yeast Bread Flour Mix" for you to use as a starting point to creating your own perfect mix.

> **A Place to Start Yeast Bread Flour Mix (10 Cups)**
> **6 cups Flour Group 1:** use one or a combination of flours
> **1 cup Flour Group 3** (Millet Flour);
> **1¼ cups Flour Group 4:** use one or a combination of flours from this group
> **¾ cup Flour Group 9** (Defatted Nut and Seed Flours, Cocoa Powder);
> **1 cup Starch Group 1** (Tapioca Starch): if using arrowroot, increase starch to 1½ cup

LIQUID

Really, it does not matter which liquid you use. Generally, watery "liquidy" liquids are better than semi-solid liquids (e.g. yogurt). The liquid in bread can be either a protein liquid or a non-protein liquid or combinations of the liquid groups. Protein liquids create a softer crumb that stays softer longer.

HYDROPHILIC BINDER

Yeast breads use the highest quantities of hydrophilic binders of all the baked goods. There should be between 3-4 tsp strong hydrophilic binder (xanthan gum and methylcellulose) per two (2) 8x4x2 inch pan which is the small standard-sized loaf. This may vary since you know that the liquid, binders, foams, sweeteners, and leaveners all have to work together and be in proportion. So depending on the other ingredients in the bread, this volume may change slightly which is why there is a 1 tsp variance noted above. If you can foam a hydrophilic binder such as methylcellulose with some of the liquid volume, do that as it adds to leavening and lightening of the bread. Small amounts of psyllium is effective also.

PROTEIN BINDER

Protein Binders Group 1 (Eggs), Group 2 (Gelatin), or Group 3 (Agar) all work as protein binder in yeast breads. An approximate place to start for volume is about 4 egg whites, or 3 packages of gelatin in 1 cup of water, or 3 tsp agar to ¾ cup water per two (2) 8x4x2 inch loaves.

Agar in combination with methylcellulose foam works better than agar on its own.

FOAM

Structural Foam Groups 1-3 are required in yeast breads – either alone or in combination. Methylcellulose foam in combinations with either egg white or gelatin foams produce superior results.

SWEETENER

Any carbohydrate-containing sweetener will work. Do not use xylitol or stevia on their own as they do not feed the yeast. If you decide that you wish to use xylitol or stevia, then you need to feed your yeast with sugar and add a small amount to the dough for best results.

Recipes, Ingredients, Tools, & Techniques

LEAVENING Yeast comes in traditional (regular) or quick rise. We find that both work. Personally we like to use traditional yeast. Quick rise yeast speeds up the rising time but does not result in as great a rise. Use a good amount of yeast. Generally you need 1½ to 2 times the amount needed in wheat bread recipe. Also, resist the urge to raise the dough twice. The structure does not benefit from a second rise. Only raise dough once. This is one area where we encourage you to cut corners.

FAT Small amounts of fat are generally used in yeast bread. Fat Group 1 (Butter) and Fat Group 3 (Lard) interferences less with the binding agents. That being said we used small amounts of oil to produce a quality product. The greater the fat content of the bread, the more we would recommend choosing from Fat Groups 1 (Butter) or 3 (Lard) because fat really challenges the binding power and compromises the rise. Oils however, do increase the moisture of the bread.

TOOLS An electric mixer of some sort is essential. It is important to thoroughly beat hydrophilic binders. Your efforts will be highly rewarded if you use a mixer. The dough tends to be too stiff for a hand mixer; making a stand mixer your best option. The great thing is that gluten-free yeast dough is not as tough to mix, so a less powerful stand mixer does the job well.

For best results accurately measure ingredients by using proper measuring tools (cups, scoops, and spoons, etc.)

Use a high-sided, round bottomed bowl for beating foam to reach maximum volume.

Have the right pans for the right dough – bread pans, pizza pan or stone, flat baking pans, bundt pans, and a few more. A French bread pan really helps to pull off the look and feel of the bread when making baguette-style bread for instance.

TECHNIQUES Pay attention to technique. Take time when creating the foams, proofing the yeast, sifting the flours, beating the dough, and letting it rise in a warm place. All lead to better end results. Anyone of these things helps, but together is best.

Remember, do not double rise your bread. That technique works well when working with gluten, but getting gluten-free dough to rise once is a trick. From our experience, it will not rise as well the second time.

TROUBLE SHOOTING If your bread is heavy and the top is bumpy and misshaped, generally that means that your dough does not have enough liquid in it.

If your bread does not rise well it is likely due to the yeast. Make sure that it is fresh and active. Feed the yeast before you add it to your bread by placing it in some water with some carbohydrate-containing sweetener. If your yeast is active, try increasing the amount of yeast used the recipe.

If your bread did not rise as well as you thought, check to make sure you added a carbohydrate-containing sweetener.

If your bread is not as light and airy as expected, check to ensure that you used structural foam (such as egg white) in your bread. Also, make sure that you sifted the flours after they were measured prior to adding to the dough.

If your bread is not as strong or chewy as you would like, check to make sure you added chewy flour mix (one that contains millet flour or oat flour and tapioca starch, for example), enough hydrophilic binder, and beat the dough well for several minutes to agitate and activate the hydrophilic binders. We like to beat bread dough for 4-5 minutes on high speed.

If your bread rises beautifully when baked, but then falls during cooling, you likely need to add more defatted protein flour or powder and increase the hydrophilic binders slightly.

If your bread is too "wet", it is likely that you have too much flour from Flour Group 4 (Quinoa, Lentil, Bean and Pea Flours). Or if you added Flour Group 5 (Amaranth Flour) or 6 (Coconut Flour) to your bread, these two groups have a tendency to create that wet texture. It also may be that your dough just had too much liquid in it and reducing the liquid volume slightly may help.

If you are using gelatin foam and the bread is too sticky or gummy, you likely have too much gelatin foam in the bread.

Recipes, Ingredients, Tools, & Techniques

RECIPE GROUP 2

FLOUR AND STARCH

FLAT BREADS, TORTILLA, CHIPATI, NAAN AND PANINI-STYLE FLAT BREADS

Getting the right flour mix for flat breads is important because you want to be able to roll them out and fry them in a pan. They need to have a good chew factor as well - otherwise they may be like a pancake - and that is not the goal! Flat breads do not need the strength to rise like yeast breads, but they do need stretch and chew. You do not need as much of Flours Group 1 (Brown Rice, Corn, Buckwheat, or Pure Oat* Flours) as yeast breads, but still about half is good. You are going to want to include a "chewier" flour such as Flour Group 3 (Millet Flour), a flour that is higher in protein and holds more moisture such as Flours group 4 (Quinoa and Bean Flours) and Flour Group 9 (Defatted Nut and Seed Flours or Protein Powders). To assist stretch and chew, you want to add Starch Group 1 (Tapioca Starch).

From our experience, everyone has their own preferences for flours and starches used – either for taste or ability to eat them. Below is "A Place to Start Flat Bread Flour Mix" for you to use as a starting point to creating your own perfect mix.

Place to Start Flat Bread Flour Mix (10 Cups)
4¼ **cups Flour Group 1:** use one or a combination of flours from Flour Group 1;
2 **cups Flour Group 3** (Millet Flour);
1⅔ **cups flour Group 4:** use one or a combination of flours;
¾ **cups Flour Group 9** (Defatted Nut and Seed Flour or Protein Powders): these work well in naan or flat breads but tend to decrease the stretch in tortillas;
1⅓ **cups Starch Group 1** (Tapioca Starch): Use tapioca. If using arrowroot, increase starch to 1¾ cup

LIQUID

Generally the liquid is water; however, the liquid can be either a protein liquid or a non-protein liquid.

HYDROPHILIC BINDER

Hydrophilic binders from Groups 1 (Xanthan and Guar Gums) and 2 (Methylcellulose) create the desired chew factor that is characteristic of flat breads. Like yeast bread, flat breads contain larger quantities. Again, we are not talking cup measures, but teaspoons. For a recipe that makes about 6 flat breads, about 2 tsp of Hydrophilic Binder Group 1 (Xanthan and Guar Gums) and/or Hydrophilic Binder Group 2 (Methylcellulose) is required. You will need to play with your recipe to get the volume correct. Hydrophilic binders work with the liquids and the other binders in the recipe. Remember that fats, particularly oil, take away from the strength, stretch and chew factor of the hydrophilic binder.

PROTEIN BINDER	Protein binders may or may not be used. Generally if a protein binder is used, it is egg white. However, adding gelatin or agar can be useful. Flat breads are supposed to be flat so do not foam the protein binder that is being incorporated. We have found that if using gelatin or agar, reconstituting the protein powder into some of the liquid volume first yields better results.
FOAM	Foams are not desired in flat breads as the goal is to keep them flat. If using methylcellulose, you need to mix it with a small amount of liquid to create very loose foam. This helps its action as a hydrophilic binder.
SWEETENER	Generally no sweetener is added unless the flat bread is intended for dessert.
LEAVENING	There may be no leavening agent in flat bread to keep it flat like tortillas. Sometimes small amounts of baking powder and/or baking soda may be present in thicker flat bread such as Panini-style flat bread.
FAT	Small amounts of fat are generally used in flat bread. Fat Group 1 (Butter) or Fat Group 3 (Lard) interferes less with the binding agents making it possible to roll out the dough.

Tortilla-style flat breads roll best when no fat is added to the recipe. When making thicker flat bread like Naan, the fat adds moisture, improves texture and does not take away from the ability to roll out.

It is best not to use oil; if oil is used, the flat bread dough will crack and break during rolling. A way to manage handling and transferring the flat bread is to roll it out on parchment paper that has been floured with sweet rice flour and then flip it into the frying pan. |
| **TOOLS** | The best way to make this dough is in a food processor with the "S" blade for beating. The dough is too stiff to beat with a hand beater. It is possible with a stand mixer, but really the food processor is the best and easiest.

For best results accurately measure your ingredients by using proper measuring tools (cups, scoops and spoons, etc.).

You also need a rolling pin and a surface for rolling. Parchment paper on the counter that is floured with sweet rice flour works well. The sweet rice flour tends not to dry out the dough as much as some of the other flours and does not add additional flavour. |
| **TECHNIQUES** | The most important thing you need to do is beat the dough using the "S" blade of your food processor. |

Another technique for enhancing elasticity is using boiling liquid. Gently pour boiling liquid in through the drop shoot of the food processor, onto the other ingredients while the food processor is running. While the ingredients mix into dough, the hot liquid cooks the starches creating a more elastic consistency.

TROUBLE SHOOTING

If your dough is crumbly, it is likely that there is not enough liquid in the dough or there is not enough strong hydrophilic binders, or if you used oil, your dough may not hold together.

If your dough cracks or breaks apart when rolling, it may be that you do not have enough hydrophilic binder, or your dough is slightly too dry. If you used oil as your fat, you are more likely to have your dough break. It also may be that you did not use boiling liquid or knead your dough long enough.

If your dough is too gummy, it is likely that you have too much strong hydrophilic binder in the dough and you may need to reduce the volume slightly.

If the flat bread has a bitter bean-like taste it could be that the cooking time of the flatbread was too short to cook out the bean flavour associated with raw bean flour. Use quinoa flour in place of bean flour.

RECIPE GROUP 3

PASTA DOUGH

FLOUR AND STARCH

Pasta has to have some chew factor. No one likes soft mushy noodles. Pasta is also supposed to be firm and moist. So, you want to choose a flour mix that enhances the chew factor and produces the wet squishy chew of pasta. For this I like to use Flour Group 1 (Brown Rice, Corn, Buckwheat, Pure Oat* Flours), Flour Group 3 (Millet Flour), Flour Group 4 (Quinoa and Bean Flours), Flour Group 5 (Amaranth Flour), and Starch Group 1 (Tapioca Starch.) Our experience is that corn flour needs to be finely ground as it tends to breakdown the elasticity of the dough and produce a mushier noodle.

From our experience, everyone has their own flour and starch preferences – either for taste or ability to eat them. Below is "A Place to Start Pasta Flour Mix" for you to use as a starting point to creating your own perfect mix.

A Place to Start Pasta Flour Mix (10 cups)
4¼ cups Flour Group 1: use one or a combination of flours;
1 cup Flour Group 3 (Millet Flour);
1 cup Flour Group 4: use one or a combination of flours;
1¼ cups Flour Group 5 (Amaranth Flour);
2½ cups Starch Group 1 (Tapioca Starch): If using arrowroot, increase starch to 3 1/4 cup

---

LIQUID

Generally the liquid in pasta is either water or juiced vegetable liquid. The liquid you use in your pasta recipe should not contain fat. Fat interferes with the binding agents and makes your dough harder to roll because it cracks and breaks more easily.

HYDROPHILIC BINDER

Pasta dough is like yeast breads and flat breads in that you need to use a healthy amount of hydrophilic binders from Groups 1 (Xanthan and Guar Gums) or 2 (Methylcellulose). Don't skimp on hydrophilic binders in pasta as they really help to create the chewy factor that is needed and are stable in the moist environment of pasta.

PROTEIN BINDER

Protein binders such as eggs are not always used in pasta. The hydrophilic binders are most important. If you are creating "egg noodles", the eggs in your dough are important.

FOAM

Foams are not used in pasta.

SWEETENER

Sweeteners are generally not used in pasta unless you are making dessert pasta such as chocolate noodles, then any crystalline or powdered sweetener will work. If using a liquid sweetener, adjust the liquid volume as found in the table on sweeteners.

LEAVENING	Leavening agents are not used in pastas.
FAT	Many wheat pasta recipes call for oil, but in gluten-free pasta, the oil breaks down the elastic structure too much making it difficult to work with. Do not add fat to gluten-free pasta.
TOOLS	To make pasta dough, a food processor with an "S" blade for beating the dough together is essential. The quantities of hydrophilic binder create stiff dough that cannot be beaten with a hand beater or even a stand mixer.
	For best results accurately measure ingredients using proper measuring tools (cups, scoops, spoons, etc.).
	A rolling pin can roll the pasta dough out or you can use a pasta maker.
	Using a stuffed pasta cutter is quicker than cutting by hand.
TECHNIQUES	Beat the ingredients in the food processor with an "S" blade.
	To create more elastic dough, slowly pour boiling liquid onto the mixed ingredients while beating.
	Once the dough is made and cooled, divide it into smaller balls and wrap each ball in plastic wrap to prevent dough from drying out.
TROUBLE SHOOTING	If your pasta does not hold together, it is likely that there is not enough hydrophilic binder present or that you used oil as your fat.
	If your pasta is too crumbly, it is likely that you do not have enough liquid in your dough. When you increase your liquid, you will likely need to increase the hydrophilic binder, not the flour, to create the right dough consistency.
	If the dough is too gummy, there is probably too much hydrophilic binder and liquid and you should reduce them both slightly or add more flour mix.

RECIPE GROUP 4 | CRÊPES

FLOUR AND STARCH

The flour mix in crêpes has more room for adjustment because the main structure of crêpes comes from eggs and milk. However, to get the right crêpe consistency we have found that a mixed gluten-free flour mix works better than any one of the flours on its own. Mixing flours encourages stability when rolled and creates the right chew factor. Using elastic flours and starches assists in reducing cracking when rolling with filling. Crêpes are thin and do not require much rise. The rise and structure comes from the egg and liquid mixture. Thus the need for Flour Group 1 (Brown Rice, Corn, Buckwheat, or Pure Oat* Flours) is reduced. We find that about one third of the flour mix from Flours Group 1 (Brown Rice, Corn, Buckwheat, or Pure Oat* Flours); one third of the flour mix from Flour Group 3 (Millet Flour) a small portion can be mixture of flours from Flour Group 9 (Defatted Nut and Seed or Protein Powders), and the remaining flour mix from Starch Group 1 (Tapioca Starch) works best.

From our experience, everyone has their own preferences for flours and starches used – either for taste or ability to eat them. Below is "A Place to Start Crêpe Flour Mix" for you to use as a starting point to creating your own perfect mix.

A Place to Start Crêpe Flour Mix (10 cups)
3 ⅔ cups Flour Group 1 use one or a combination of flours;
3 ⅔ cups Flour Group 3 (Millet Flour);
⅔ cups Flour Group 9 (Defatted Nut and Seed Flour or Protein Powder);
2 cups Starch Group 1 (Tapioca Starch) : if using arrowroot, increase starch to 2 1/3 cup

LIQUID

Protein liquids work best for crêpes.

HYDROPHILIC BINDER

Small amounts of hydrophilic binder from Hydrophilic Binder Groups 1 (Xanthan and Guar Gums) and/or 2 (Methylcellulose) work the best. The hydrophilic binder enhances the elasticity of the crêpe. Small amounts of hydrophilic binder are needed so that the crêpe batter remains runny enough to circle around in the bottom of the hot crêpe pan.

PROTEIN BINDER

Eggs are the protein binder of choice for crêpes.

FOAM

No foams are used in crêpes.

SWEETENER

Savoury crêpes do not use any sweetener. Dessert crêpes may use sweetener, it does not matter what sweetener you choose.

LEAVENING

Leaveners are not used in crêpes. The eggs act to leaven the crêpe the desired amount.

Recipes, Ingredients, Tools, & Techniques

FAT

Oil can be used successfully in crêpes because the egg is the binding agent that holds the crêpe together and it is not impacted by oil like hydrophilic binders are. If you find that your crêpes are cracking, you may want to reduce the oil or change to melted butter or lard.

TOOLS

You will need a hand beater or a blender to make crêpe batter. The small amount of hydrophilic binder really benefits from a minute or two of beating from an electric source.

For best results, accurately measure ingredients using proper measuring tools (cups, scoops, and spoons, etc.).

You will also need a crêpe pan or a small non-stick fry pan and ladle to pour the correct amount of batter into your pan. A small 6-inch pan and a ⅛ cup scoop works beautifully.

Heat resistant brush for brushing fat onto the pan.

Flipper to turn the crêpe over.

TECHNIQUES

Sift the flour after measuring. Sifting the flour adds air between the granules making your crepes lighter.

Blend or beat the batter.

Portion out the batter when pouring into the frying pan so that your crêpes are not too thick or too thin.

Ensure that your pan is hot and that you have only very lightly brushed it with melted butter or oil. If the pan is too greasy the batter will not stick to the pan and will slide around making it difficult to coat the bottom of the pan with batter thinly.

TROUBLE SHOOTING

If your crêpe batter does not run and cover the bottom of the pan, it is likely that your batter is too thick. Dilute it using a bit more liquid and blend it in for consistent batter.

If your batter is too thin and crêpes do not hold together, it is likely that you do not have enough eggs in the batter. Increasing the number of eggs helps solve this issue.

If your batter does not stick to the bottom of the pan so that you can get an even layer of crêpe batter when you circle the pan, it is likely that your pan is either too well greased or your pan is not hot enough.

RECIPE GROUP 5 | NON-YEAST BREAD LOAVES

Such as Irish Soda Bread, Pumpkin Bread, Zucchini Bread, Banana Bread, and Muffins

FLOUR AND STARCH

- The flour mixture for these breads and muffins needs to have more capacity for structure. There is not the same expectation of chewiness as with yeast bread. However, there is an expectation that the bread will be moist, yet firm enough to be sliced and buttered. There is a difference between this style of loaf and that of a cake loaf, which has an even softer crumb and is generally sweeter, and is eaten as cake.

- A good portion of the flour mix needs to come from Flour Group 1 (Brown Rice, Corn, Buckwheat, Pure Oat* Flours), and about equal amounts of a combination of Flour Groups 2 (Sorghum, Teff and Fonio Flours), 3 (Millet Flour) and 4 (Quinoa and Bean Flours), Flour Group 9 (Defatted Nut and Seed Flours and Protein Powders), and Starch Group 1 (Tapioca Starch.)

- From our experience, everyone has their own preferences for flours and starches used – either for taste or ability to eat them. Below is "A Place to Start Non-Yeast Bread Flour Mix" for you to use as a starting point to creating your own perfect mix.

A Place to Start Non-Yeast Bread Flour Mix (10 Cups)
3½ cups Flour Group 1: use one or a combination of flours;
2½ cups Flour Group 2: use one or a combination of flours;
1 cup Flour Group 3:
2 cups Flour Group 4: use one or a combination of flours;
½ cup Flour Group 9: use a combination or a single protein flour/powder of your choice;
½ cup Starch Group 1 (Tapioca Starch): If using arrowroot, increase starch to 3/4 cup

---

LIQUID

- The liquids are generally protein-based liquid. If you cannot use a protein-based liquid, use a non-protein based liquid and add some additional protein. Usually an additional tablespoon of protein powder or a teaspoon of protein binder such as gelatin or agar will work.

HYDROPHILIC BINDER

- You will need to use hydrophilic binders although not in the same quantities used in yeast breads. It is also best to use a combination of strong hydrophilic binders that require agitation and soft hydrophilic binders that require time. Our favourite combination is xanthan gum and psyllium. The amount of hydrophilic binders is determined by the liquid measure not the flour measure. If you have mashed fruit in the bread, you will need slightly more hydrophilic binder – generally the stronger group – Hydrophilic Binder Groups 1 (Xanthan and Guar Gums) or 2 (Methylcellulose).

Recipes, Ingredients, Tools, & Techniques

PROTEIN BINDER
- Include a protein binder. Egg, gelatin or agar all work. If using agar, also include methylcellulose foam to enhance lightness of the loaf. Often the protein binder also acts as your foam.

FOAM
- Foams are required for assisting with leavening and creating a lighter and more desirable product. Egg white foams, gelatin foams and methylcellulose foams all work well. If you are using agar as the protein binder to replace egg white, methylcellulose foam is a good combination to assist in leavening.

SWEETENER
- Any sweetener may be used with this recipe. A liquid sweetener adds to the moisture content so you may need to decrease the liquid ingredients of your recipe slightly if using a liquid sweetener.

LEAVENING
- Leavening agents are very important. Baking powder and baking soda in combination with an acid like buttermilk or vinegar are often used as the leavening agents. You may increase the baking powder volume compared to that of a wheat recipe. Increasing the baking soda often takes away from taste in the end product as it has a slight metallic taste.

FAT
- For best results use a solid fat (butter, lard or shortening) with a small amount of liquid fat (oil). Larger amounts of liquid fat will impede the binding capacity of the hydrophilic binders and impact the structure and rise. Adding oil will reduce dryness and produce a moister and softer crumb.

TOOLS
- You will need to have a hand beater or a stand mixer to beat the batter adequately to activate the strong hydrophilic binders from Groups 1 (Xanthan and Guar Gums) and 2 (Methylcellulose).
- High-sided, narrow bottomed bowl for beating the foam to maximum volume.
- For best results, accurately measure ingredients by using proper measuring tools (cups, scoops, and spoons, etc.).
- Loaf pans. An 8x4x2 inch pan is the preferred size for loaves. A 9x5x2 inch pan can also work.

TECHNIQUES
- Sift all flour after measuring to separate flour granules and incorporate air to improve lightness of product and leavening.
- Beating is very important to activate the hydrophilic binders that require agitation for maximum effectiveness e.g. Hydrophilic Binder Groups 1 (Xanthan and Guar Gums) and 2 (Methylcellulose).

- Beat the protein binder into a foam and incorporate it into the recipe to increase rise and enhance bread airiness.

- Replace oil with melted butter or lard. To reduce saturated fat content consider replacing small amounts of butter or lard with oil. Whip together prior to adding to batter or dough. This results in a satisfactory product.

- After placing batter into the loaf pan, allow the batter to sit for 10-15 minutes to let the hydrophilic binders that require time maximize their effectiveness e.g. Hydrophilic Binder Groups 3 (Psyllium Husk), 4 (Whole and Ground Chia Seeds) and 5 (Whole and Ground Flax Seeds). It also allows the leavening agents to get a head start in producing gas to rise the baked good.

TROUBLE SHOOTING

If your bread is lumpy and bumpy on top when baked, the dough or batter did not contain enough liquid. Increasing the liquid volume can eliminate this issue. It also could be that you have slightly too much hydrophilic binder. If you reduce the hydrophilic binder, this may resolve the issue.

If your bread is too dry and crumbly, you likely have too much flour mixture compared to liquid and binders. You need either to decrease the quantities of flour mixture or increase the quantities of liquid and binders. Another reason may be changing sweetener from a carbohydrate-containing sweetener to an alternate sweetener. Alternate sweeteners do not melt and create liquid volume or tenderize like carbohydrate-containing sweeteners.

If your bread is too wet in texture, you likely have too much liquid and binder compared to flour mixture and you need to increase the portion of flour in the mixture. Another reason may be that you included amaranth or coconut flour into the flour mix in too great a volume. Both these flours create a wet and "uncooked" end product.

If your bread does not rise like you thought it would, review the quantity of leavening agents in the bread recipe to see if you have maximized air inclusion through use of ingredients that foam. Adding a combination of baking soda and an acid can also assist.

If your bread rises and then falls, check that the loaf is cooked all the way through. This can also be due to the structure of the bread not being strong enough to support the rise. Increasing the protein content using Flour Group 9 (Defatted Nut and Seed Flour and Protein Powders), increasing the flour content from Flour Group 1 (Brown Rice, Buckwheat, Corn and Pure Oat* Flours), and increasing the hydrophilic and/or protein binders should correct this issue.

Recipes, Ingredients, Tools, & Techniques

RECIPE GROUP 6 | WAFFLES AND OTHER ITEMS MADE IN ELECTRIC MAKERS

FLOUR AND STARCH

- There are a number of electric makers on the market, including waffle irons, cake ball makers, cupcake makers and others. The flour mix for items made in electric makers must have enough strength and elasticity to withstand being removed piping hot from the maker. They may also have to endure rolling around in other ingredients or mixes while hot (for example, many cake balls are then rolled in sugar or cocoa powder or topped with glaze and so on). You will need to have a good percentage of your flour mix from Flour Group 1 (Brown Rice, Corn, Buckwheat and Pure Oat* Flours). You will also want to combine it with flours from Flour Group 2 (Sorghum, Teff and Fonio Flours), Flour Group 3 (Millet Flour), Flour Group 4 (Quinoa and Bean Flours), and Flour Group 9 (Defatted Nut and Seed Flours and Protein Powders).

- From our experience, everyone has their own preferences for flours and starches used – either for taste or ability to eat them. Below is "A Place to Start Waffle Flour Mix" for you to use as a starting point to creating your own perfect mix.

A Place to Start Waffle Flour Mix (10 Cups)
4¼ **cups Flour Group 1**: use one or a combination of flours;
3¼ **cups Flour Group 2**: use one or a combination of flours;
¾ **cup Flour Group 4**: use one or a combination of flours;
1 cup Flour Group 9: (defatted nut and seed flours or protein powder);
¾ **cup Starch Group 1** (Tapioca Starch): if using arrowroot starch, increase starch to 1⅓ cups.

LIQUID

- Liquids in these items vary depending on the flavour of the item being created. Predominantly they are protein based liquids or combinations of protein and non-protein based liquids. If the recipe calls for a protein based liquid and you are replacing it with a non-protein based liquid, you need to add some additional protein such as 1 tbsp protein powder or 1 tsp gelatin or agar.

HYDROPHILIC BINDER

- Hydrophilic binders are important! The items need to be able to come out of the electric makers while hot. So, using a combination of hydrophilic binders from Hydrophilic Binder Groups 1 (Xanthan or Guar Gums) or 2 (Methylcellulose) and from Group 3 (Psyllium) creates a strong enough bind and allows for a softer crumb and texture.

PROTEIN BINDER

- All batters in this group require a protein binder. If the protein binder can be turned into foam, it will create even stronger and airier products.

FOAM

- All strong foams can be used in batters for electric makers. Airy foams such as whipping cream can also be incorporated into the batter. Airy foam cannot replace structural foam. The airy foam is an addition to assist with leavening.

The New
Gluten-free

SWEETENER
- Any sweetener can be used with success. If you use a liquid sweetener, it will add to the moisture content and you may need to decrease the liquid ingredients of your recipe slightly.

LEAVENING
- Leavening agents are very important. Baking powder and baking soda in combination with an acid are often used as the leavening agents. You will want to increase the baking powder volume compared to a wheat recipe. Increasing the baking soda often takes away from taste in the end product.

FAT
- For best results use a solid fat (butter, lard or shortening) with a small amount of liquid fat (oil). Adding oil will reduce dryness and produce a moister and softer crumb. Larger amounts of liquid fat will impede the binding capacity of the hydrophilic binders, impact the structure and rise and will result in the item falling apart when removed from the electric maker.

TOOLS
- You need to have a hand beater or a stand mixer to beat the batter adequately to activate the strong hydrophilic binders from Hydrophilic Binder Groups 1 (Xanthan or Guar Gums) or 2 (Methylcellulose).
- A high-sided, narrow-bottomed bowl for beating the foam to maximum volume.
- For best results, accurately measure ingredients using proper measuring tools (cups, scoops, and spoons, etc.).
- Spatula.
- Scoop or ladle for placing batter into maker.
- Electric maker(s).

TECHNIQUES
- Items made in electric makers need to have a strong enough structure to be pulled out of the mold hot.
- Beating is very important to activate the hydrophilic binders that require agitation for maximum effectiveness e.g. Hydrophilic Binder Group 1 (Xanthan and Guar Gums) and 2 (Methylcellulose).
- Beat the protein binder into a foam and incorporate it into the recipe to increase rise and enhance bread airiness.
- Replace oil with melted butter or lard. To reduce saturated fat content consider replacing small amounts of butter or lard with oil. Whip together prior to adding to batter or dough. This results in a satisfactory product.
- Rest the batter for 10-15 minutes prior to cooking to let the hydrophilic binders that require time maximize their effectiveness e.g. Hydrophilic Binder Groups 3 (Psyllium Husk), 4 (Whole and Ground Chia Seeds) and 5 (Whole and Ground Flax Seeds). This also allows the leavening agents to get a head start in producing gas to rise the baked good.

TROUBLE SHOOTING

- If your items fall apart when removing from maker, you likely do not have enough binding ingredients or you have used oil as your fat.

- If the item does not rise in the maker, this may be the result of a few different issues:
    - You do not have enough leavening agent in the batter.
    - The dough does not have enough structure to let the leavening agent work. Adding more flour from Flour Groups 1 (Brown Rice, Buckwheat, Corn and Pure Oat* Flours) and 9 (Defatted Nut and Seed Flours and Protein Powders) will assist.
    - You may need to increase your hydrophilic and/or protein binders.

- If batter is exploding out of the maker, which can happen, you are over filling the maker or you have too much leavening agent in the batter.

- The items are not cooked all the way through – this may be for several reasons:
    - You are removing the item too soon from the maker.
    - Your batter has too much liquid in proportion to flour and binders.
    - You have included amaranth or coconut flour in your flour mix in too high a quantity.

RECIPE GROUP 7

FLOUR AND STARCH

PANCAKES

- The flour and starch mix for pancakes is much more forgiving. Lisa has made countless batches of gluten-free pancakes in the last 20 years and some of those batches were so much better than others. The ideal pancake is soft to bite into, but has enough firmness and chew so that it does not get soggy with syrup or fruit sauce. We have discovered that having some of Flour Group 1 (Brown Rice, Corn, Buckwheat and Pure Oat* Flours) is important for getting a slightly firmer texture. A small amount of Starch Group 1 (Tapioca Starch) helps to give pancakes the chew factor that is required. By combining Flour Group 1 (Brown Rice, Corn, Buckwheat and Pure Oat* Flours) and Starch Group 1 (Tapioca Starch), the pancakes will have firmness and chew without being cake-like or soggy with toppings.

The rest of the flour mix can be any flour you like from Flour Groups 2 (Sorghum, Teff and Fonio Flours), Flour Group 3 (Millet Flour), Flour Group 4 (Quinoa and Bean Flours), or Flour Group 9 (Defatted Nut and Seed Flours and Protein Powders). Flour Group 8 (Nut and Seed Meals) can be used in pancakes, but it needs to be added at the last minute because of the increased fat content. Remember that flours in Flour Group 8 (Nut and Seed Meals) do not have a long shelf life.

- From our experience, everyone has their own preferences for flours and starches used – either for taste or ability to eat them. Below is "A Place to Start Pancake Flour Mix" for you to use as a starting point to creating your own perfect mix.

A Place to Start Pancake Flour Mix (10 Cups)
3¼ **cups Flour Group 1**: use one or a combination of flours;
2½ **cups Flour Group 2**: use one or a combination of flours;
1¼ **cups Flour Group 3** (Millet Flour);
1¾ **cups Flour Group 4**: use one or a combination of flours;
⅔ **cup Flour Group 9:** (defatted nut or seed flour or protein powder); you can use a combination as desired;
⅔ **cup Starch Group 1** (Tapioca Starch): if using arrowroot, increase starch to 1 cup

Recipes, Ingredients, Tools, & Techniques

LIQUID
- The liquid used in a pancake mix tends to be a protein based liquid. If you are not using a protein-based liquid, you should replace the protein with a substitute such as protein powder or a protein binder. If you have added defatted nut or seed flour or alternate protein powder to your flour mix, you may not need to add additional protein to make up for that lost in the substitution of liquid. If you are replacing the protein in the liquid, use gelatin, agar or defatted nut/seed flour or protein powders. The quantity of liquid can be adjusted to get the right thickness of pancake that you desire. Some people like thinner pancakes where others prefer thick and fluffy pancakes.

HYDROPHILIC BINDER
- You need to add some hydrophilic binders to your pancakes. A combination of Hydrophilic Binders Group 1 (Xanthan and Guar Gums) or 2 (Methylcellulose) and Group 3 (Psyllium) or 4 (Whole and Ground Chia Seeds) results in the best outcome. Groups 1 (Xanthan and Guar Gums) or 2 (Methylcellulose) or Groups 3 (Psyllium) or 4 (Whole and Ground Chia Seeds) on their own do not produce the soft firm texture pancakes are supposed to have compared to when hydrophilic binders are combined.

PROTEIN BINDER
- Protein binders are important in pancakes. Most pancakes use egg protein. Small amounts of gelatin or agar can be used in combination with methylcellulose foam.

FOAM
- Foams are not always used in pancakes. If you want a fluffy pancake, beating the egg white creates a fluffier pancake. Also incorporating airy foams from whipped cream, coconut cream or evaporated milk enhances the lightness and fluffiness of the pancake.

SWEETENER
- You can use any sweetener in your pancakes with success. Because pancakes require a more liquid batter, the difference between sweeteners is less noticeable.

LEAVENING
- You will need to add leavening agents to your pancakes. Typically baking powder and baking soda are used. Adding an acid such as buttermilk to your pancakes enhances the gas production from the baking soda and increases the rise in the pancake. If your goal is a thinner pancake you may not want to enhance the leavening agents or add as much leavening agent to the batter mix.

FAT
- Any fat will work in pancakes. Oil and melted butter tend to be the most popular. We suggest you use oil here because it works well and lets you save the butter for other baking where butter really counts.

TOOLS
- Hand beaters are needed to beat your batter and possibly the foam in fluffier pancakes.

- High-sided, round-bottomed bowl for beating the foam if using.
- For best results, accurately measure ingredients using proper measuring tools (cups, scoops, spoons, etc.).
- An electric griddle or fry pan.
- Brush for brushing oil or butter onto the pan.
- Scoop for ladling batter onto grill or into fry pan.
- Flipper for turning pancakes over.

TECHNIQUES

- Beating the pancake batter is important to activate the hydrophilic binders that require agitation from Groups 1 (Xanthan and Guar Gums) and 2 (Methylcellulose).
- Letting the batter sit for 10 minutes to reach greater thickness for the hydrophilic binders from Groups 3 (Psyllium) and 4 (Whole or Ground Chia Seeds) is also beneficial.

TROUBLE SHOOTING

If your pancakes are too soft or cake-like and they absorb the syrup or the sauce so much that they get soggy, it is likely that you do not have enough structure in your flour mix. Increasing the content of flours from Flour Groups 1 (Brown Rice, Buckwheat, Corn and Pure Oat* Flours) and 9 (Defatted Nut and Seed and Protein Powders) as well as starch from Starch Group 1 (Tapioca Starch) may assist in resolving this issue. You can also look at the protein binder content. Increasing the number of eggs in the batter by one may also help.

If your pancakes are too dry, this could be because there is too much flour mix for the amount of liquid added. It also could be from too much of Flour Group 1 (Brown Rice Buckwheat, and Pure Oat* Flours) and Starch Group 1 (Tapioca Starch) in the flour mix. Flours from Flour Groups 2 (Sorghum, Teff and Fonio Flours), 4 (Quinoa, Lentil, Beans and Pea Flours) and 8 (Nut and Seed Meals) help to increase moisture content in the pancake.

If your pancakes look cooked on the outside and have been on the grill for a long time but are not cooking properly in the inside, it could be because you have added too much amaranth or coconut flour or other nut or seed meals. Amaranth and coconut flours do not have the right characteristics or properties to work well in pancakes. We suggest you use other flours.

Recipes, Ingredients, Tools, & Techniques

RECIPE GROUP 8 | **MUFFINS, CAKES, CUPCAKES, AND CAKE-STYLE LOAVES**

FLOUR AND STARCH

- The goal for this group of baked goods is to have a soft and moist crumb that melts in your mouth. These products should not be mushy, pasty or crumbly. The flour mix needs to have enough structure to hold the rise and be comprised of flours that create a softer crumb. Lisa has found that using flours from Flour Groups 2 (Sorghum, Teff and Fonio Flours), 4 (Quinoa, Lentil, Beans and Pea Flours), 8 (Nut and Seed Meals), and 9 (Defatted Nut and Seed Flours and Protein Powders) as the flour mix combination works well. Baked items that contain mashed fruit or grated or diced fruit or vegetables such as apple, pear, carrot, or zucchini need to have flours from Flour Group 1 (Brown Rice, Buckwheat, Corn and Pure Oat* Flours) and starch from Starch Group 1 (Tapioca Starch). If you prefer a more "cakey" or pudding-like product with less "chew" factor replace some Starch Group 1 (Tapioca Starch) with Starch Group 3 (Potato Starch) or Starch Group 4 (Corn Starch).

- From our experience, everyone has their own preferences for flours and starches used – either for taste or ability to eat them. Below is "A Place to Start Cake Flour Mix" for you to use as a starting point to creating your own perfect mix.

A Place to Start Cake Flour Mix (10 Cups)
2 cups flour from Flour Group 1: use one or a combination of flours;
4 ⅛ cups flour from Flour Group 2: use one or a combination of flours;
2 ⅔ cups flour from Flour Group 4: use one or a combination of flours;
¼ cup Flour Group 9; (Defatted Nut and Seed Flours, Cocoa Powder);
1 cup Starch Group 1 (Tapioca Starch): if using arrowroot, increase starch to about 1 1/3 cup

---

LIQUID

- The liquid in cakes can be either protein liquid or non-protein liquid. Generally they are liquids that contain protein, fat, and carbohydrate. If substituting one liquid for another, look at the label and try to add back to what the substituting liquid is missing. For example, when substituting cows milk for rice milk, you need to add some fat (in the form of oil) and some protein (added gelatin, agar or protein powder can be used).

HYDROPHILIC BINDER

- Hydrophilic binders are required. You want to use only a small amount of hydrophilic binders from Group 1 (Xanthan and Guar Gums) and 2 (Methylcellulose) and greater amounts from Groups 3 (Psyllium) and 4 (Whole or Ground Chia Seeds). The hydrophilic binders from Groups 3 (Psyllium) and 4 (Whole or Ground Chia Seeds) tend to produce a softer crumb texture that is desired in cake and cake-like baked goods.

PROTEIN BINDER

- Protein binders are required in some form. Eggs tend to be the most often used. Adding agar or gelatin and a methylcellulose foam work to replace eggs if needed.

FOAM

- Foams are often used in cakes to add air to lighten and moisten in order to achieve the desired texture. Structure foams are used alone or in combination with airy foam. When making a cake, if it calls for eggs and you are using eggs, foam the white and the yolk separately. Foaming of these ingredients assists you in getting a great end product. For some cakes you could have three bowls of foams that you fold together with the other ingredients (egg white foam, egg yolk foam, and perhaps whipped cream foam).

SWEETENER

- The sweetener adds to the tenderness of the cake. The sugar melts and forms a binder and softens the texture of the cake. When exchanging liquid sugar for a crystal sugar the moisture content of the cake needs to be adjusted slightly. Also, some liquid sugars have more water as part of their composition than others, and this can impact the texture and moisture of the cake. If using stevia, you will need to add liquid to the batter as stevia does not melt to form liquid and add moisture. Stevia also does not add to binding. When using stevia, you need to think about how to add moisture and binding to the liquid. Adding an additional egg or liquid egg product might work well depending on the recipe and volume of liquid and binding required.

LEAVENING

- Generally comes from baking powder and baking soda in combination with an acid such as fruit juice or buttermilk. Cream of tartar is also added to change chemical composition to assist in gas production and leavening.

FAT

- Butter always makes great cakes. For best results use a solid fat (butter, lard or shortening) with a small amount of liquid fat (oil). Larger amounts of liquid fat will impede the binding capacity of the hydrophilic binders and impact the structure and rise. Adding oil will reduce dryness and produce a moister and softer crumb. Whipping a combination of butter with a very small amount of oil can create moister cake.

Recipes, Ingredients, Tools, & Techniques

TOOLS
- Hand beater or stand mixer.
- For best results, accurately measure ingredients using proper measuring tools (cups, scoops, and spoons, etc.).
- Spatula.
- Brush for greasing.
- Appropriate baking pans – cake pan, muffin pan, or loaf pan.

TECHNIQUES
- Beating the batter is important to activate the binders from Flour Group 1 (Brown Rice, Buckwheat, Corn and Pure Oat* Flours) and 2 (Sorghum, Teff and Fonio Flours). Beating also assists in incorporating air into the batter. The additional air helps to lighten the texture of the cake.
- Using foams in the batter is very helpful to lighten the baked good.
- Letting the batter sit and rest in the pan for about 10-15 minutes prior to baking helps to let the hydrophilic binders become more effective and gives the leavening agents a head start.

TROUBLE SHOOTING
- If your cakes or muffins rise and fall, it means that there is not enough structure in the batter to hold up the rise. Adjusting the amount of flour from Flour Group 1 (Brown Rice, Buckwheat, Corn and Pure Oat* Flours) and starch from Starch Groups 1 (Tapioca Starch) or 3 (Potato Starch) may resolve this issue. You may also have to look at the binders that have been added. Increasing the protein binders and/or the hydrophilic binders may also help to resolve the issue.
- If the baked good does not rise at all, increase the leavening agents and you may also need to look at the point above. Including foam into the batter will assist in leavening.
- If you have added nut/seed meals to your cake and the cake does not rise or is too heavy in texture, reduce the amount of nut/seed meal in the flour mix. Nut/seed meals are heavy due to the increased fat content. By adding a defatted nut/seed product, you can benefit from the protein content without the additional fat.
- If your baked good is too dry, then you may need to look at the fat content, sweetener and flour volumes of your cake. If you have too much flour to liquid ratio, the cake will be drier. If you have too much of the flours from Flour Group 1 (Brown Rice, Buckwheat, Corn and Pure Oat* Flours) in your flour mix, it may be too dry. Sweeteners help to provide moisture, binding and assists in creating the desired crumb. If you have reduced the volume of sweetener in the cake, it may result in a drier cake. Increasing the sweetener is not usually what you want to do if the cake is sweet enough. But increasing the liquid and the binding capacity often resolves this issue.

- If your cake is cooked but feels too "wet" when chewed or the crumb turns to a mushy, pudding consistency in your mouth, reminding you of undercooked dough or batter, it is likely that you have too much flour from Flour Group 4 (Quinoa, Lentil, Beans and Pea Flours) in the flour mix.

- If your cake is too crumbly it is likely that you do not have enough binders in the cake or that you have used oil that has broken down the binding capacity of the binders. Changing oil to butter or lard may resolve this issue. If you used butter or lard and the cake is still crumbly, it is likely that you have added more flour to absorb the liquid and less binder. Reducing the flour and increasing the binder should resolve this issue.

CHAPTER 2:
FAT-BASED AND/OR EGG-BASED BATTERS AND DOUGH

RECIPE GROUP 9

FLOUR AND STARCH

BISCUITS, SCONES, AND SOFT COOKIES

- The desired texture for this group is to be somewhat firm, moist with a softer crumb, but it also has to have a bit of a chew factor. The flour mix needs to have flours and starch that adds to the chew factor – such as millet flour and tapioca starch. The flour mix needs to have flour that adds to a firmer structure such as flours from Flour Group 1 (Brown Rice, Corn, Buckwheat, and Pure Oat* Flours). The flour mix needs to have flours that contribute to a moist and soft crumb such as the flours from Flour Group 4 (Quinoa, Bean and Legume Flours).

- From our experience, everyone has their own preferences for flours and starches used – either for taste or ability to eat them. Below is "A Place to Start Biscuits, Scones and Soft Cookies Flour Mix" for you to use as a starting point to creating your own perfect mix.

A Place to Start: Biscuits, Scones, and Soft Cookies Flour Mix (10 Cups)
2½ **cups flour from Flour Group 1**: use one or a combination of flours;
2½ **cups flour from Flour Group 3** (Millet Flour);
3¾ **cups flour from Flour Group 4**: use one or a combination of flours;
1¼ **cups starch from Starch Group 1** (Tapioca Starch): if using arrowroot, increase starch to 2 cups

LIQUID	• Generally smaller amounts of liquid are used and the liquid generally is a protein based liquid that is higher in fat such as full fat milk or cream. Canned coconut milk also tends to work well as it is high in fat. Other liquids can also work. When substituting, look at the composition of the liquid you are replacing and try to add components to make it more ideal for your purpose. For example, if you have skim milk and not cream, adding a couple of teaspoons of melted butter will increase the fat content closer to cream.
HYDROPHILIC BINDER	• A combination of hydrophilic binders from Hydrophilic Binder Groups 1 (Xanthan and Guar Gum) and Group 2 (Methylcellulose) with binders from Groups 3 (Psyllium) and 4 (Whole or Ground Chia Seed) tend to work best. The hydrophilic binders from the first 2 groups add to firmness and chew and the ones from the Hydrophilic Binder Groups 3 and 4 assist in binding but lead to a softer bind hence softer crumb.
PROTEIN BINDER	• Protein binders are important to this group of baking. Generally egg is used as the protein binder. Gelatin or agar in combination with methylcellulose foam can also work well.
FOAM	• Structure foams or airy foams tend not to be used in this group. Methylcellulose foam is important to use if the protein binder is gelatin or agar. The methylcellulose foam assists in adding air, which assists in leavening and in creating a lighter texture to the end product.
SWEETENER	• Sweeteners will vary from product to product. Baked goods that are savoury may have no sweetener or very little sweetener. Those that are sweeter in nature will have more such as a soft cookie like pumpkin cookies. If substituting sweeteners, you need to account for the moisture content and adjust up or down depending on what sweetener you are using. For example, if the recipe calls for sugar and you are using honey, you will have to use less honey. If you are using stevia, you will need to add liquid and a bit of binder from either the protein binder groups or the hydrophilic binder groups.
LEAVENING	• Leavening agents generally used are baking powder and baking soda. Cream of tartar is also used to change the pH (i.e. increase the acid content) of the batter to assist in leavening.
FAT	• The type of fat used makes a difference for this group. Butter or lard really helps produce better products. If you want to reduce the butter or lard content, cutting half with avocado, full fat cream cheese or macadamia nut butter can lead to great end products with reduced butter and fat content and healthier nutrient profile.
TOOLS	• Food processor for biscuits and scones and stand mixer for soft cookies. • For best results you want to accurately measure your ingredients using proper measuring tools (cups, scoops, and spoons, etc.).

- Cutters for biscuits.
- Scoop for soft drop cookies. Two spoons can also work for a two-spoon drop method.
- Baking sheets.

TECHNIQUES

- Cutting the fat into the flour mixture using a food processor evenly coats the flour mixture with fat resulting in a softer crumb.
- Beating the batter with either the "S" blade of the food processor or the cookie paddle in the stand mixer fully activates the hydrophilic binders from Hydrophilic Binder Groups 1 (Xanthan and Guar Gums) and 2 (Methylcellulose).
- Letting the dough rest before rolling and cutting into biscuits or dropping batter onto a pan lets the hydrophilic binders from Hydrophilic Binder Groups 3 (Psyllium) and 4 (Ground Chia Seeds) work to full capacity.
- Gluten-free biscuit dough is going to be stickier and wetter than wheat-based biscuit dough. Resist the urge to add more flour. Sprinkle with sweet rice flour to keep from sticking to the board or your hand. Dust the cutter with sweet rice flour as well.
- Rolling dough in sweet rice flour increases the ease of the task and does not tend to dry out the dough.

TROUBLE SHOOTING

- If the biscuits, scones or cookies are too dry you likely have too much flour mix in the dough. Decreasing the flour mix and increasing the liquid and the binders assists in moistening the final product. It also could be that the flour mix has too much flour from Flour Group 1 (Brown Rice, Corn, Buckwheat, and Pure Oat* Flours). If you exchange more flour from Flour Group 4 (Quinoa, Legume and Bean Flours), it will assist in bringing a more moist texture to your baked item.
- If the biscuit, scone or cookie is too cake-like, it is likely that you do not have enough ingredients such as millet flour and tapioca starch to add to the chew factor. Adding these will increase the chew factor of the baked item.
- If the biscuit when baked feels too "wet" in your mouth, you likely need to add more flour or you need to reduce the amount of flour from Flour Group 4 (Quinoa, Lentil, Bean and Pea Flours) and increase flours from Flour Groups 1 (Brown Rice, Buckwheat, Corn and Pure Oat* Flours) or 3 (Millet Flour).

RECIPE GROUP 10

BISCUIT OR FOAM CAKES, SPONGE OR POUND CAKES (JELLY ROLLS OR TORTES WHERE THE MAIN BASE OF THE CAKE IS EGG WHITE FOAM)

FLOUR AND STARCH

- You can pretty much use any flour or combinations of flours that you like for these cakes. The flour is suspended in egg white foam. The egg white foam cooks and forms the structure more so than the flour does. You can use flours from all groups alone or in combination. Some people prefer some combinations better than others. The flavour of the flour usually makes more difference than the flour itself.

- From our experience, everyone has their own preferences for flours and starches used – either for taste or ability to eat them. Below is "A Place to Start Biscuit or Foam Cake Flour Mix" for you to use as a starting point to creating your own perfect mix.

Place to Start Biscuit or Foam Cake Flour Mix (10 Cups)
1 ⅔ cups flour from Flour Group 1: use one or a combination of flours;
3 ⅓ cups flour from Flour Group 2: use one or a combination of flours;
1 ⅔ cups flour from Flour Group 4: use one or a combination of flours;
3 ⅓ cups flour from Flour Group 5: use one or a combination of flours;
⅔ cup starch from Starch Group 1 (Tapioca Starch): If using arrowroot starch, increase starch to 3/4 cup

NOTE: You can add flour from Flour Group 8 (nut/seed meal) to Foam Cakes but you cannot add it to the mix unless you are going to refrigerate or freeze your mix. If using nut/seed meal 2/3 - 3/4 (66-75%) of your 10 cup mix needs to be flour mix, the remaining 1/4 - 1/3 (25-33%) can be ground nut meal. Almond flour works well and can be used in greater volumes e.g. 50% flour mix and 50% almond flour.

LIQUID

- There are no liquids in these biscuit or foam cakes.

HYDROPHILIC BINDER

- There are no hydrophilic binders in biscuit or foam cakes.

PROTEIN BINDER

- These cakes need to be created with egg white foam and/or egg yolk foam. Other protein binders will not work or turn out the same.

FOAM

- Egg white foam and/or egg yolk foam.

SWEETENER

- Crystal or powdered sweetener is best as the added "water" found in liquid sweeteners negatively impacts the foamy texture of the cooked baked good.

LEAVENING

- Cream of tartar is used to help stabilize the egg white foam. The egg white foam creates the rise.

Recipes, Ingredients, Tools, & Techniques

FAT
- There is no added fat in many foam style cakes. The only fat in these cakes comes from the egg yolks. Pound cake is the exception.

TOOLS
- Electric hand beater or stand mixer.
- High-sided, narrow-bottomed bowl.
- For best results accurately measure ingredients using proper measuring tools (cups, scoops, and spoons, etc.).
- Spatula.
- Parchment paper.
- Sided cookie sheet.

TECHNIQUES
- Beat egg whites to stiff peak stage and egg yolks until light yellow and about 3 times the volume.
- Gently fold the dry ingredients and the foams together so as not to reduce the volume of the foam.

TROUBLE SHOOTING
- From our experience, this type of cake rarely goes sideways or doesn't work out. So, really we do not have much to say here. If your cake doesn't turn out as expected; be sure that the egg whites and egg yolks were beaten properly and that the ingredients were folded together gently, but thoroughly. The age of the eggs you use may impact the foam quality. Old egg whites create greater volume, but tend to be less stable and that may impact the final product.

RECIPE GROUP 11

FLOUR AND STARCH

CRISPY COOKIES AND CHEWY COOKIES

- The flours that stand out for cookies are Flour Group 5 (Amaranth Flour), Flour Group 6 (Coconut Flour) and Flour Group 8 (Nut and Seed Meals). These groups tend to do less well in water-based baking, but flourish in fat-based mixtures. Flour Group 8 (Nut and Seed Meals) can stand alone when creating cookies. We prefer to combine flours from Flour Groups 6 (Coconut) and 8 (Nut and Seed Meals) with other flours, such as Flour Group 3 (Millet Flour), 4 (Quinoa, Lentil, Bean and Pea Flours), 5 (Amaranth Flour), and 9 (Defatted Nut and Seed Flours and Protein Powders). Gingerbread houses or some cut out cookies have a different composition and need a different flour mix, one more similar to that of tortilla and pasta dough.

- From our experience, everyone has their own preferences for flours and starches used – either for taste or ability to eat them. Below is "A Place to Start Crispy Cookie Flour Mix" and "A Place to Start Chewy Cookie Flour Mix" for you to use as starting points to creating your own perfect mixes.

A Place to Start Crispy Cookie Flour Mix (10 Cups)
4 cups flour from Flour Group 2: use one or a combination of flours;
4¼ cups flour from Flour Group 5 (Amaranth);
1¾ cups flour from Flour Group 8: use one or a combination of nut or seed meals.

NOTE: that this flour mix needs to be stored in the fridge or freezer due to the addition of nut and/or seed meal.

A Place to Start Chewy Cookie Flour Mix (10 Cups)
2 cups flour from Flour Group 2: use one or a combination of flours;
2 cups flour from Flour Group 3 (Millet Flour);
2 cups flour from Flour Group 4: use one or a combination of flours;
2¼ cups flour from Flour Group 5 (Amaranth Flour);
1¼ cups flour from Flour Groups 6 and/or 8 and/or 9: combinations of these flours or any one flour from these groups will work;
½ cup starch from Starch Group 1 (Tapioca Starch): if using arrowroot starch, increase starch to ⅔ cup

NOTE: this flour mix needs to be stored in the fridge or freezer if nut and/or seed meal is used.

LIQUID

- Generally no liquid is added.

HYDROPHILIC BINDER	• Hydrophilic binders are required to hold these cookies together. Binders can be used alone or in combination and vary depending on what the desired end texture is supposed to be. If wanting a chewier texture, use hydrophilic binders from Hydrophilic Binders Groups 1 (Xanthan and Guar Gum) and 2 (Methylcellulose). If a crispier texture is desired, use a combination of a small amount of hydrophilic binder from Hydrophilic Binder Groups 1 and 2 and larger amounts of hydrophilic binder from Groups 3 (Psyllium) and 4 (Whole or Ground Chia Seeds). Because crispy and chewy cookie recipes are fat-based cookie dough, the hydrophilic binders are not as strong as they would be in water-based dough because of the absence of water and the fat interferes with binding.
PROTEIN BINDER	• Generally cookies have egg as a binder. Methylcellulose foams can be used as a binder in replacement for egg.
FOAM	• Foams are not generally used in cookies, except for methylcellulose foam as a binder or egg replacer.
SWEETENER	• A crystal or powdered sweetener is used in crispy cookies. Some chewier cookies use honey or other liquid sweetener but generally crystal sugars are used. If using stevia, it is hard to create a crisp or chewy cookie. Cookies made with stevia tend to be more dense and firm.
LEAVENING	• Generally baking powder or baking soda is used.
FAT	• Butter or lard.
TOOLS	• A stand mixer.
	• For best results, accurately measure ingredients using proper measuring tools (cups, scoops, spoons, etc.).
	• Cookie sheet.
TECHNIQUES	• Beating the dough with an electric stand mixer helps to thoroughly combine the ingredients and work the hydrophilic binders that require agitation.
	• Flattening the cookies prior to baking assists in getting the correct texture. The hydrophilic binders reduce the "melting" characteristic of most wheat-based cookies; flattening them assists in this process.
TROUBLE SHOOTING	• If your cookie is not as short or crisp as you desired, you need to increase the ingredients that result in that outcome. Flours such as amaranth and nut meals help to produce a richer crispy cookie. Also reduced fat or reduced sweetener cookies will not be as crisp since these ingredients assist in creating that texture.

TROUBLE SHOOTING

- If you are looking for a chewier cookie, you need to look at the ingredients that create chew, such as millet flour and tapioca starch. Increasing these components may assist in achieving this texture. Reduced fat and sweetener in a recipe can also impact this texture. The other thing that can impact chewiness in a cookie is over cooking. A chewy cookie becomes a hard cookie if over cooked, so, you want to "just" cook the dough.

- If the cookie is crumbly, it could be that there is not enough binder in the cookie or that there is too much flour to fat ratio in the cookie. If the cookie is a reduced sweetener cookie, then it could be that the cookie needs more moisture and more binding.

Recipes, Ingredients, Tools, & Techniques

RECIPE GROUP 12	**PASTRY**
FLOUR AND STARCH	The quest for the perfect gluten-free pastry is an object of desire for many. The flour mix is very important. The other thing with pastry is that many people are trying to make it "better" for you than traditional pastry. From Lisa's experience it takes a mix of flours to create the perfect pastry crust. Pie dough has to be short and flakey; it needs to hold together when rolled; and it needs to be strong enough to hold its shape when baked. This is a tall order in the gluten-free baking world. Amaranth and the nut flours help to create a short and flakier texture, millet flour and tapioca starch help to add stretch and chew, and brown rice flour assists in strength and structure. A combination of these flours work together to create great pastry.

- From our experience, everyone has their own preferences for flours and starches used – either for taste or ability to eat them. Below is a "Place to Start: Pastry Flour Mix" for you to use as a starting point to creating your own perfect mix.

A Place to Start Pastry Flour Mix (10 Cups)
1 cup flour from Flour Group 1: use one or a combination of flours;
2¾ cup flour from Flour Group 3 (Millet Flour);
2½ cup flour from Flour Group 5 (Amaranth Flour);
1¾ cup flour from Flour Group 6 or 8 one or a combination of flours or meals;
2 cups starch from Starch Group 1 (Tapioca Starch): if using arrowroot, increase starch to 2½ cups

NOTE: Flour Group 6 (Coconut Flour) is best for rolled pastry. Flour Group 8 (Nut and Seed Meals) is better for press pastry. This flour mix needs to be stored in the fridge or freezer if nut and/or seed meal is used.

LIQUID
- Generally the liquid used is water.

HYDROPHILIC BINDER
- Binders from Hydrophilic Binder Groups 1 (Xanthan and Guar Gums) and 2 (Methylcellulose) work best to accomplish the stretch required for rolling.

PROTEIN BINDER
- Eggs are added to some pastries to help with binding. If egg cannot be used, a methylcellulose foam is a good replacement.

FOAM
- Foams are not used in pastry. The exception is a lightly foamed methylcellulose to replace egg.

SWEETENER
- Small amounts of sweetener may be added to sweet pastry. Sweetener is not a required ingredient. Crystal or powder sweeteners are better than liquid sweeteners.

LEAVENING	• Not used in pastry.
FAT	• If you want to roll your pastry, you need to use butter or lard. Oil interferes with binding and you will not be able to create dough that rolls and holds together. Oil can be used in pastry that is pressed into the pan.
	• We have found that you can substitute half the solid fat with avocado and the pastry works well. This is best suited for complementary flavours as there is a slight avocado flavour. Usually with ½ an avocado you do not notice it.
	• Full fat cream cheese can be used to replace half the fat with great success.
	• Macadamia nut butter can be used to replace half the fat. The pastry dough made with macadamia nut butter tends not to roll as well, but presses very well. You can also roll it out into smaller shapes and transfer it successfully. Rolling on parchment paper and flipping over on top of the pie and fixing the cracks may also be acceptable.
TOOLS	• Food processor.
	• For best results, accurately measure ingredients using proper measuring tools (cups, scoops, spoons, etc.).
	• Rolling pin.
	• Cutters.
	• Parchment paper – roll on parchment paper and then lift and transfer – prevents breaking.
	• Pie plate, tart pan.
TECHNIQUES	• Blend the fat with the flour ingredients using the "S" blade of the food processor.
	• While blending the dry ingredients in the food processor, add the liquid ingredients slowly and just until the dough is formed.
TROUBLE SHOOTING	• Pastry dough is very finicky and slight adjustments to ingredients can change an ideal pastry (flakey) to a disappointing pastry (tough, crumbly, and greasy). Pastry needs to have the right proportions of flour, fat, binders, and liquid to make it right. If it is too tough, you likely have too much liquid and binder. If the dough is too crumbly and dry, you likely do not have enough liquid and binder. The use of egg in the pastry is very helpful.

SECTION 5
Putting It All Together

CHAPTER 1:
GLUTEN-FREE BAKING – PUTTING IT ALL TOGETHER

Gluten-free baking is unlike wheat-based baking. Gluten-free baking demands that we identify the desired outcome, understand the ingredients required and the tools and techniques to achieve it! We have summarized the information provided in this resource guide into one table in hopes that you may find it useful as a quick reference chart. A "kitchen-proof" inside-your-cupboard-door poster is available on the The New Gluten-Free™ website at: www.thenewgluten-free.ca

SUMMARY TABLE: PUTTING IT ALL TOGETHER

MOISTURE BASE = TEXTURE: CHEW, SOFT, MOIST WATER-BASED LIQUID								MOISTURE BASE = FAT-BASED &/OR EGG TEXTURE: CRISP, CRUNCHY, TENDER BASED LIQUID			
RECIPE GROUP 1	RECIPE GROUP 2	RECIPE GROUP 3	RECIPE GROUP 4	RECIPE GROUP 5	RECIPE GROUP 6	RECIPE GROUP 7	RECIPE GROUP 8	RECIPE GROUP 9	RECIPE GROUP 10	RECIPE GROUP 11	RECIPE GROUP 12
Yeast Bread Pizza Dough	Flat Breads Tortilla Some Cut Out Cookies	Pasta	Crêpes	Non-Yeast Breads	Waffles Snack Balls	Pancakes	Muffins Loaves Cake Cupcakes	Biscuits Scones Soft Cookies	Foam Cakes Sponge Cakes Pound Cakes	Crispy Cookies Chewy Cookies	Pastry

SECTION 1: GLUTEN-FREE FLOUR AND STARCHES

RECIPE GROUP 1	RECIPE GROUP 2	RECIPE GROUP 3	RECIPE GROUP 4	RECIPE GROUP 5	RECIPE GROUP 6	RECIPE GROUP 7	RECIPE GROUP 8	RECIPE GROUP 9	RECIPE GROUP 10	RECIPE GROUP 11	RECIPE GROUP 12

FLOUR GROUPS 1, 2, 3, 4, 7, 9.	**FLOUR GROUPS 1, 2, 3, 4, 5, 6, 7, 8, 9.**
Use small amounts of Starch Group 1 Starches. Starch Groups 3 and 4 do not add desired texture. Roll out using Starch Group 5.	Use small amounts of Starch Group 1 and/or Starch Group 2. For moist pudding-like crumb in cakes Starch Groups 3 and 4 may be preferred. Roll out using Starch Group 5.

SECTION 2: LIQUIDS, BINDERS, FOAMS, LEAVENING AGENTS, AND SWEETENERS

RECIPE GROUP 1	RECIPE GROUP 2	RECIPE GROUP 3	RECIPE GROUP 4	RECIPE GROUP 5	RECIPE GROUP 6	RECIPE GROUP 7	RECIPE GROUP 8	RECIPE GROUP 9	RECIPE GROUP 10	RECIPE GROUP 11	RECIPE GROUP 12
Non-Protein and Protein Liquids from Groups 1 through 11 can be used successfully.								Small amount of Protein Liquids Groups 7, 8, 9, 10, 11.	No Liquid Groups	Small amount Liquid Group 1 and/or 7.	
Hydrophilic Binders (HB) - Groups 1 & 2 are often both used in combination in higher % to liquids; to create stretch, add to strength, & chew factor.		HB Group 1 used alone.	Smaller amount of strong HB from Groups 1 and 2 are used in combination with softer HB from Groups 3 and 4.						Use soft HB from Groups 3 and 4.	Use a strong HB from Groups 1 and 2.	
Protein Binders (PB) Groups 1, 2 and 3 can all be used successfully.		PB Group 1.	PB Groups 1, 2 and 3 can all be used successfully.						PB Group 1.		
Strong Structure Foams from Groups 1, 2 and 3.	Foam Group 2 (Methylcellulose) may be used for these groups.	No Foams used in Crêpes	Structure Foams and Airy Foams from Groups 1, 2, 3, 4 5, 6 and potentially 7 can be used. Once Foam Group 7 foams are foamed it is better combined with stronger foam such as egg white or gelatin.					Foam Group 2 (Methylcellulose). Foam Group 1 (Egg White) and Foam Group 4 (Egg Yolk) for RECIPE GROUP 10 recipes.			
Yeast and/or yeast with baking powder.	Often will not have any leavening agents included in the recipe. Some flat bread may include small amounts of leavening agent.		Will contain leavening agents alone or in combination to maximize the rise.								In general no leavening agents in pastry.
Sweetener Groups 1, 2, 3 and 4 are suitable options to "feed" the yeast.	Most savory flat breads, pasta, and crêpes do not contain sweeteners. Dessert flat breads, cut out cookies, pasta and crêpes contain sweetener: Groups 1, 2, 3, 4 and 6. Group 5 may be added as a flavouring.		Sweetener Groups 1, 2, 3 and 4 work best. Sweetener Group 5 can be used with recipe modifications.					Sweeteners from Groups 3 and 4 for best results.	Sweeteners from Groups 3 and 4 for best results. Recipes can be modified to incorporate Groups 1, 2 and 5.	Sweeteners from Groups 3 and 4 for best results.

SECTION 3: SOLID AND LIQUID FAT

RECIPE GROUP 1	RECIPE GROUP 2	RECIPE GROUP 3	RECIPE GROUP 4	RECIPE GROUP 5	RECIPE GROUP 6	RECIPE GROUP 7	RECIPE GROUP 8	RECIPE GROUP 9	RECIPE GROUP 10	RECIPE GROUP 11	RECIPE GROUP 12
	Group 1 (Butter) Butter is very versatile and creates great products every time. It can be used effectively for all groups; works in solid or melted form. When using other fats, it is important to choose a fat that will work effectively.										
Groups 1, 3, 9	Group 1, 2, 3, 5, 6.		Groups 1, 9.	Groups 1, 2, 3, 5, 6, 9.				Groups 1, 3.	Group 1, except for foam cakes which do not use any fat	Groups 1, 2, 3, 5, 6.	Groups 1, 2, 3, 5, 6.

SECTION 6: TOOLS AND TECHNIQUES

RECIPE GROUP 1	RECIPE GROUP 2	RECIPE GROUP 3	RECIPE GROUP 4	RECIPE GROUP 5	RECIPE GROUP 6	RECIPE GROUP 7	RECIPE GROUP 8	RECIPE GROUP 9	RECIPE GROUP 10	RECIPE GROUP 11	RECIPE GROUP 12
Stand Mixer Stick beater	Food Processor S-blade Stick beater	Food Processor S-blade Stick beater, Rolling pin, pasta cutters or pasta maker	Hand Beater crêpe pan	Stand mixer or hand beaters Stick beater, Correct pan	Hand Beaters or stand mixer Stick beater, Electric maker - waffle, cake ball maker, etc.	Hand Beaters Stand Mixer Stick beater, Electric grill or fry pan	Hand Beaters or Stand Mixer Stick beater Correct Pan Scoop	Food Processor S-blade Stick beater, Biscuit cutter, cookie scoops	Stand Mixer or hand beater	Stand Mixer Might need Cookie scoop, cookie cutters, cookie press.	Food Processor S-blade Stick beater, Rolling pin Cutters Correct pans
Time, Heat Beating, Sifting	Boiling liquid, Beating, Sifting	Boiling liquid, beating, Sifting	Beating, Sifting	Time, Beating, Sifting				Beating, Sifting			Beating, Sifting

LEGEND

FLOUR GROUPS

1. Brown rice, white rice, buckwheat, corn, pure oat*
2. Sorghum, teff, fonio
3. Millet
4. Quinoa, black, white and whole bean, lentil, garfava, chickpea, soy
5. Amaranth
6. Coconut
7. Rice bran
8. Nut/seed meals
9. Cocoa powder and defatted nut/seed flour

STARCH GROUPS

1. Tapioca
2. Arrowfoot
3. Potato
4. Cornstarch
5. Sweet rice flour

LIQUID GROUPS

1. Water
2. Juice
3. Grain "milk"
4. Nut "milk"
5. Seed "milk"
6. Mashed fruit
7. Cream
8. Legume "milk"
9. Dairy milk
10. Partially-solid dairy
11. Partially-solid dairy-free

BINDER GROUPS

HYDROPHILIC

1. Xanthan, guar
2. Methylcellulose
3. Psyllium
4. Whole/ground chia
5. Whole/ground flax

PROTEIN

1. Egg white, egg white powder
2. Gelatin
3. Agar

FOAMS GROUPS

STRUCTURAL

1. Egg white
2. Methylcellulose
3. Gelatin
4. Egg Yolk

AIRY

5. Whipping cream
6. Coconut cream
7. Evaporated milk

SWEETENERS GROUPS

LIQUID

1. Corn, cane and brown rice syrups, honey, molasses
2. Maple and agave syrup
6. Liquid stevia

CRYSTAL

3. White sugar
4. Brown, raw, demerara, coconut
5. Date sugar
6. Xylitol, stevia

FATS/OILS GROUPS

SOLID

1. Butter
2. Macadmaia nut butter
3. Lard, shortening
4. Hard margarine
5. Cream Cheese
6. Avocado
7. Soft Margarine
8. Low fat soft margarine

LIQUID

9. Vegetable, nut and seed oils

CHAPTER 2:
RECIPES THAT DEMONSTRATE GLUTEN-FREE INGREDIENTS, TOOLS AND TECHNIQUES

Nutrient analysis of the following recipes *Powered by the ESHA Research Nutrient Database*©. All ingredients listed in the recipe, including those listed as optional, have been included in the analysis.

BASIC YEAST BREAD
EGG WHITE FOAM

This bread recipe uses egg white foam to assist in lightening and leavening the loaf. It also uses methylcellulose foam which doubles as a hydrophilic binder and foam to assist in chew, stick, and leavening. To achieve maximum texture use a stand mixer as the strong beating enhances the chewy texture. Warmth and time to let the bread rise is also important.

YIELD: Two (2) 8x4 loaves

METHOD:

1. Separate eggs. Beat egg whites until stiff peaks form.
2. Beat yolks until light yellow and foamy, if using.
3. Place yeast and teaspoon of sugar into a bowl. Add first amount (½ cup) of warm water.
4. Place ¾ cup of warm water into a high-sided bowl. Add methylcellulose. With a stick beater, beat until thick and foamy.
5. Place ½ c water and 1 tbsp psyllium in a small bowl. Let gel. Add 2 tbsp oil and mix until fully combined.
6. Measure all flours and starches and place into a sifter. Sift all flours prior to adding to mixing bowl. Do not sift, then measure - measure first.
7. Place the flours, starches, xanthan gum, salt, sugar, and butter or lard into a mixer. Mix until the butter or lard is combined with the flour and it resembles cornmeal.
8. Add dissolved yeast, psyllium gel, vinegar, methylcellulose foam and beaten egg whites and yolks (if using yolks) to the dry ingredients. Beat on high speed for approximately 5 minutes, scraping sides as needed.
9. Spray two (2) 8 x 4 inch loaf pans. Spoon dough equally between the two pans. Let rise in a warm place until double in volume. Warming up the oven by turning on the oven light may be a good option. Time will vary depending on yeast and temperature of the environment.
10. Preheat oven to 400°F (200°C or Gas Mark 6). Bake for 5 minutes. Turn oven down and bake at 350°F (180°C or Gas Mark 4) for 20 minutes.
11. Loaf is done when it pulls away from the sides and sounds hollow when tapped. If the loaf is getting too brown, cover with tin foil.
12. Remove from oven. Let sit in the pan for 5-8 minutes. Remove to a cooling rack.

PER 36G SERVING: calories 70, fat 2.5 g, carbohydrate 11 g, fibre 2 g, protein 2 g

IMPERIAL		METRIC		INGREDIENT	IMPERIAL		METRIC		INGREDIENT
4	Lg	4	Lg	Egg whites, beaten	4¼	tsp	21	ml	Xanthan gum
2	Lg	2	Lg	Egg yolks, beaten (optional)	1¼	tsp	6	ml	Salt
4	tsp	20	ml	Yeast	⅛	c	30	ml	Sugar or honey
1	tsp	5	ml	Sugar	2	tbsp	30	ml	Butter, lard or vegetable shortening
½	c	125	ml	Warm water	1	tsp	5	ml	Methylcellulose
1¼	c	300	ml	Brown rice flour	¾	c	180	ml	Warm water
½	c	125	ml	Corn flour, pure oat* flour or buckwheat flour	1	tsp	5	ml	Vinegar
6	tbsp	90	ml	Millet flour	½	c	125	ml	Warm water
½	c	80	ml	White bean flour	1	tbsp	30	ml	Psyllium
3	tbsp	60	ml	Defatted nut/seed flour or protein powder	2	tbsp	30	ml	Oil
¼	c	60	ml	Tapioca starch					

BASIC YEAST BREAD
GELATIN FOAM

This recipe uses gelatin foam to provide structure and strength to the bread. It also uses methylcellulose to assist with binding and leavening. Gelatin foam is a good alternative to egg white foam especially for people who do not eat eggs. To achieve maximum texture use a stand mixer. The strong beating enhances the chewy texture. Warmth and time to let the bread rise is also important.

YIELD: Two (2) 8x4 loaves

METHOD:

1. Dissolve gelatin in ¼ c cold water. Add boiling water and stir until well combined and gelatin has completely dissolved.

2. Beat gelatin mixture with an electric hand beater for about 10-15 minutes or until thick and peaks form. The time will vary depending on the beater you are using.

3. Place ¾ cup warm water into a high-sided bowl. Add methylcellulose. With a stick beater, beat until thick and foamy.

4. Place yeast and 1 tsp of sugar into a bowl. Add ½ cup warm water. The yeast mixture should start to foam as the yeast activates.

5. Place ½ c water and 1 tbsp psyllium in a small bowl. Let gel. Add 2 tbsp oil and mix until fully combined.

6. Measure all flours and starches and place into a sifter. Sift all flours prior to adding to mixing bowl. Do not sift, then measure - measure first.

7. Place the flours, starch, xanthan gum, salt, honey, and butter or lard into a mixer. Mix until the butter or lard is combined with the flour and resembles cornmeal.

8. Add dissolved yeast, psyllium gel, vinegar, methylcellulose foam, and gelatin foam onto dry ingredients. Beat on high speed for approximately 5 minutes, scraping sides of bowl as required.

9. Spray two (2) 8x4 inch bread loaf pans. Divide batter equally between the prepared pans. Place in a warm place and let rise until double in volume. Warming the oven up by turning on the oven light is always a good option. Time will vary depending on yeast and temperature of the environment.

10. Preheat oven to 400°F (200° C or Gas Mark 6). Bake for 5 minutes. Turn oven down and bake at 350°F (180° C or Gas Mark 4) for 20 minutes.

11. Loaf is done when it pulls away from the sides and sounds hollow when tapped. If the loaf becomes too brown, cover with tin foil.

12. Remove from oven. Let sit in the pan for 5-8 minutes. Remove to a cooling rack.

PER 37G SERVING: calories 70, fat 2 g, carbohydrate 12 g, fibre 2 g, protein 2 g

IMPERIAL		METRIC		INGREDIENT	IMPERIAL		METRIC		INGREDIENT
1½	c	375	ml	Brown rice flour	½	c	125	ml	Boiling water
½	c	125	ml	Buckwheat, corn flour or pure oat* flour	4	tsp	20	ml	Yeast
6	tbsp	90	ml	Millet flour	1	tsp	5	ml	Sugar
3	tbsp	45	ml	Defatted nut/ seed flour or protein powder	½	c	125	ml	Warm water
½	c	125	ml	White bean flour	⅛	c	30	ml	Sugar or honey
¼	c	80	ml	Tapioca starch	¾	c	180	ml	Warm water
4¼	tsp	21	ml	Xanthan gum	1	tsp	5	ml	Methylcellulose
1¼	tsp	6	ml	Salt	1	tsp	5	ml	Vinegar
2	tbsp	30	ml	Butter, lard or vegetable shortening	½	c	125	ml	Warm water
3	pkg	3	pkg	Unflavoured gelatin	1	tbsp	15	ml	Psyllium
¼	c	60	ml	Cold water	2	tbsp	30	ml	Oil

BASIC YEAST BREAD
AGAR AND METHYLCELLULOSE FOAM

This recipe uses agar and methylcellulose foam to provide the structure and strength of the bread. Agar does not create foam, but does work as a binding agent. To get the maximum texture the use of a stand mixer and strong beating enhances the chewy texture. Warmth and time to let the bread rise is important. Agar is a good alternative to egg white especially for people who do not eat eggs or who follow a vegan diet. For vegan bread substitute the butter with vegetable shortening to eliminate all animal-based products from the recipe.

YIELD: Two (2) 8x4 loaves

METHOD:

1. Dissolve agar in ¼ cold water. Add the boiling water. Stir until well combined and agar has completely dissolved. Let cool to warm.
2. Place yeast and 1 tsp of sugar into a bowl. Add warm water. The yeast mixture should start to foam as the yeast activates.
3. Place ¾ cup warm water into a high-sided bowl. Add Agar solution to warm water and mix to combine. Add methylcellulose. With a stick beater, beat until thick and foamy.
4. Place ½ c water and 1 tbsp psyllium in a small bowl. Let gel. Add 2 tbsp oil and mix until fully combined.
5. Measure all flours and starches and place into a sifter. Sift all flours prior to adding to mixing bowl. Do not sift, then measure - measure first.
6. Place the flours, starch, xanthan gum, salt, sugar, and butter or lard into a mixer. Mix until the butter/lard is combined with the flour and it resembles cornmeal.
7. Add dissolved yeast, psyllium gel, vinegar, methylcellulose foam, and dissolved agar onto dry ingredients. Beat on high speed for approximately 5 minutes, scraping sides of bowl as required.
8. Spray two (2) 8x4x2 inch bread loaf pans. Divide batter equally between the prepared pans. Place in a warm place and let rise until double in volume. Warming the oven up by turning the oven light on is always a good option. Time will vary depending on yeast and temperature of the environment.
9. Preheat oven to 400°F (200° C, Gas Mark 6). Bake for 10 minutes. Turn oven down and bake at 350° F (180° C, Gas Mark 4) for 20-25 minutes.
10. Loaf is done when it pulls away from the sides and sounds hollow when tapped. If the loaf becomes too brown, cover with tin foil.
11. Remove from oven. Let sit in the pan for 5-8 minutes. Remove to a cooling rack.

PER 33 G SERVING: calories 70, fat 2 g, carbohydrate 12 g, fibre 2 g, protein 2 g

IMPERIAL		METRIC		INGREDIENT	IMPERIAL		METRIC		INGREDIENT
2	tsp	30	ml	Agar	¼	c	60	ml	Tapioca starch
¼	c	60	ml	Cold water	4¼	tsp	21	ml	Xanthan gum
½	c	125	ml	Boiling water	1¼	tsp	6	ml	Salt
4	tsp	20	ml	Yeast	2	tbsp	30	ml	Butter, lard or vegetable shortening
1	tsp	5	ml	Sugar	2	tsp	10	ml	Methylcellulose
½	c	125	ml	Warm water	¾	c	180	ml	Warm water
1½	c	375	ml	Brown rice flour	⅛	c	30	ml	Honey or sugar
½	c	125	ml	Buckwheat, corn flour or pure oat* flour	1	tsp	5	ml	Vinegar
6	tbsp	90	ml	Millet flour	½	c	125	ml	Water
½	c	125	ml	White bean flour	1	tbsp	15	ml	Psyllium
3	tbsp	45	ml	Defatted nut/ seed flour or protein powder	2	tbsp	30	ml	Oil

TORTILLAS

Tortillas are an example of using the food processor and boiling water as a way to increase the gluey stretch and strength of dough. This enhances the ability to roll the dough and prevents the dough from cracking after cooking. This recipe also uses strong hydrophilic binders to assist with the stretch and structure. Protein binders are not important as the strong hydrophilic binders in these products. As you can see from this recipe, no protein binders are used. Kneading dough is essential to enhancing the stretch and elastic quality. The longer you knead the dough the better the stretch.

YIELD: 10

METHOD:

1. Measure all flours and starches and place into a sifter. Sift all flours prior to adding to mixing bowl. Do not sift, then measure - measure first.
2. Place all dry ingredients into a food processor and pulse to mix.
3. With food processor on, slowly add boiling water to form a dough ball. Process 1 minute, add additional water if needed.
4. Lightly flour a surface with sweet rice flour. Knead dough on surface for approximately 10 minutes. Add additional flour to surface if dough is sticky and continue kneading. Dough should be tacky but not sticky. Do not dry out with flour as it will lose its elastic quality.
5. Divide dough into 10 dough balls. Place dough ball onto a clean surface lightly sprinkled with sweet rice flour. Roll dough as thin as possible using a rolling pin until you get an approximate 7-inch circle. If you like your tortillas completely round use a cutter to cut the edges (the rim of a lid can work).
6. Heat a large heavy-bottomed skillet over medium heat until hot (takes about 4 minutes).
7. One at a time, cook the tortillas in the hot skillet until brown spots start to form. Flip and cook the other side. Each tortilla will take about 3 minutes to cook. Set cooked tortillas aside. Tortillas are best eaten fresh.

PER 44 G SERVING: calories 100, fat 1 g, carbohydrate 19 g, fibre 3 g, protein 4 g

IMPERIAL		METRIC		INGREDIENT	IMPERIAL		METRIC		INGREDIENT
¾	c	180	ml	Brown rice flour	½	tsp	2	ml	Salt
½	c	125	ml	Millet flour	2	tsp	2	ml	Xanthan gum
¼	c	60	ml	Quinoa flour	¾	c	190	ml	Boiling water
2	tbsp	30	ml	Whey protein powder (unflavoured)	2	tbsp	30	ml	Boiling water
3	tbsp	45	ml	Tapioca starch					

PASTA DOUGH

Pasta is another example of how a food processor, boiling water, a strong hydrophilic binder and the use of gluey flours can create dough that can be rolled and cut out into shapes. The use of amaranth flour in water-based dough is unusual and strategic as it will add to the moist and chewy texture desired in pasta. Like all pasta, this pasta is best when rolled as thin as possible.

YIELD: Seventy (70) 1-inch cut outs for tortellini or ravioli

METHOD:

1. Measure all flours and starches and place into a sifter. Sift all flours prior to adding to mixing bowl. Do not sift, then measure - measure first.
2. Place all flours, starch, salt, and xanthan gum in a food processor. Pulse to mix.
3. While food processor is running, add boiling water in a steady stream to the flour mixture. Process for about 1-2 minutes to form a dough ball. Drip additional boiling water in as needed to get a tacky (but not sticky) dough ball.
4. Remove dough from food processor to a clean smooth surface. Knead for about 10 minutes until dough has cooled and is smooth and elastic. If the dough is sticky lightly flour surface with sweet rice flour (do not add too much flour as it will dry out the dough).
5. Break dough into 6 pieces. Place pieces in a re-sealable plastic bag.
6. Roll out one of the dough pieces on a clean surface until desired thickness is reached or press dough through a pasta maker. If using a pasta maker roll dough out into a flat strip then press through pasta maker guiding strip from the top. Once dough is through the maker support the dough with your hand and guide it out to reduce breaking. Support the dough with your hand as it is run through the pasta maker. If the dough is breaking, it is likely too dry, wet hands and knead dough until tacky and then run through the pasta maker again.
7. Cut the pressed dough into desired shape(s). Once shapes are cut from the flattened dough, pick up the leftover pieces, knead and re-roll to flatten. If making filled pasta, place filling in center of pasta cut out, wet edges, place top and seal edges.
8. Bring a large pot of water to a boil. Add pasta and cook until desired tenderness, 3-4 minutes.

PER 55 G SERVING: calories 160, fat 4.5 g, carbohydrate 29 g, fibre 3 g, protein 3 g

IMPERIAL		METRIC		INGREDIENT
¾	c	180	ml	Brown rice flour
⅓	c	80	ml	Millet flour
¼	c	60	ml	Amaranth flour
¼	c	60	ml	Chickpea or lentil flour
⅓	c	80	ml	Tapioca starch
1	tsp	5	ml	Salt
4	tsp	20	ml	Xanthan gum
⅔	c	160	ml	Boiling water
2-3	tbsp	30-45	ml	Boiling water, added as needed

BASIC CRÊPES

Crêpes provide an example of egg white protein acting as the binder that holds the structure together. The use of xanthan gum, millet flour and tapioca starch provide an elastic quality to the crêpe so that it will continue to hold its shape and not split when rolled. These crêpes are perfect for sweet or savoury fillings. These crêpes are soft, moist, and hold their shape.

YIELD: Twelve (12) 6-inch crêpes

METHOD:

1. In a bowl, beat milk, eggs, and oil together using a hand beater.
2. Measure all flours and starches and place into a sifter. Sift all flours prior to adding to mixing bowl. Do not sift, then measure - measure first.
3. Add remaining ingredients and beat for 1 minute. Let sit for 5 minutes.
4. Lightly brush a crêpe pan with melted butter. Pour ⅛ cup of batter into a hot 6-inch crêpe pan. Tilt pan in a circle to spread batter evenly over bottom of crêpe pan. Cook until golden brown. Flip and cook other side until golden brown.
5. Once cooked remove from pan immediately.
6. Fill with desired filling.

PER 32 G SERVING: calories 50, fat 2.5 g, carbohydrate 6 g, fibre 0 g, protein 2 g

IMPERIAL		METRIC		INGREDIENT
¼	c	60	ml	Brown rice flour
¼	c	60	ml	Millet flour
1	tsp	5	ml	Defatted nut/seed flour or protein powder
5	tsp	25	ml	Tapioca starch
¼	tsp	1	ml	Xanthan gum
⅛	tsp	1	pinch	Salt
½	tsp	2	ml	Sugar
1	tbsp	15	ml	Oil
2	Lg	2	Lg	Eggs
¾	c	190	ml	Milk

IRISH SODA BREAD

Irish soda bread is an example of non-yeast bread that uses leavening agents in combination with an acid to assist in leavening. The hydrophilic binding agents are used in combination – one strong binder that requires agitation and another that requires time. The use of foams assist in leavening and creating a light texture. The technique of beating the batter and letting the dough sit help the binders and the leavening agents reach maximum potential. The flour mixture used has strength and stretch elements as well as flours that hold moisture and create a softer crumb.

YIELD: Two (2) 8x4 loaves

METHOD:

1. Measure all flours and starches and place into a sifter. Sift all flours prior to adding to mixing bowl. Do not sift, then measure - measure first.
2. Place all dry ingredients, except raisins, into a bowl of a mixer.
3. Separate eggs. Using a hand beater beat egg whites until stiff peaks form. Set aside. Beat the yolks until light yellow and triple in volume.
4. Place ½ c water and 3/4 tsp methylcellulose into a high-sided bowl. Beat with a stick beater until thick and foamy.
5. Add buttermilk, lemon juice, honey, methylcellulose foam, and egg yolk foam to dry ingredients. Beat for 1-2 minutes on high speed, until smooth, stopping mixer to scrape sides as needed.
6. Add melted butter and oil and beat until just combined.
7. Fold in raisins and pulse until distributed equally.
8. Grease two (2) 8x4x2 inch loaf pans. Divide batter equally between the prepared pans and smooth the top with the back of a spoon. Let sit approximately 15 minutes.
9. Preheat oven to 325°F (160° C, Gas Mark 3) and bake for 30-35 minutes or until golden and the bread begins to crack and pull away from the sides. A toothpick pushed through the center of the loaf should come out clean.
10. Let sit for 5-8 minutes. Remove from pan and let cool completely.
11. When cool, wrap in tinfoil and then place in an airtight container or plastic bag. The tinfoil will enhance the soda bread flavour.

NOTE: If using whey protein powder to replace the defatted nut/seed flour add equal amounts of quinoa or bean flour.

PER 41 G SERVING: calories 100, fat 2.5 g, carbohydrate 18 g, fibre 2 g, protein 3 g

IMPERIAL		METRIC		INGREDIENT
1	c	250	ml	Brown rice flour
¾	c	180	ml	Sorghum flour
½	c	125	ml	Millet flour
½	c	125	ml	Quinoa flour
⅓	c	80	ml	White bean flour
2	tbsp	30	ml	Defatted nut/seed or protein powder
2	tbsp	30	ml	Tapioca starch
1	tsp	5	ml	Xanthan gum
2	tbsp	30	ml	Psyllium
1¼	tsp	6	ml	Baking soda
3½	tsp	17	ml	Baking powder
1	tsp	5	ml	Salt
2	Lg	2	Lg	Eggs, separated and beaten
¾	tsp	7	ml	Methylcellulose
½	c	125	ml	Water
¼	c	60	ml	Honey
1½	c	375	ml	Buttermilk
1	tbsp	15	ml	Lemon Juice
2	tbsp	30	ml	Butter, melted
2	tbsp	30	ml	Oil
1	c	250	ml	Raisins (optional)

BASIC BUTTERMILK WAFFLES

Waffles are an example of an item that is made in an "electric maker". The batter needs to have enough structure to be able to be removed while hot without being too firm or tough. The flour mixture has structure and moisture flours as well as stretchy starch, and uses a strong hydrophilic binder for binding in combination with protein binders. Foaming the protein binder results in a lighter product that remains strong. Leavening comes from gas producing leavening agents in combination with an acid. In this case, letting the batter sit is not for the hydrophilic binders but for the leavening agents to get a "head start". This is necessary as electric makers cook batters very quickly.

YIELD: 12-14 4x4 inch waffle fingers

METHOD:

1. Separate eggs. Place yolks into a small high-sided bowl and set aside.
2. Place egg whites into a high-sided narrow bottomed bowl. With an electric hand beater, beat egg whites until stiff peaks form.
3. Beat egg yolks until light yellow and triple in volume.
4. Measure all flours and starches and place into a sifter. Sift all flours prior to adding to mixing bowl. Do not sift, then measure - measure first.
5. Mix all dry ingredients together in a mixing bowl.
6. Add egg yolk foam, vanilla, honey, buttermilk and milk to the flour mixture. Beat with a hand beater for 1-2 minutes. Add melted butter and oil and beat with a hand beater until combined.
7. Fold in egg white foam until well combined.
8. Allow batter to sit for approximately 5 minutes.
9. Heat waffle iron to medium high heat as directed by the waffle iron manufacturer.
10. Spray iron with spray oil. Pour batter into heated waffle iron in the volume specified by the waffle iron manufacturer. Cook until cooked through. Remove immediately.

NOTE: Most waffle irons beep when waffles are cooked. If your waffle maker does not beep, time how long it takes to cook the waffles to desired doneness and record for future reference.

PER 68 G SERVING: calories 140, fat 6 g, carbohydrate 18 g, fibre 2 g, protein 5 g

IMPERIAL		METRIC		INGREDIENT	IMPERIAL		METRIC		INGREDIENT
½	c	125	ml	Brown rice flour	½	tsp	2	ml	Gelatin powder
3	tbsp	45	ml	Buckwheat flour	2	tsp	10	ml	Psyllium husk
⅔	c	160	ml	Sorghum flour	2	Lg	2	Lg	Eggs, separated
3	tbsp	45	ml	White bean flour	1½	tsp	7	ml	Vanilla powder or 3 tsp vanilla extract
2	tbsp	30	ml	Defatted nut/ seed flour or protein powder	2	tbsp	30	ml	Honey or sugar
2	tbsp	30	ml	Tapioca starch	1	c	250	ml	Buttermilk
1	tbsp	15	ml	Baking powder	½	c	125	ml	Milk
¾	tsp	4	ml	Baking soda	3	tbsp	45	ml	Butter, melted
¼	tsp	1	ml	Salt	1	tbsp	15	ml	Oil
½	tsp	2	ml	Xanthan gum					

CORNMEAL CHEDDAR LUNCH WAFFLES

This recipe utilizes cornmeal, calls for added nutritional enhancers and uses a waffle iron. Using the textures and flavours inherent to the base ingredients, the nutritional yeast and the hemp hearts blend in and add nutrition benefit as well as enhance the end product. This waffle has great texture and can be used as the base to a pizza, a side dish to chili, as sandwich bread or enjoyed on its own!

YIELD: Eleven (11) 4x4 waffles

METHOD:

1. Sift corn flour, sorghum flour, garfava bean flour/chickpea flour, and tapioca starch.
2. In a medium-sized high-sided bowl, place all dry ingredients and mix well.
3. Separate eggs. Place egg yolks into a small high-sided round-bottomed bowl. Place egg whites in a high-sided bowl. Beat until stiff peaks form. Beat egg yolks until light yellow and triple in volume.
4. Add milk, buttermilk, egg white and egg yolk foams to dry ingredients. Beat on high speed for 1-2 minutes.
5. Melt butter. Add oil and mix. Add butter/oil mixture to batter and mix until combined.
6. Add grated cheese, green onions, and parsley. Mix until combined and distributed evenly.
7. Heat waffle iron to high heat as directed by the manufacturer.
8. Spray waffle iron with cooking spray. Pour waffle mix onto iron in quantities specified by the manufacturer.
9. Cook until golden brown and cooked through. Remove immediately.

NOTE: Many irons beep when waffles are cooked. If not, you may want to time how long it takes to cook a batch once your iron is hot.

PER 91 G SERVING: calories 230, fat 10 g, carbohydrate 24 g, fibre 2 g, protein 10 g

IMPERIAL		METRIC		INGREDIENT	IMPERIAL		METRIC		INGREDIENT
½	c	125	ml	Brown rice flour	½	tsp	2	ml	Powdered garlic (optional)
1	c	250	ml	Corn meal	½	tsp	2	ml	Gelatin powder
¼	c	60	ml	Corn flour	1	tbsp	15	ml	Sugar
¼	c	60	ml	Sorghum flour	2	Lg	2	Lg	Eggs, separated
¼	c	60	ml	Garfava bean or chickpea flour	2	tbsp	30	ml	Butter, melted
3	tbsp	45	ml	Tapioca starch	2	tbsp	30	ml	Oil
1	tbsp	15	ml	Baking powder	¾	c	180	ml	Milk
½	tsp	2	ml	Baking soda	1	c	250	ml	Buttermilk
½	tsp	2	ml	Salt	4	oz	110	g	Aged sharp cheddar cheese
1	tsp	5	ml	Xanthan gum	¼	c	60	ml	Fresh green onions or chives, finely chopped
¼-½	tsp	1-2	ml	Fresh ground pepper	2-3	tbsp	30	ml	Fresh parsley, finely chopped
¼	c	60	ml	Nutritional yeast flakes					

CHOCOLATE SNACK BALLS

This recipe uses an electric cake ball maker for cooking the batter into perfect balls. The batter has to be strong enough to be removed when hot and soft enough to be cake-like. An electric mixer is essential to get the light, airy and strong structure that is required for snack balls to be removed from the maker. We use butter in this recipe, however, we have been successful using a combination of butter and oil in snack balls. If you choose to use oil, you have to be very gentle in removing them from the maker so that they do not fall apart when hot. Snack balls made with oil alone do not roll well in sugar as they tend to break but can be iced when cooled.

YIELD: 21 3-inch (using a 1-ounce scoop)

METHOD:

1. Measure all flours and starches and place into a sifter. Sift all flours prior to adding to mixing bowl. Do not sift, then measure - measure first.
2. Place all dry ingredients in a bowl and mix well.
3. Separate eggs. Place egg yolks into a small high-sided round-bottomed bowl. Place egg whites into a large high-sided round-bottomed bowl. Beat egg whites into foam until stiff peaks form. Beat yolks until light yellow and triple in volume.
4. Combine milk, buttermilk and vanilla. Pour onto dry ingredients.
5. Add egg white and yolk foams onto wet ingredients and beat with electric hand beaters until ingredients are combined. Beat scraping sides until all ingredients are mixed thoroughly. Beat for 1-2 minutes on high.
6. Heat cake ball maker as directed. Spray with spray oil.
7. Using a 1-ounce scoop, scoop batter into cake ball maker.
8. Cook for approximately 4-5 minutes or until cooked all the way through.
9. Eat plain, coat with glaze or roll in a mixture of cocoa powder and icing sugar.

OPTION: Use 2 tbsp melted butter and 1 tbsp oil to improve nutrient profile of the fat.

PER 16 G SERVING: calories 35, fat 1 g, carbohydrate 5 g, fibre 1 g, protein 1 g

IMPERIAL		METRIC		INGREDIENT	IMPERIAL		METRIC		INGREDIENT
¼	c	60	ml	Teff flour	¼	tsp	60	ml	Baking soda
¼	c	60	ml	Sorghum flour	¼	tsp	1	ml	Salt
¼	c	60	ml	Buckwheat or Pure oat* flour	½	tsp	2	ml	Xanthan gum
3	tbsp	45	ml	Brown rice flour	1½	tsp	7	ml	Psyllium husk
3	tbsp	45	ml	Black bean flour	2	tsp	10	ml	Vanilla
2	tbsp	30	ml	Defatted nut/seed flour or protein powder	1	c	250	ml	Milk
2	tbsp	30	ml	Tapioca starch	⅓	c	80	ml	Buttermilk
⅓	c	80	ml	Sugar	2	Lg	2	Lg	Eggs, separated
½	c	125	ml	Cocoa powder	2	tbsp	30	ml	Melted butter
1½	tsp	7	ml	Baking powder	1	tbsp	15	ml	Oil

BASIC BUTTERMILK PANCAKES

Pancakes are an example of a baked good that uses a flour mix containing structure flours from Flour Group 1, flours that provide stretch and chew, and flours that soften and add moisture. Pancakes need to be soft yet firm enough to hold syrup or a sauce without becoming soggy or chewy like bread. The combination of hydrophilic binders that require agitation and as well as those that require time creates this texture as well. Protein binders are helpful in strengthening the structure. Oil works well in pancakes as it used in a small volume and strong chew is not desired. Pancakes can be of different thickness depending on preference. Some people like thick and fluffy pancakes where others prefer them thin. If you prefer pancakes on the thin side do not beat the egg white, instead add unbeaten egg white to wet ingredients.

YIELD: 21 3-inch Pancakes

METHOD:

1. Measure all flours and starches and place into a sifter. Sift all flours prior to adding to mixing bowl. Do not sift, then measure - measure first.
2. Place all dry ingredients in a bowl and mix well.
3. Separate egg. Place egg yolk into a small high-sided bowl. Place the egg white into a high-sided bowl. Using an electric mixer beat egg white until stiff peaks form. Beat egg yolk until light yellow and triple in volume.
4. In a high-side bowl add oil, buttermilk, milk, and egg yolk. Add all dry ingredients at once and beat with an electric hand beater for 1- 2 minutes.
5. Add egg white foam to pancake batter with beater on low beat until combined.
6. Let sit for 5 minutes, meanwhile heat and grease griddle lightly with oil or spray with spray oil.
7. When griddle has reached temperature, spoon batter onto grill. Cook until underside is golden and batter bubbly looking and cooked enough to flip. Flip pancakes and cook the other side until that side is golden and pancake is cooked all the way through.

NOTE: If using whey protein powder to replace the defatted nut/seed flour add equal amounts of quinoa or bean flour.

NOTE: If you like thinner pancakes, add slightly more milk until desired consistency is reached.

PER 73 G SERVING: calories 80, fat 3 g, carbohydrate 12 g, fibre 1 g, protein 3 g

IMPERIAL		METRIC		INGREDIENT	IMPERIAL		METRIC		INGREDIENT
⅔	c	160	ml	Brown rice flour	2	tsp	10	ml	Baking powder
½	c	125	ml	Sorghum flour	½	tsp	2	ml	Baking soda
¼	c	60	ml	Millet flour	½	tsp	2	ml	Salt
6	tbsp	90	ml	Quinoa flour	⅛	c	30	ml	Sugar (white, brown, coconut or date)
2	tbsp	30	ml	Garfava bean flour	2	tbsp	30	ml	Oil
2	tbsp	30	ml	Defatted nut/seed flour or protein powder	2	Lg	2	Lg	Eggs, separated
2	tbsp	30	ml	Tapioca starch	1	c	250	ml	Buttermilk
¼	tsp	1	ml	Xanthan gum	1	c	250	ml	Milk
2	tbsp	30	ml	Psyllium husk					

MOCK BRAN MUFFINS

Mock bran muffins are a good example of how to incorporate nutritious ingredients such as brown rice flakes, rice bran, hemp hearts, and flax seeds in a traditional muffin. This recipe also uses the technique of soaking ingredients for an extended period of time which helps soften and blend the ingredients while producing a more desirable end texture. The use of foams assist in structure and leavening. In addition to the protein binder, a combination of hydrophilic binders are used to create the muffin texture. The other ingredients assist in creating structure, texture and increasing the nutrient content of the muffin.

YIELD: 36 medium-sized muffins

METHOD:

1. In a bowl combine the first 6 ingredients and mix thoroughly. Cover and place in the fridge for 8 hours or overnight.
2. Remove the muffin batter from the fridge. Use electric hand beaters or a stand mixer to lightly beat the mixture.
3. Place ⅓ c water and 3/4 tsp methylcellulose into a high-sided bowl and beat with a stick beater until thick and foamy. Let gel. Add 2 tbsp oil and mix until fully combined.
4. Separate eggs and place whites and yolks into two separate high-sided bowls. With a hand beater beat egg whites until stiff peaks form and set aside. Beat egg yolks until light yellow and triple in volume.
5. Measure all flours and starches and place into a sifter. Sift all flours prior to adding to mixing bowl. Do not sift, then measure - measure first.
6. Add sifted flour, remaining dry ingredients (except raisins or dates), methylcellulose foam, and egg yolk foam to the batter. Using electric hand beaters or stand mixer beat batter for 1-2 minutes.
7. Add 3 tbsp melted butter and 2 tbsp oil to batter and mix until combined.
8. Add egg white foam to mixture and lightly beat into batter until incorporated.
9. Fold in raisins or chopped dates until distributed equally.
10. Spoon batter into greased muffin cups. Let sit for approximately 10 minutes.
11. Bake at 350°F (180°C, Gas Mark 4) for 18-20 minutes or until golden and toothpick comes out clean.
12. Let cool for 3-5 minutes before removing from pan to cooling rack.

PER 50 G SERVING: calories 140, fat 4.5 g, carbohydrate 22 g, fibre 3 g, protein 4 g

IMPERIAL		METRIC		INGREDIENT	IMPERIAL		METRIC		INGREDIENT
1½	c	375	ml	Brown rice flakes	½	tsp	2	ml	Xanthan gum
1	c	250	ml	Rice bran	3	tbsp	45	ml	Chia seeds, ground
¾	c	180	ml	Boiling water	1	tsp	5	ml	Baking soda
⅔	c	160	ml	Molasses	1	tbsp	15	ml	Baking powder
2	c	500	ml	Buttermilk	½	tsp	2	ml	Salt
⅓	c	80	ml	Brown sugar or coconut sugar	¼	c	60	ml	Hemp hearts
2	Lg	2	Lg	Eggs	⅓	c	80	ml	Flax seeds, ground
⅔	c	160	ml	Buckwheat flour	⅓	c	80	ml	Water
¾	c	180	ml	Sorghum flour	¾	tsp	7	ml	Methylcellulose
¼	c	60	ml	Black bean flour	2	tbsp	30	ml	Oil
⅛	c	30	ml	Defatted nut/seed flour or protein powder	3	tbsp	45	ml	Melted butter
¼	c	60	ml	Tapioca starch	½-⅔	c	125-160	ml	Raisins or chopped dates (optional)

BANANA MUFFINS

This recipe demonstrates the use of mashed fruit. Mashed fruit is heavy and moist and requires a higher proportion of xanthan gum in the hydrophilic binder combination than muffins made without mashed fruit. Maximizing the leavening agents to assist in rising is required. Using baking powder and baking soda, together with an acid, results in a better end product. Coupled with beaten egg white and the use of butter over oil, the texture and rise comes together to yield a most desirable end product. It is very important to beat the batter to maximize the effect of the xanthan gum and then let the batter sit to maximize effectiveness of the psyllium husk.

YIELD: 21 muffins (using a 2-ounce scoop).

METHOD:

1. Measure all flours and starches and place into a sifter. Sift all flours prior to adding to mixing bowl. Do not sift, then measure - measure first.
2. Place all dry ingredients in a bowl and mix well.
3. Separate eggs. Place egg whites and egg yolks into separate high-sided bowls. With an electric hand beater, beat egg whites until stiff peaks form. Beat egg yolks until light yellow and triple in volume.
4. Peel and mash bananas until smooth.
5. In a bowl combine vanilla, buttermilk, lemon juice and mashed banana and beat until combined.
6. In a separate bowl, melt butter. Add oil and mix. Set aside.
7. Add milk and banana mixture and egg white and egg yolk foams to dry ingredients. With an electric hand beater, beat on high speed for 1-2 minutes.
8. Beat in melted butter/oil mixture until just combined.
9. Stir in chocolate chips and nuts if desired.
10. Spray medium-sized muffin cups with spray oil.
11. Spoon batter into muffin cups. Let sit for approximately 10 minutes.
12. Bake at 350°F (180°C or Gas Mark 4) for 18 minutes or until golden and inserted toothpick comes out clean.
13. Let cool for 3-5 minutes remove from pan to cooling rack.

PER 52 G SERVING: calories 140, fat 6 g, carbohydrate 21 g, fibre 2 g, protein 3 g

IMPERIAL		METRIC		INGREDIENT	IMPERIAL		METRIC		INGREDIENT
⅔	c	160	ml	Brown rice flour	⅛	tsp	1	pinch	Nutmeg
½	c	125	ml	Sorghum flour	1½	c	325	ml	Mashed banana
¼	c	60	ml	Millet flour	2	Lg	2	Lg	Eggs, separated
2	tbsp	30	ml	Chickpea or garfava flour	1	tsp	5	ml	Vanilla
2	tbsp	30	ml	Defatted nut/seed powder or protein powder	⅓	c	80	ml	Buttermilk
2	tbsp	30	ml	Tapioca starch	1	tbsp	15	ml	Lemon juice
¾	tsp	4	ml	Xanthan gum	6	tbsp	90	ml	Honey or sugar
1	tbsp	15	ml	Psyllium	3	tbsp	45	ml	Melted butter
2	tsp	10	ml	Baking powder	1	tbsp	15	ml	Oil
½	tsp	2	ml	Baking soda	⅔	c	160	ml	Chocolate chips, raisins or chopped dates, optional
½	tsp	2	ml	Salt	⅔	c	160	ml	Chopped nuts (walnuts, pecans or hazelnuts), optional

BASIC BISCUITS

Biscuits are one of the hardest gluten-free items to make - they need to have the correct light and moist texture. The right combination and balance of structure flours, moisture flours, butter, liquid, and binders (protein and hydrophilic binders, in particular the methylcellulose foam) are the keys to making great biscuits. The dough will be much wetter than traditional wheat-based biscuit dough. Letting the dough sit to let the hydrophilic binders stiffen the dough is an important step to be successful in cutting out biscuits. Resist the urge to add flour, additional flour will produce a dry biscuit.

YIELD: 16 biscuits

METHOD:

1. Measure all flours and starches and place into a sifter. Sift all flours prior to adding to bowl of food processor. Do not sift, then measure - measure first.
2. Place all dry ingredients, except methylcellulose into a food processor with "S" blade in place. Pulse to mix ingredients.
3. Cut in cold butter and process until flour and butter mixture resembles cornmeal.
4. In a high-sided mixing bowl beat the methylcellulose and water using a stick beater until thick and foamy. Foam should measure ⅔ cup.
5. Add foam, cream, and eggs to the dry ingredients. Process until smooth. Scrape the sides of the bowl and process for 1 minute.
6. Generously sprinkle sweet rice flour onto the counter or board. Scoop biscuit dough into rice flour. The dough will be sticky and closer to thick muffin batter than biscuit dough. With floured hands pat into a circle about ½ inch thick. Let sit for 5-10 minutes until to firms up a bit.
7. Cut out biscuits with biscuit cutter coated with sweet rice flour.
8. Place on a parchment paper lined cookie sheet.
9. Bake at 375°F (180°C, Gas Mark 4) for 10-12 minutes or until golden and cooked all the way through.

PER 48 G SERVING: calories 140, fat 7 g, carbohydrate 15 g, fibre 2 g, protein 3 g

IMPERIAL		METRIC		INGREDIENT	IMPERIAL		METRIC		INGREDIENT
½	c	125	ml	Brown rice flour	2	tbsp	30	ml	Sugar, depending on desired sweetness
¾	c	180	ml	Millet flour	½	tsp	2	ml	Salt
½	c	125	ml	Quinoa flour	½	c	125	ml	Butter
¼	c	60	ml	Garfava flour	1	tsp	5	ml	Methylcellulose
¼	c	60	ml	Tapioca starch	½	c	125	ml	Water
1	tsp	5	ml	Xanthan gum	½	c	125	ml	Cream
2	tbsp	30	ml	Chia seeds, ground	2	Lg	2	Lg	Eggs
4	tsp	20	ml	Baking powder					

CHOCOLATE BISCUIT OR FOAM CAKE

In this recipe egg white foam forms the structure for the cake. These cakes are easy to make and quick to bake. The flours used have more to do with flavour than structure.

YIELD: One (1) 12x17 inch jelly roll pan (1 log or one (1) 4-layer cake

METHOD:

1. Preheat oven to 450°F (230°C, Gas Mark 8).
2. Measure all flours and starches and place into a sifter. Sift all flours prior to adding to mixing bowl. Do not sift, then measure - measure first.
3. Dissolve cocoa in boiling water. Set aside to cool.
4. Separate 3 of the eggs. Set aside the egg whites. Place the egg yolks into a high-sided bowl or into the bowl of a mixer. Add the remaining eggs and ½ cup of sugar. Beat on high speed for 5 minutes or until the eggs are thick and fluffy, light yellow and tripled in volume. Add vanilla to cocoa mixture. Beat into egg yolks in three portions.
5. In a separate bowl combine the flours and starches. Sift half the mixture over the egg mixture and fold in. Fold in the remaining flour.
6. Beat the egg whites until frothy. Add the cream of tartar. Continue to beat until soft peaks form then add the remaining 1 tbsp of sugar. Continue to beat until stiff peaks form. Fold egg whites into the batter.
7. Line a cookie sheet with parchment paper. Spread the batter over the parchment paper. If wishing to make smaller rounds or squares, draw the number of circles in the size desired on parchment paper. Divide batter evenly between the circles. Spread out within the lines (makes four (4) 8-inch circles).
8. Bake at 450°F (230°C, Gas Mark 8) for 7 minutes or until the tester comes out clean and the cake springs back.
9. Remove from oven. Allow to cool if shaped into squares or circles for torte. Once cool, fill with desired filling or icing.

OR

1. If using for jelly roll or log cake remove cake on parchment paper to a flat surface. Sprinkle top with powdered sugar. Flip onto a clean tea towel and remove parchment paper. Sprinkle with powdered sugar. Roll biscuit in the towel to form a log. Place on a cooling rack to cool.
2. Gently unroll the cake and fill with desired filling (custard, jam, icing, *ganache*, ice cream or whipped cream) and roll back up into a log. Decorate as desired.

PER 40 G SERVING: calories 90, fat 2.5 g, carbohydrate 14 g, fibre 1 g, protein 3 g

IMPERIAL		METRIC		INGREDIENT	IMPERIAL		METRIC		INGREDIENT
1	tbsp	15	ml	Brown rice flour	¼	c	60	ml	Cocoa powder
1	tbsp	15	ml	Sorghum flour	5	Lg	5	Lg	Eggs
1	tbsp	15	ml	Teff flour	½	c	125	ml	Sugar
1	tbsp	15	ml	Amaranth flour	1	tsp	5	ml	Vanilla
1	tbsp	15	ml	White bean flour	¼	tsp	1	ml	Cream of tartar
2	tsp	10	ml	Tapioca starch	1	tbsp	15	ml	Sugar
3	tbsp	45	ml	Boiling water					

GINGER SPICE COOKIES

Cookies are fat-based batters that use sweeteners to assist in creating structure and create a crisp and chewy texture. The hydrophilic binder and egg help to hold the cookie together and prevent it from crumbling apart. Amaranth flour works great in fat-based baked goods as the fat and the amaranth create a more tender texture.

YIELD: 40 cookies using a 1-ounce scoop

METHOD:

1. Cream butter and sugar. Add egg and beat on high again until smooth and fluffy.
2. Add molasses and beat on high for 1 minute.
3. Measure all flours and starches and place into a sifter. Sift all flours prior to adding to mixing bowl. Do not sift, then measure - measure first.
4. Add all dry ingredients and beat on high for 1 minute.
5. Line a cookie sheet with parchment paper. Drop dough by the spoonful onto the cookie sheet.
6. Grease the bottom of a flat-bottomed glass. Dip into sugar and press a dough ball flat. Dip into sugar again and repeat, adding grease to the bottom of the glass as needed.
7. Bake at 375°F (180°C, Gas Mark 4) for 8-10 minutes.
8. Remove from oven. Allow to cool slightly before removing to a cooling rack.

PER 22 G SERVING: calories 90, fat 4 g, carbohydrate 12 g, fibre 1 g, protein 2 g

NOTE: Increase the sugar by ¼ c/60 ml to ⅓ c/80 ml to increase crunchiness and sweetness if desired.

IMPERIAL		METRIC		INGREDIENT	IMPERIAL		METRIC		INGREDIENT
½	c	125	ml	Teff flour	1	tbsp	15	ml	Ground ginger
¾	c	180	ml	Sorghum flour	1	tsp	5	ml	Ground cinnamon
1	c	250	ml	Amaranth flour	¼	tsp	1	ml	Ground cloves
3	tbsp	45	ml	Tapioca starch	½	tsp	2	ml	Salt
¼	c	60	ml	Rice bran	¾	c	180	ml	Butter
2	tbsp	30	ml	Black bean flour	¾	c	180	ml	Brown or coconut sugar
⅓	c	80	ml	Defatted nut/seed flour or protein powder or nut/seed meal	1	Lg	1	Lg	Egg
¾	tsp	4	ml	Xanthan gum	½	c	125	ml	Molasses
2	tsp	10	ml	Baking soda					

QUINOA FLAKE BARS

Quinoa flake bars are an example of a sweetener as the sole binder. When sugar heats to boiling it hardens. The length of time you cook the bar determines how chewy or crispy the bar will be. The bars are not set when removed from the oven as the sugar has to cool to harden – much like making candy.

YIELD: 56 bars (cut from a 12x17 sided cookie sheet)

METHOD:

1. In a microwave-safe bowl place the butter. Melt in the microwave.
2. Add honey and vanilla and stir until well combined.
3. Add all other ingredients and stir until thoroughly coated.
4. Add chocolate chips and/or dried fruit.
5. Place on a parchment lined pan. Bake at 325°F (160°C, Gas Mark 3) for 18-20 minutes. Allow to cool for about 3 minutes. Cut into bars. Do not remove from the pan. Allow to cool completely before removing.

NOTE: do not try to make this recipe without parchment paper. The bars do not come off the pan once cooled and do not maintain their shape when warm.

PER 12 G SERVING: calories 90, fat 5 g, carbohydrate 9 g, fibre 2 g, protein 2 g

NOTE: If desired, add the optional sugar to increase crunchiness and sweetness.

IMPERIAL		METRIC		INGREDIENT	IMPERIAL		METRIC		INGREDIENT
⅔	c	160	ml	Honey	⅓	c	80	ml	Hemp hearts
½	c	125	ml	Butter, melted	⅓	c	80	ml	Psyllium husk
1½	tsp	7	ml	Vanilla	⅓	c	80	ml	Chia seeds, ground
2½	c	625	ml	Quinoa flakes	⅔	c	160	ml	Walnuts or pecans, chopped, or sunflower seeds
½	tsp	2	ml	Salt	½	c	125	ml	Coconut, shredded
⅓	c	80	ml	Ground flax meal	¾	c	175	ml	Chocolate chips or chopped dried fruit
¼	c	60	ml	Pumpkin seed protein powder	¼	c	60	ml	Brown Sugar, optional

TRADITIONAL PIE DOUGH

Making good pastry is difficult regardless of the flour used. We are not pastry fans unless it is great pasty. This recipe works exceptionally well for both savoury and sweet items. The trick with pastry is that you need to have stretch, strength, and tenderness all wrapped into one. Using flours that have strength and stretch, as well as those that tenderize, help to achieve this desired texture. Also adding xanthan gum as the hydrophilic binder assists in rolling. Butter has the least impact on the hydrophilic binding capacity so using butter assists in rolling. Mashed avocado makes great pie dough, particularly for savoury crusts like those used in meat pies. Macadamia nut butter is also good fat substitute.

YIELD: 2 crusts or 36 tart shells

METHOD:

1. Set up a food processor with the bowl and the "S" blade.
2. Measure all flours and starches and place into a sifter. Sift all flours prior to adding to mixing bowl. Do not sift, then measure - measure first.
3. Place all the dry ingredients into the food processor and pulse to mix.
4. Add the cold butter. Process until the mixture is well combined.
5. Add the egg, vinegar, and water. Process until dough forms. Beat with the "S" blade for at least 1 minute to activate the xanthan gum and form a ball of dough. Dough will be soft and smooth.
6. Remove dough from food processor to parchment paper. Press dough into tart or pie shells. If having a top crust flip pie pan over onto parchment paper prior to lining and draw a circle onto parchment. Flip parchment so drawn circle is on back. Press dough into circle following outline. Place on firm surface such as cutting board and place in fridge or freezer to firm up. Fill pie once dough is firm. Remove from fridge and flip onto top of pie. Peel off parchment paper and pinch edges to seal. Slit top of crust and brush with milk. If sweet pie, you can sprinkle with sugar.
7. If a baked crust is required (as with banana cream pie) bake at 375°F (190°C, Gas Mark 5) for 12-14 minutes or until golden brown. Cool and fill with pie filling.
8. For filled pie (such as apple pie) bake at 375°F (190°C, Gas Mark 5) for 30-40 minutes for cooked filling and up to 1 hour for uncooked fillings.

NOTE: Below are a few options to alter the fat in the pastry if needed. Traditional pastry is more tender with butter or butter, lard and vegetable shortening combinations. Pastry made with avocado and/or macadamia nut butter produce a high quality, more sturdy and hearty, less tender pastry for savory pies.

USE:

- ½ cup butter and ½ cup mashed avocado; or
- ½ cup butter and ½ cup macadamia nut butter; or

- 1 cup macadamia nut butter; or
- ½ cup macadamia nut butter and ½ cup mashed avocado.

NOTE: the following breakdown is for the crust or shells only and does not account for filling

PER 37G SERVING (based on 10 slices from a double crusted pie): calories 300, fat 21 g, carbohydrate 25 g, fibre 4 g, protein 4 g

PER 15G TART SHELL (based on 45 tart shells): calories 70, fat 4.5 g, carbohydrate 6 g, fibre 1 g, protein 1 g

IMPERIAL		METRIC		INGREDIENT
⅓	c	90	ml	Brown rice flour
⅔	c	160	ml	Millet flour
⅔	c	160	ml	Amaranth flour
½	c	125	ml	Coconut flour
½	c	125	ml	Tapioca starch
¾	tsp	4	ml	Xanthan gum
1	tbsp	15	ml	Sugar
½	tsp	2	ml	Salt
1	c	250	ml	Cold butter
1	Lg	1	Lg	Egg
½	tsp	2	ml	Vinegar
3	tbsp	45	ml	Very cold water

NUTRITION FACT LABELS

BASIC YEAST BREAD EGG WHITE FOAM

Nutrition Facts

Serving Size (36g)
Servings Per Container 32 slices

Amount Per Serving

Calories 70   Calories from Fat 20

% Daily Value*

Total Fat 2.5g	4%
Saturated Fat 1g	5%
Trans Fat 0g	
Cholesterol 25mg	8%
Sodium 115mg	5%
Total Carbohydrate 11g	4%
Dietary Fiber 2g	8%
Sugars 2g	
Protein 2g	

Vitamin A 2%   •   Vitamin C 0%
Calcium 0%   •   Iron 2%

*Percent Daily Values are based on a 2,000 calorie diet. Your daily values may be higher or lower depending on your calorie needs:

	Calories:	2,000	2,500
Total Fat	Less than	65g	80g
Saturated Fat	Less than	20g	25g
Cholesterol	Less than	300mg	300mg
Sodium	Less than	2,400mg	2,400mg
Total Carbohydrate		300g	375g
Dietary Fiber		25g	30g

Calories per gram:
 Fat 9   •   Carbohydrate 4   •   Protein 4

BASIC YEAST BREAD GELATIN FOAM

Nutrition Facts

Serving Size (37g)
Servings Per Container

Amount Per Serving

Calories 70   Calories from Fat 15

% Daily Value*

Total Fat 2g	3%
Saturated Fat 1g	5%
Trans Fat 0g	
Cholesterol 5mg	2%
Sodium 105mg	4%
Total Carbohydrate 12g	4%
Dietary Fiber 2g	8%
Sugars 2g	
Protein 2g	

Vitamin A 0%   •   Vitamin C 0%
Calcium 0%   •   Iron 2%

*Percent Daily Values are based on a 2,000 calorie diet. Your daily values may be higher or lower depending on your calorie needs:

	Calories:	2,000	2,500
Total Fat	Less than	65g	80g
Saturated Fat	Less than	20g	25g
Cholesterol	Less than	300mg	300mg
Sodium	Less than	2,400mg	2,400mg
Total Carbohydrate		300g	375g
Dietary Fiber		25g	30g

Calories per gram:
 Fat 9   •   Carbohydrate 4   •   Protein 4

BASIC YEAST BREAD AGAR AND METHYLCELLULOSE FOAM

Nutrition Facts

Serving Size (33g)
Servings Per Container

Amount Per Serving

Calories 70	Calories from Fat 15
	% Daily Value*
Total Fat 2g	3%
Saturated Fat 1g	5%
Trans Fat 0g	
Cholesterol 5mg	2%
Sodium 105mg	4%
Total Carbohydrate 12g	4%
Dietary Fiber 2g	8%
Sugars 2g	
Protein 2g	

Vitamin A 0%	•	Vitamin C 0%
Calcium 0%	•	Iron 2%

*Percent Daily Values are based on a 2,000 calorie diet. Your daily values may be higher or lower depending on your calorie needs:

	Calories:	2,000	2,500
Total Fat	Less than	65g	80g
Saturated Fat	Less than	20g	25g
Cholesterol	Less than	300mg	300mg
Sodium	Less than	2,400mg	2,400mg
Total Carbohydrate		300g	375g
Dietary Fiber		25g	30g

Calories per gram:
Fat 9 • Carbohydrate 4 • Protein 4

TORTILLAS

Nutrition Facts

Serving Size (44g)
Servings Per Container

Amount Per Serving

Calories 100	Calories from Fat 10
	% Daily Value*
Total Fat 1g	2%
Saturated Fat 0g	0%
Trans Fat 0g	
Cholesterol 0mg	0%
Sodium 120mg	5%
Total Carbohydrate 19g	6%
Dietary Fiber 3g	12%
Sugars 0g	
Protein 4g	

Vitamin A 0%	•	Vitamin C 0%
Calcium 0%	•	Iron 8%

*Percent Daily Values are based on a 2,000 calorie diet. Your daily values may be higher or lower depending on your calorie needs:

	Calories:	2,000	2,500
Total Fat	Less than	65g	80g
Saturated Fat	Less than	20g	25g
Cholesterol	Less than	300mg	300mg
Sodium	Less than	2,400mg	2,400mg
Total Carbohydrate		300g	375g
Dietary Fiber		25g	30g

Calories per gram:
Fat 9 • Carbohydrate 4 • Protein 4

PASTA DOUGH

Nutrition Facts

Serving Size (55g)
Servings Per Container

Amount Per Serving

Calories 140   Calories from Fat 35

% Daily Value*

Total Fat 4g	**6%**
Saturated Fat 2g	**10%**
Trans Fat 0g	
Cholesterol 10mg	**3%**
Sodium 370mg	**15%**
Total Carbohydrate 26g	**9%**
Dietary Fiber 3g	**12%**
Sugars 0g	
Protein 2g	

Vitamin A 2% • Vitamin C 0%
Calcium 2% • Iron 6%

*Percent Daily Values are based on a 2,000 calorie diet. Your daily values may be higher or lower depending on your calorie needs:

		2,000	2,500
Total Fat	Less than	65g	80g
Saturated Fat	Less than	20g	25g
Cholesterol	Less than	300mg	300mg
Sodium	Less than	2,400mg	2,400mg
Total Carbohydrate		300g	375g
Dietary Fiber		25g	30g

Calories per gram:
Fat 9 • Carbohydrate 4 • Protein 4

BASIC CRÊPES

Nutrition Facts

Serving Size (32g)
Servings Per Container

Amount Per Serving

Calories 50   Calories from Fat 20

% Daily Value*

Total Fat 2.5g	**4%**
Saturated Fat 0g	**0%**
Trans Fat 0g	
Cholesterol 30mg	**10%**
Sodium 70mg	**3%**
Total Carbohydrate 6g	**2%**
Dietary Fiber 0g	**0%**
Sugars 1g	
Protein 2g	

Vitamin A 2% • Vitamin C 0%
Calcium 2% • Iron 2%

*Percent Daily Values are based on a 2,000 calorie diet. Your daily values may be higher or lower depending on your calorie needs:

		2,000	2,500
Total Fat	Less than	65g	80g
Saturated Fat	Less than	20g	25g
Cholesterol	Less than	300mg	300mg
Sodium	Less than	2,400mg	2,400mg
Total Carbohydrate		300g	375g
Dietary Fiber		25g	30g

Calories per gram:
Fat 9 • Carbohydrate 4 • Protein 4

IRISH SODA BREAD

Nutrition Facts

Serving Size (41g)
Servings Per Container

Amount Per Serving

Calories 90	Calories from Fat 20
	% Daily Value*
Total Fat 2.5g	4%
Saturated Fat 1g	5%
Trans Fat 0g	
Cholesterol 15mg	5%
Sodium 150mg	6%
Total Carbohydrate 16g	5%
Dietary Fiber 1g	4%
Sugars 6g	
Protein 2g	

Vitamin A 2%	•	Vitamin C 0%
Calcium 2%	•	Iron 4%

*Percent Daily Values are based on a 2,000 calorie diet. Your daily values may be higher or lower depending on your calorie needs:

	Calories:	2,000	2,500
Total Fat	Less than	65g	80g
Saturated Fat	Less than	20g	25g
Cholesterol	Less than	300mg	300mg
Sodium	Less than	2,400mg	2,400mg
Total Carbohydrate		300g	375g
Dietary Fiber		25g	30g

Calories per gram:
Fat 9 • Carbohydrate 4 • Protein 4

MOCK BRAN MUFFINS

Nutrition Facts

Serving Size (50g)
Servings Per Container

Amount Per Serving

Calories 140	Calories from Fat 40
	% Daily Value*
Total Fat 4.5g	7%
Saturated Fat 1g	5%
Trans Fat 0g	
Cholesterol 15mg	5%
Sodium 170mg	7%
Total Carbohydrate 22g	7%
Dietary Fiber 3g	12%
Sugars 8g	
Protein 4g	

Vitamin A 0%	•	Vitamin C 2%
Calcium 4%	•	Iron 15%

*Percent Daily Values are based on a 2,000 calorie diet. Your daily values may be higher or lower depending on your calorie needs:

	Calories:	2,000	2,500
Total Fat	Less than	65g	80g
Saturated Fat	Less than	20g	25g
Cholesterol	Less than	300mg	300mg
Sodium	Less than	2,400mg	2,400mg
Total Carbohydrate		300g	375g
Dietary Fiber		25g	30g

Calories per gram:
Fat 9 • Carbohydrate 4 • Protein 4

BASIC BUTTERMILK WAFFLES

Nutrition Facts

Serving Size (68g)
Servings Per Container

Amount Per Serving

Calories 140	Calories from Fat 50

% Daily Value*

Total Fat 6g	9%
Saturated Fat 2.5g	13%
Trans Fat 0g	
Cholesterol 40mg	13%
Sodium 190mg	8%
Total Carbohydrate 18g	6%
Dietary Fiber 2g	8%
Sugars 4g	
Protein 5g	

Vitamin A 4% • Vitamin C 0%
Calcium 6% • Iron 4%

*Percent Daily Values are based on a 2,000 calorie diet. Your daily values may be higher or lower depending on your calorie needs:

		Calories:	2,000	2,500
Total Fat	Less than		65g	80g
Saturated Fat	Less than		20g	25g
Cholesterol	Less than		300mg	300mg
Sodium	Less than		2,400mg	2,400mg
Total Carbohydrate			300g	375g
Dietary Fiber			25g	30g

Calories per gram:
  Fat 9 • Carbohydrate 4 • Protein 4

CORNMEAL CHEDDAR LUNCH WAFFLES

Nutrition Facts

Serving Size (91g)
Servings Per Container

Amount Per Serving

Calories 220	Calories from Fat 90

% Daily Value*

Total Fat 10g	15%
Saturated Fat 4.5g	23%
Trans Fat 0g	
Cholesterol 50mg	17%
Sodium 280mg	12%
Total Carbohydrate 24g	8%
Dietary Fiber 2g	8%
Sugars 3g	
Protein 10g	

Vitamin A 8% • Vitamin C 2%
Calcium 15% • Iron 10%

*Percent Daily Values are based on a 2,000 calorie diet. Your daily values may be higher or lower depending on your calorie needs:

		Calories:	2,000	2,500
Total Fat	Less than		65g	80g
Saturated Fat	Less than		20g	25g
Cholesterol	Less than		300mg	300mg
Sodium	Less than		2,400mg	2,400mg
Total Carbohydrate			300g	375g
Dietary Fiber			25g	30g

Calories per gram:
  Fat 9 • Carbohydrate 4 • Protein 4

CHOCOLATE SNACK BALLS

Nutrition Facts

Serving Size (16g)
Servings Per Container

Amount Per Serving

Calories 35 — Calories from Fat 10

	% Daily Value*
Total Fat 1g	2%
Saturated Fat 0.5g	3%
Trans Fat 0g	
Cholesterol 10mg	3%
Sodium 35mg	1%
Total Carbohydrate 5g	2%
Dietary Fiber 1g	4%
Sugars 2g	
Protein 1g	

Vitamin A 0% • Vitamin C 0%
Calcium 2% • Iron 2%

*Percent Daily Values are based on a 2,000 calorie diet. Your daily values may be higher or lower depending on your calorie needs:

		Calories:	2,000	2,500
Total Fat	Less than		65g	80g
Saturated Fat	Less than		20g	25g
Cholesterol	Less than		300mg	300mg
Sodium	Less than		2,400mg	2,400mg
Total Carbohydrate			300g	375g
Dietary Fiber			25g	30g

Calories per gram:
  Fat 9 • Carbohydrate 4 • Protein 4

BASIC BUTTERMILK PANCAKES

Nutrition Facts

Serving Size (73g)
Servings Per Container

Amount Per Serving

Calories 140 — Calories from Fat 45

	% Daily Value*
Total Fat 5g	8%
Saturated Fat 1g	5%
Trans Fat 0g	
Cholesterol 20mg	7%
Sodium 190mg	8%
Total Carbohydrate 21g	7%
Dietary Fiber 2g	8%
Sugars 4g	
Protein 4g	

Vitamin A 2% • Vitamin C 0%
Calcium 6% • Iron 4%

*Percent Daily Values are based on a 2,000 calorie diet. Your daily values may be higher or lower depending on your calorie needs:

		Calories:	2,000	2,500
Total Fat	Less than		65g	80g
Saturated Fat	Less than		20g	25g
Cholesterol	Less than		300mg	300mg
Sodium	Less than		2,400mg	2,400mg
Total Carbohydrate			300g	375g
Dietary Fiber			25g	30g

Calories per gram:
  Fat 9 • Carbohydrate 4 • Protein 4

BANANA MUFFINS

Nutrition Facts

Serving Size (52g)
Servings Per Container

Amount Per Serving

Calories 140	Calories from Fat 60

% Daily Value*

Total Fat 6g	9%
Saturated Fat 2g	10%
Trans Fat 0g	
Cholesterol 20mg	7%
Sodium 115mg	5%
Total Carbohydrate 21g	7%
Dietary Fiber 2g	8%
Sugars 9g	
Protein 3g	

Vitamin A 2%	•	Vitamin C 2%
Calcium 2%	•	Iron 6%

*Percent Daily Values are based on a 2,000 calorie diet. Your daily values may be higher or lower depending on your calorie needs:

	Calories:	2,000	2,500
Total Fat	Less than	65g	80g
Saturated Fat	Less than	20g	25g
Cholesterol	Less than	300mg	300mg
Sodium	Less than	2,400mg	2,400mg
Total Carbohydrate		300g	375g
Dietary Fiber		25g	30g

Calories per gram:
Fat 9 • Carbohydrate 4 • Protein 4

BASIC BISCUITS

Nutrition Facts

Serving Size (48g)
Servings Per Container

Amount Per Serving

Calories 130	Calories from Fat 70

% Daily Value*

Total Fat 7g	11%
Saturated Fat 4g	20%
Trans Fat 0g	
Cholesterol 40mg	13%
Sodium 140mg	6%
Total Carbohydrate 14g	5%
Dietary Fiber 2g	8%
Sugars 2g	
Protein 3g	

Vitamin A 4%	•	Vitamin C 0%
Calcium 4%	•	Iron 4%

*Percent Daily Values are based on a 2,000 calorie diet. Your daily values may be higher or lower depending on your calorie needs:

	Calories:	2,000	2,500
Total Fat	Less than	65g	80g
Saturated Fat	Less than	20g	25g
Cholesterol	Less than	300mg	300mg
Sodium	Less than	2,400mg	2,400mg
Total Carbohydrate		300g	375g
Dietary Fiber		25g	30g

Calories per gram:
Fat 9 • Carbohydrate 4 • Protein 4

CHOCOLATE BISCUIT OR FOAM CAKE

Nutrition Facts

Serving Size (40g)
Servings Per Container

Amount Per Serving

Calories 90	Calories from Fat 20

	% Daily Value*
Total Fat 2.5g	4%
Saturated Fat 1g	5%
Trans Fat 0g	
Cholesterol 80mg	27%
Sodium 30mg	1%
Total Carbohydrate 14g	5%
Dietary Fiber 1g	4%
Sugars 10g	
Protein 3g	

Vitamin A 2%	•	Vitamin C 0%
Calcium 2%	•	Iron 4%

*Percent Daily Values are based on a 2,000 calorie diet. Your daily values may be higher or lower depending on your calorie needs:

	Calories:	2,000	2,500
Total Fat	Less than	65g	80g
Saturated Fat	Less than	20g	25g
Cholesterol	Less than	300mg	300mg
Sodium	Less than	2,400mg	2,400mg
Total Carbohydrate		300g	375g
Dietary Fiber		25g	30g

Calories per gram:
Fat 9 • Carbohydrate 4 • Protein 4

GINGER SPICE COOKIES

Nutrition Facts

Serving Size (22g)
Servings Per Container

Amount Per Serving

Calories 90	Calories from Fat 35

	% Daily Value*
Total Fat 4g	6%
Saturated Fat 2.5g	13%
Trans Fat 0g	
Cholesterol 15mg	5%
Sodium 130mg	5%
Total Carbohydrate 12g	4%
Dietary Fiber 1g	4%
Sugars 6g	
Protein 2g	

Vitamin A 2%	•	Vitamin C 0%
Calcium 2%	•	Iron 4%

*Percent Daily Values are based on a 2,000 calorie diet. Your daily values may be higher or lower depending on your calorie needs:

	Calories:	2,000	2,500
Total Fat	Less than	65g	80g
Saturated Fat	Less than	20g	25g
Cholesterol	Less than	300mg	300mg
Sodium	Less than	2,400mg	2,400mg
Total Carbohydrate		300g	375g
Dietary Fiber		25g	30g

Calories per gram:
Fat 9 • Carbohydrate 4 • Protein 4

QUINOA FLAKE BARS

Nutrition Facts

Serving Size (12g)
Servings Per Container

Amount Per Serving

Calories 90   Calories from Fat 45

	% Daily Value*
Total Fat 5g	8%
Saturated Fat 2g	10%
Trans Fat 0g	
Cholesterol 5mg	2%
Sodium 35mg	1%
Total Carbohydrate 9g	3%
Dietary Fiber 2g	8%
Sugars 5g	
Protein 2g	

Vitamin A 2% • Vitamin C 0%
Calcium 2% • Iron 4%

*Percent Daily Values are based on a 2,000 calorie diet. Your daily values may be higher or lower depending on your calorie needs:

		Calories:	2,000	2,500
Total Fat	Less than		65g	80g
Saturated Fat	Less than		20g	25g
Cholesterol	Less than		300mg	300mg
Sodium	Less than		2,400mg	2,400mg
Total Carbohydrate			300g	375g
Dietary Fiber			25g	30g

Calories per gram:
Fat 9 • Carbohydrate 4 • Protein 4

TRADITIONAL PIE DOUGH

Nutrition Facts

Serving Size (67g)
Servings Per Container Double Crust Pie - 10 servings

Amount Per Serving

Calories 300   Calories from Fat 180

	% Daily Value*
Total Fat 21g	32%
Saturated Fat 13g	65%
Trans Fat 0.5g	
Cholesterol 65mg	22%
Sodium 300mg	13%
Total Carbohydrate 25g	8%
Dietary Fiber 4g	16%
Sugars 2g	
Protein 4g	

Vitamin A 10% • Vitamin C 0%
Calcium 2% • Iron 6%

*Percent Daily Values are based on a 2,000 calorie diet. Your daily values may be higher or lower depending on your calorie needs:

		Calories:	2,000	2,500
Total Fat	Less than		65g	80g
Saturated Fat	Less than		20g	25g
Cholesterol	Less than		300mg	300mg
Sodium	Less than		2,400mg	2,400mg
Total Carbohydrate			300g	375g
Dietary Fiber			25g	30g

Calories per gram:
Fat 9 • Carbohydrate 4 • Protein 4

SECTION 6
About Tools And Techniques

CHAPTER 1:
TOOLS

MIXERS AND BEATERS

- **ELECTRIC HAND BEATER:** Electric hand beaters are a quick and easy way to beat liquid ingredients or soft batters. Electric hand beaters generally have 2 beaters that rotate more quickly and beat more efficiently, and in less time than what people can do with a whisk. Most electric hand beaters come with different speeds and range in power. Any electric hand beater will do the trick. Use an electric hand beater for the following things:

    - Beating ingredients such as egg whites, egg yolks, gelatin, whipping cream, coconut cream, and evaporated milk into foams.

    - Beating soft batters (cake, pancake, crêpes, waffles, and some muffin batters) to activate hydrophilic binders that require agitation.

    - Beating fat such as butter to incorporate air to lighten baked goods.

- **STAND MIXERS:** A stand mixer is much stronger than an electric hand beater and is required for stiffer batters such as breads, cookie dough, thick and quick bread batters. Stand mixers come in different sizes and range of motor strength. Gluten-free breads do not require the motor power that yeast breads do; so low-powered stand mixers work just fine without the risk of the motor burning out. The size of the mixer is personal – generally a mixer that will hold up to 6 cups of flour or two loaves of bread is plenty big. Stand mixers come with different attachments. The beater and the cookie paddle are very useful in gluten-free baking. The dough hook does not work as well in gluten-free baking. Use a stand mixer for the following things:

    - Beating yeast dough such as any yeast bread or pizza dough.

    - Beating cookie dough.

    - Beating quick bread batters, such as muffins and loaves.

    - Beating anything that cannot be beaten with an electric hand beater using the wire whisk attachment.

- **STICK BEATERS:** Stick beaters have a single shaft with a small blade at the bottom surrounded by a protective half shell. Stick beaters come in different sizes and motor power as well. Any standard stick beater will work well. Use a stick beater for the following things:

  - Beating hydrophilic binders that require agitation such as methylcellulose into liquid prior to beating into foam.

  - Puréeing mashed fruits or vegetables into a smooth uniform consistency.

- **FOOD PROCESSOR:** Food processors come in all different sizes and motor power as well. They can have different attachments for puréeing, mixing, grating/shredding, slicing, and dicing. In gluten-free baking the "S" blade and a grater or shredder blade are very useful. Use a food processor for the following things:

  - "S" blade

    - Cutting fat into flour for biscuits, pastries, flat bread, and pasta.

    - Mixing and "kneading" dough for biscuits, pastries, flat bread, and pasta.

    - Puréeing fruits, vegetables, legumes, nuts and seeds until smooth or desired consistency.

    - Grinding nuts and seeds into fine meals for use in flour mixes.

    - Chopping fresh herbs such as basil or pesto into small pieces.

  - Grater or Shredder blade

    - Grating vegetables or fruits such as carrot, zucchini, or apple for muffins, cakes or loaves.

BOWLS, MEASURING TOOLS AND BAKING PANS

Everyone has their own preferences when it comes to the tools to do the job. The important things to know are; what kind of baker you are and to match the equipment or tools to your style. One thing that is true about most jobs, crafts, sports, or art is that having the right equipment makes the task easier and/or more enjoyable and you more successful. Inferior equipment leads to frustration and poor products. A favourite story comes to Lisa's mind when we thought about this topic. The following is written in Lisa's words and it is a story about one of Lisa's good friends and a cake baking experience.

A friend of mine was telling me that she was trying to make a bundt cake. The cake never turned out right – burnt on the outside and undercooked on the inside. She made several attempts with failures. I happened to be over at her house and she was telling me about her latest bundt cake failure and I asked if I could see her bundt pan. My friend went to the kitchen and brought out a jelly mold pan! Yes, she was using a jelly mold pan that was metal, but really not meant to be baked in. After recovering from a fit of laughter we switched her pan for a "real" bundt pan and the cake turned out beautifully. She was not familiar with jelly molds and found the pan at a garage sale and bought it thinking it was a cake pan. The moral of the story is that if you are unsure do not be afraid to ask questions to confirm whether your thinking is correct. Small things can make a big difference!

- **BOWLS:** Having the right bowl for the job is important. The bowls used should have the following properties: be able to have metal beaters grazing their surface, be the appropriate size, be easy to hang onto, and have high sides with smaller bases. These properties combine to assist in creating perfect foams. To keep things simple we like to have a variety of metal or glass bowls that fit inside one another. This makes them multi-purpose, and easy to store and wash. Glass is best if you want to adjust the temperature in the microwave and metal is better if you want to chill things down fast in the fridge or freezer.

- **LIQUID MEASURE CUPS OR BOWLS:** Having different sized liquid measuring cups or bowls is great for accurate liquid volume measurements and they double as great mixing bowls. There are many different brands of glass liquid measuring cups and bowls that work well and come in multiple sizes. Most fit inside one another to assist in storage.

- **DRY MEASURE CUPS OR SCOOPS:** Having measures in multiple sizes allow better accuracy. Whether you acquire cups or scoops depends on your preference. Most brands make measuring cups or scoops that stack inside one another for easy storage.

- **MEASURING SPOONS:** Again, acquire measures in multiple sizes – the more sizes the better your accuracy. Try to get ones that have an ⅛ of a teaspoon. I find that useful when small amounts of hydrophilic binder such as xanthan gum are required. You can also get measures for a "pinch" or a "dash". Lisa was given some of these as a gag gift. But she actually does find them useful as she can now measure small volumes and be consistent every time. These are not necessary, but can be useful if you bake in a rush as we do often and desire consistent results each and every time.

- **SCALES:** Scales are helpful in getting amounts exact. When recipes are increased past household volume to commercial volume, weights are even more critical. For items such as solid fat, chocolate, or grated cheese a scale can be very handy for improved accuracy.

- **BAKING PANS:** Get good baking pans! The pan can make all the difference to the end result. Baking pans can be made from glass, metal, anodized aluminum, non-stick or silicon. Pan size also makes a difference. Changing the size of the pan can result in changes to the end product. Choosing the right pan for the job and the correct pan preparation is important for success.

    - Choose the size required by the recipe.

    - "Pan" generally indicates metal and "plate" or "dish" generally indicates glass. If you choose to use a glass dish over a metal pan, you should reduce the oven temperature by 25 degrees.

    - Metal pans can be made out of different materials such as anodized aluminum, stainless steel or cast iron. Each conducts heat uniquely and requires different maintenance. You may need to adjust the oven temperature or the pan preparation based on the baking pan that you are using.

        - Stainless steel and cast iron pans need to be seasoned before use. The quality of the pan and degree to which the pan is seasoned can make a difference to the end result. These pans also tend to be heavy.

        - Anodized aluminum pans are light, efficient at conducting heat, and are naturally more "non-stick". Anodized aluminum baking pans often produce more desirable results. Anodized aluminum pans should not be placed into a dishwasher as harsh cleansers breakdown the surface. Maintain them by lightly washing with mild soap and water. If they start to dull, place a good amount of white vinegar and boiling water into the baking pan and let sit for 20-30 minutes.

        - Non-stick pans have a non-stick surface of either aluminum or stainless steel. The non-stick surface can be damaged so bakers need to follow manufacturer's directions for care and use.

        - Silicon pans are the modern day non-stick. They are safe in temperatures between 76°F and 500°F that are not direct flame. Silicon bakeware is made from 100 % platinum silicon. The advantage is that its non-stick surface does not breakdown. They are light, non-breakable and flexible, transfer heat efficiently, cool quickly, allow for easy release of the cooked baked good to a rack, can be washed in the dishwasher, and are easy to store.

ELECTRIC MAKERS

These include waffle irons, cake ball makers, cupcake makers, tart and pie makers, and others. There are "makers" of all kinds of shapes and sizes. The great news is that gluten-free baked goods turn out really well in electric makers - simple, fast, and delicious. With greater availability of electric makers, even those bakers without a full kitchen can enjoy some homemade baking.

BREAD MACHINES

Bread machines can be used. However, for best results, prepare the dough in a stand mixer and then place the dough into the bread maker for finishing off. If you have an oven, we recommend using an oven. But if you want to make your own bread and do not have an oven, a bread machine is a good alternative.

STORAGE

Most home bakers of gluten-free products that we talk to do not want to have to store multiple flours, binders or other ingredients. Storage of ingredients is a hurdle to get over. Some ingredients need refrigeration and others can be stored in the pantry. Many storage systems have containers in multiple sizes but do not provide enough of the right size for a gluten-free storage system. Most, if not all, gluten-free ingredients come in small bags, many of which do not re-seal or stand up nicely on the pantry shelf, refrigerator or freezer. All of them are better when kept in airtight containers. After many years of using different systems, Lisa has settled on glass canning jars with plastic screw-top lids. The largest and mid-size are great for flours, seeds, and fibres and the jam jar sizes are great for binders and leaveners. Canning jars are uniform in size and shape, are easy to find and are cost-effective. They sit well in the pantry and in the fridge or freezer. Canning jars also are easily washed in the dishwasher between fill-ups. Canning jars can be labeled with permanent marker on the lid and the jar or by cutting off the label from the gluten-free package and taping it onto the jar. We find that ingredients stay fresh longer in glass canning jars than in their original packaging. We no longer wonder what ingredients we have on hand or where they are and the desire for organization and simplicity has been met. Don't shy away from having multiple ingredients on hand. A case of canning jars goes a long way to simplifying the variety!

CHAPTER 2:
TECHNIQUES

- **BEATING**: Beating does two main things: fully activates the hydrophilic binders that require agitation, and incorporates air. Both significantly improve the final product and it is worth getting the proper equipment and taking the time to use it.

- **TIME**: Time is also so important. Waiting the required time for processes to occur greatly enhances success in your baking ventures. It requires time for leavening agents, such as yeast, to ferment and produce gas. Hydrophilic binders require time to gel and fully absorb liquid to form the binding gel. Hydrophilic binders that require agitation need enough time under the beater to fully activate to produce more desirable baked goods. Do not rush or cut corners on time.

- **TIMING**: When ingredients are added to batter or dough can make a difference to the final product. For example, adding oil to the batter after the hydrophilic binders have been incorporated is best as the fat impacts the binding capacity less resulting in a more desirable baked good.

- **HEAT**: Heat changes ingredients. Fat, carbohydrates or sugar, and protein all change how they behave under heat. For example:

    - Boiling sugar in liquid enhances its binding and sticking power and can even make hard crystals;

    - Boiling water poured into a dough while beating it cooks the starches and enhances the elasticity of the dough;

    - Deep fat frying something creates a different outcome than when it is baked in the oven;

    - Adjusting oven temperature for browning and baking as well as fast or slow baking create different end products using the same batter. Some recipes use combinations of temperatures to capture the best of both temperature ranges in a baked product. For instance, yeast bread is often started hot and turned down;

    - Room temperature egg whites produce a stronger structure of foam than cold egg whites.

- **COLD**: Cold changes the ingredients and dough as well. For example:

    - Chilling whipping cream, coconut cream, and evaporated milk creates greater volumes in airy foams;

- Chilling yeast dough slows down the growth of the yeast and the fermentation process. This is used in "over-night" yeast dough items such as buns or cinnamon buns;

- Chilling higher fat pastry or cookie dough makes the dough easier to roll and cut than room temperature dough;

- Chilling "sets", gels, or thickens ingredients such as dissolved gelatin and liquid to create a semi-solid liquid that when incorporated into dessert items produce a different texture.

- **CHOP SIZE:** The size of a chopped ingredient affects how it behaves in a product. For instance, chopped nuts are added as an addition to add texture and nutrition into a baked good. Nut flour is added into the flour mixture as part of the dry ingredient and it impacts structure and crumb consistency and texture. Nut butters tend to be added as part of the fat component for moistening and emulsifying.

- **SIFTING:** Most gluten-free recipes call for unsifted flour. For improved accuracy and ease, recipes in The New Gluten Free™ state volumes for unsifted flour. For this reason it is important to measure the flour first and then sift. Sifting will separate the flour granules thereby expanding the volume by incorporating air. This will help lighten and leaven your baked item.

SECTION 7
Baking Beyond The Guide

BAKING BEYOND
THE GUIDE

It is our hope that *The Guide* brings a new quality standard to gluten-free baked goods in terms of availability, taste, nutrition, and health benefits both at home and in the food industry. The greater number of people who know how to create gluten-free baking, the greater the capacity we have to do it well – conveniently, nutritiously, deliciously, and cost effectively.

We encourage you to incorporate the ingredients, tools and techniques in *The Guide* to create delicious gluten-free baked goods using a variety of gluten-free ingredients. With greater understanding of the science and art of gluten-free baking, you will be able to create your own recipes from family favourites or your own ideas as well as to critique existing gluten-free recipes for success.

Use The Recipe Equation below to tailor your recipes to your individual tastes and preferences as well as to any secondary ingredient restrictions you may have.

The Recipe Equation

Although *The Guide* is large and detailed *The Recipe Equation* is simple and speaks to the principles of gluten-free baking.

THE RECIPE EQUATION

Determine what it is you want to bake: is it crunchy, chewy, tender? **+** Consider the moisture base of the recipe: is fat- or water-based moisture being added? **+** Build on the moisture base with the "right" combination and proportion of the 7 key components: flours, starches, liquids, binders, foams and leavening agents, sweeteners, and fats. **+** The right equipment, tools and some very important techniques. **=** Gluten-Free products that turn out every time!

THE LAST "AH-HA"...
FOR NOW!

It is never too late to learn or make new discoveries. While in the final editing stages of The Guide, we were developing a coffee cake recipe for a local natural market when we were forced to re-look at the relationship between fat and hydrophilic binders. In Lisa's words here is what happened.

I took one of my tried-and-true coffee cake recipes and made some adjustments to meet the specifications desired by the market. As I was making the test cake I decided to change the melted butter to oil – thinking that it was likely going to be a mistake. Normally when I add melted butter to a batter, I add it in after I have beaten the wet and dry ingredients together to ensure that I have fully activated the hydrophilic binders. On the other hand when I add oil to a batter, I add it to the wet ingredients before I add the dry ingredients and beat the batter. In this case, I switched from melted butter to oil after I had beaten the batter together. So, I had to add the oil to the batter like I would have done if I were using melted butter. The result was surprising. The cake rose beautifully, the crumb was excellent and moist, and the cake held together without crumbling. Hmmm. I found myself asking many questions – does it matter when the oil is added to the batter? Should it be added before the hydrophilic binders have a chance to activate or after the hydrophilic binders have been activated? If the answer is yes, it does matter if it is before or after – then, do hydrophilic binders that require agitation to bind react differently from those that require time to bind?

Back to my kitchen laboratory I went. I decided to start with hydrophilic binders that require agitation and try an experiment with xanthan gum and methylcellulose. I created a xanthan gum gel with xanthan gum and water and then I added oil to the gel. I also combined oil and water and tried to create a xanthan gum gel. The oil impacted the integrity of the gel with both approaches. The gel integrity was slightly better when the oil was added after the gel had formed. The overall conclusion confirmed what I had already known – oil impacts gums effectiveness. Next I created a stiff methylcellulose foam. I divided the foam in half and added a dose of oil to one of the foams and beat the oil into the foam. The foam softened and would not hold a peak. I added another dose of oil and beat it in. The foaminess reduced again. To the second bowl I added the oil to the water and methylcellulose powder and beat it into foam. The mixture did create foam with good volume, however, no matter how long I beat it I could not create foam that held a peak. The consistency and volume of the foam was comparable to that of the foam where the oil was added after the foam was created and the oil beaten in. From this I concluded that oil has some impact on methylcellulose foam but it maintains better integrity than when oil is added to xanthan gum gel.

Next I wanted to test out the hydrophilic binders that require time. I created the same consistency gels with psyllium and ground chia seeds. I divided the gels equally so that I had four bowls in front of me. I added the same volume of oil to one of the halves and vigorously stirred oil into the gel. The result was that the oil broke down the gel of the ground chia seed, but enhanced the glueyness of the psyllium gel. The psyllium gel was stronger and gluier. I then added another dose of oil to both gels containing the oil. The ground chia seed gel continued to weaken. But the psyllium gel again became stronger and more gluey. I decided to add another dose of oil to the psyllium gel and found that it again became gluier and stronger – so much so that it now formed a glue ball that was so strong it would not stretch! I decided to add the water, the oil and the psyllium at the same time. The mixture did form a gel, but the gel lacked in glueyness. From this I concluded that the strength and gluey structure of psyllium changes depending on when oil is added and that psyllium gel must be amphiphilic (both water and fat loving). I also determined that there is an ideal range for percent of oil to water-based liquid to develop desired "chew" for different baked items: 8-20% oil (8 ml to 20 ml oil in 100 ml water) in the water-based liquid is a place to start estimated range. My conclusion is that oil does not respond the same with the hydrophilic binders that require time.

This little experiment has much promise for future recipe development using oil as the fat while enhancing chew factor in baked goods through the use of psyllium husk and oil. Considering this discovery has come at the end of The Guide's creation, it has not been actively tested nor worked through the concepts of this guide. So, we leave you with this discovery to ponder and test. Good luck!

SECTION 8
Appendices

APPENDIX 1:
KITCHEN MUST-HAVES

Knowing what to buy can be tricky when first starting out. We have put together a basic list of kitchen "must-haves" that you will want to have on hand. Buying a case of wide mouth 1-litre glass canning jars with plastic screw-top lids is a great idea for storing small, opened bags of gluten-free flour. A wide mouth canning funnel allows you to pour the flour into each jar with ease. Cut the label from the bag and tape to the jar. Canning jars are cost effective, fit well into the cupboard or refrigerator, are easily washed and can be relabeled for reuse.

Recipes, Ingredients, Tools, & Techniques

EQUIPMENT	TOOLS	BAKING PANS	STORAGE
Stand mixer	High-sided, narrow-based mixing bowls	Baking pans for bread (8x4x2 inch pan preferred), muffins, cakes, and tarts	1L glass canning jars with plastic airtight screw-top lids
Hand beater	Measuring cups, spoons and scoops	Oven mitts	Wide mouth funnel to fit canning jars
Stick beater	Scale	Cooling racks	
Food processor	Spatulas, scrappers, mixing spoons. One (1) and two (2) ounce scoops as well as "dash" (⅛ tsp), "pinch" and "smidgen" measuring spoons are very useful		
Electric makers – waffle iron, cake ball maker	Cutter for biscuits, cookies, and pasta		
	Rolling pin, pasta maker		
	Sifters		

APPENDIX 2:
BASIC PANTRY LIST

Knowing what to buy can be tricky when first starting out. We have put together a basic list of items that you may need. The great thing about using a variety of flours is that you do not need very much of any one flour and glass canning jars work really well to store the leftovers from opened bags. You do not have to buy everything on list. Buy the ingredients you like and will use because ingredients are best kept fresh.

FLOURS, STARCHES, FLAKES AND GRAINS

Brown Rice Flour	Chickpea Flour	Sweet Rice Flour	Quinoa Flakes
Corn Flour	White Bean Flour	Tapioca Starch	Quinoa Grain
Buckwheat Flour	Black Bean Flour	Potato Starch	Brown Rice Flakes
Pure Oat* Flour	Garfava Bean Flour	Cocoa Powder	Pure Oat *Flakes
Sorghum Flour	Lentil Flour	Defatted Seed or Nut Flour	Brown Rice Flakes
Teff Flour	Coconut Flour	Defatted Protein Powder	Cornmeal
Millet Flour	Nut Flours of Choice		Pure Oat* Bran
Quinoa Flour			Teff Grain

BINDERS

Xanthan Gum	Chia Seeds	Eggs	Agar
Methylcellulose	Psyllium Husk	Gelatin	

LEAVENING AGENTS

Baking Powder	Baking Soda	Yeast	Carbonated Beverages

SWEETENERS

Sugar	Agave Syrup	Maple Syrup	Stevia
Honey	Molasses	Corn Syrup	Xylitol

HERBS AND SPICES

Cinnamon	Cloves	Vanilla	Rosemary
Ginger	Nutmeg	Garlic	Thyme
Allspice	Cardamom	Dill	Basil

ADDITIONAL ITEMS TO ENHANCE NUTRITION AND/OR TO ADD FLAVOUR

Hemp Hearts/Seeds		Nuts	Dried Fruit
Nutritional Yeast	Flax Seeds	Seeds	Rice Bran
Chocolate Chips	Gluten-free Flavoured Chips	Carob Chips	Berries

LIQUIDS

Buttermilk	Coconut Milk/ Beverage	Grain Milks	Soya Milk
Milk	Yogurts – Dairy and Non-dairy	Hemp Milk	Mashed/sauced Vegetables and Fruit

FATS AND OILS

| Butter | Avocado | Oil | Lard |

APPENDIX 3:
SOURCES OF INFORMATION AND REFERENCE MATERIALS

When we reflect on the writing of this reference guide, we are at a loss on how to adequately reference our materials. While one of us (Areli) is still relatively new to gluten-free baking, Lisa has gleaned the information so gradually over time that it is now part of her DNA. Lisa has read a lot, baked a lot and has thought a lot about the science of food, the process of cooking and baking and the interaction of ingredients used in baking.

The following paragraphs have been written in the first-person from Lisa's perspective.

LISA:

Over the years I have read more food and nutrition books, magazines, articles, and research papers that have informed my knowledge and practice than I can remember or list. Some of my earlier resources on gluten-free baking no longer exist today and others I have kept only a page or two with little or no information about the authors or even the name of the book from which it came. I have also spent much time reading about wheat-based baking and cooking in an effort to understand how the tools and techniques of wheat-based baking produce the results they do so that I may relate them to gluten-free baking.

My quest for developing delicious and nutritious gluten-free baking started almost 20 years ago for my own benefit. As such, I never kept formal notes or references. Before the Internet, I frequented the library and took out books on cooking and baking as well as reference books. I read all of the dietitian newsletters and journals from the Canadian Dietitians Association. Since the Internet opened up, I have opted for the ease of "googling" for quick answers. I have also written to companies and manufacturers for information about their products and processing techniques.

I have read and used recipes and flour mix combinations from *all* of Bette Hagman's books. It was great to see Bette Hagman's cookbooks in print when they first came out to know that I was on a similar track of experimentation and use of ingredients. They fueled my motivation to continue.

I appreciated *125 Best Gluten-Free Recipes* by Donna Washburn and Heather Butt when it came out. Today there are many more gluten-free cookbooks out there with their own slant on how to make great baked goods with the weird and wonderful flour options and ingredients available today.

I have reviewed the methods and recipes from the *Joy of Cooking*, *Betty Crocker*, and *How to Cook Everything* and have read and used recipes from *the America's Test Kitchen* series, *Companies Coming*, *Best of Bridge*, *Martha Stewart*, and *Rachel Ray*. Also, I have read a number of vegetarian cookbooks such as the *Moosewood Cookbooks* and *Rebar*.

I have contributed recipes to a number of the Dietitians of Canada cookbooks and have read them all and used many of their recipes.

I have read umpteen "smart-eating" cookbooks such as the *Anne Lindsay* Cook Book Series, *The Enlightened Eater* by Rosie Schwartz, *The Healthy Kitchen* by Andrew Weil and Rosie Daley, *Meals in Minutes* by the American Heart Association, and *Weekend Wonders - healthy meals for every day* by Rose Reisman, to name a few. Many more unnamed books I borrowed from the library, friends, and family.

Apparently I get sucked in at the grocery line-up as well. I have numerous food, cooking and baking magazines, including, *Canadian Living*, *Taste of Home*, *Phyllis Hoffman*, *Better Homes and Gardens*, *The Best of Fine Cooking*, *Country Home*, and more.

I have tried many "electric makers" for waffles, cake balls, mini cupcakes, and pies and have reviewed their cookbooks for ideas to understand what "they" do to get the desired wheat-based product so that I can translate it into a gluten-free version.

Specific food books such as *Pumpkin* by DeeDee Stovel was great when researching how to add mashed fruit and vegetables into my gluten-free baking; *Quinoa The Everyday Superfood 365* by Patricia Green and Carolyn Hemming, and *Full of Beans* by Violet Currie and Kay Spicer also helped.

I have read books on pasta making, muffin making, cake making, bread making, cookie making, pastry making, and biscuit making.

Recipes, Ingredients, Tools, & Techniques

I have researched Internet websites thoroughly for gluten-free flours, liquids, binders, fats, sweeteners, foams, leavening agents, baking equipment, techniques, tools, and gluten-free recipes and cookbooks.

I even branched out into cake decorating and learned how to create baked goods that look like "everyone else's". I took courses at our local cake decorating shop, "Creating Occasions," and learned all about cake decorating from the cake to icing, sugar, chocolate, tools, and techniques from Lora Lonesberry, the owner and pastry chef. My favourite book from that era is *The Cake Bible* by Rose Levy Beranbaum. I loved reading it and I have been able to glean enough knowledge to translate her beautiful cakes into delightful gluten-free versions. I have even mastered the Chocolate Basket! However, my kids would argue that the inspirations from *Hello, Cupcake!* by Karen Tack & Alan Richardson is actually the highlight.

I love books such as *Eating on the Wild Side, The Missing Link to Optimal Health* by Jo Robinson as they give me thought-provoking ideas to consider as I develop and revise my recipes.

From this you may have gathered that I am a "foodie" with an interest in food science and nutrition, and the improvement of gluten-free baking so that it will not be "just a requirement of keeping out of the emergency department" but a choice that is truly delicious and nutritious.

Post Publication Errata

Page	Change to be made
172	Basic Yeast Bread Egg White Foam: Method correction: Direction 4, change ¾ c water to ½ c water
172	Basic Yeast Bread Egg White Foam: Method correction: Direction 5, change ½ c water to ¾ c water
172	Basic Yeast Bread Egg White Foam: Method correction: Direction 5, move, add 2 tbsp oil and mix until fully combined to the end of Direction 8
173	Basic Yeast Bread Egg White Foam: Ingredient volume correction: Change 4 ¼ xanthan gum (21 ml) to 4 tsp (20 ml) xanthan gum
173	Basic Yeast Bread Egg White Foam: Ingredient volume correction: Change ½ c (125 ml) to ¾ c (180ml) warm water
174	Basic Yeast Bread Gelatin Foam: Ingredient volume correction: Change ¾ c (180 ml) to ½ c (125 ml) warm water
174	Basic Yeast Bread Gelatin Foam: Method correction: Direction 1, change ¼ c cold water to ½ c cold water
174	Basic Yeast Bread Gelatin Foam: Method correction: Direction 3, change ¾ c water to ½ c water
175	Basic Yeast Bread Gelatin Foam: Method correction: Direction 5, move, add 2 tbsp oil and mix until fully combined to the end of Direction 8
175	Basic Yeast Bread Gelatin Foam: Ingredient volume correction: Change 4 ¼ tsp (21 ml) xanthan gum to 4 tsp (20 ml) xanthan gum
175	Basic Yeast Bread Gelatin Foam: Ingredient volume correction: Change ¼ c (60 ml) cold water to ½ c (125 ml) cold water
176	Basic Yeast Bread Gelatin Foam: Ingredient volume correction: Change ¾ c (180 ml) warm water to ½ c (125 ml) warm water
176	Basic Yeast Bread Agar and Methylcellulose Foam: Method correction: Direction 4, move, add 2 tbsp oil and mix until fully combined to the end of Direction 7
188	Cornmeal Cheddar Waffles: Method modification: Direction 1. Add another sentence: Add hemp hearts (optional) to dry mix and stir to combine.
189	Cornmeal Cheddar Waffles: Ingredient addition: 3 tbsp (45 ml) Hemp Hearts (optional)
190	Chocolate Snack Balls: Yield correction: should read 36 1-inch balls

Printed in Canada